# Aging in America

# Aging
# in America

## A Cultural History

## Lawrence R. Samuel

**PENN**

UNIVERSITY OF PENNSYLVANIA PRESS

PHILADELPHIA

Copyright © 2017 University of Pennsylvania Press

Published by
University of Pennsylvania Press
Philadelphia, Pennsylvania 19104-4112
www.upenn.edu/pennpress

Printed in the United States of America on acid-free paper
1   3   5   7   9   10   8   6   4   2


Cataloging-in-Publication Data is available from the  Library of Congress
ISBN 978-0-8122-4883-8

What shall I do with this absurdity—O heart,
O troubled heart—this caricature,
Decrepit age that has been tied to me as to a dog's tail?
                              —W. B. Yeats, "The Tower"

# Contents

# Preface

"How old is your granddaughter?" the nice older woman asks me as I drop off my daughter at school. I'm fifty-eight years old and my daughter is three, making it a not unreasonable question. Still, her thinking that I look more like a grandfather than a father is a bit irritating, and a completely objective reminder that I appear to others more old than young. Children too sometimes approach me at playgrounds while I'm in the company of my daughter and ask if I'm her daddy, a sign of how embedded perceptions about age are in our youth-obsessed society.

Like most people on the north side of middle age, I find my advancing age an annoying and surprising fact of life, wondering how and when this particular inconvenient truth crept up on me. As a typical baby boomer (of the generation born approximately between the mid-1940s and the mid-1960s), I've naturally thought of myself as somehow always being young despite the obvious signs that prove otherwise. I shunned joining the AARP when it first approached me when I turned fifty, not wanting to be part of an organization made up of old people. (I later eagerly signed up when I learned I was missing out on some great discounts.) I pride myself on not putting much stock in a person's physical appearance, knowing it's mostly a genetic dealing of the cards, but occasionally I fall victim to the self-loathing many people past the half-century mark experience when I catch a glimpse of myself in the mirror. (I often try not to look.) Exactly whose body is this? I sometimes ask myself, bewildered at how I have come to occupy this not especially attractive shell. The physical signs of aging—gray and disappearing hair, need for reading glasses, spots on the skin, creaking joints, a proclivity to gain weight just by looking at food, and a host of minor ailments—are further confirmation of my lost youth, as are the ever-growing number of meds my doctor tells me I should take to stay relatively healthy. I'd like to have back my physical self from around the mid-1980s, but that's obviously not going to happen.

Conversely, however, I feel that my interior self has only improved with the years. The demons that plagued me as a young adult have largely disappeared, and I now enjoy a kind of emotional contentedness that I directly attribute to having spent more time on the planet. Call it experience, wisdom, or whatever you like, but living long enough tends to bring with it a palpable sense of well-being and satisfaction. With the compulsions of both my id and my ego mostly sated, a Freudian might say, my superego now has the ability to run free, a wonderful thing. Like many folks hovering around age sixty, I feel as though I'm playing with house money, with every day a gift to be appreciated or even savored. Having a little girl to care for and a family circus to help keep running is all the motivation I need to get out of bed in the morning and, without any exaggeration at all, to try to stay alive as long as possible.

Many people at a similar stage of life are not so lucky. When I inquire, doing some informal research for this book, friends and strangers alike who are close to my age consistently tell me they have little idea what to do with the rest of their life. For them, particularly the well to do, ironically, identifying a clear meaning and purpose for their third act of life is a struggle. Their kids out of the nest and their mortgage paid, these folks no longer really have to hold nine-to-five jobs but continue to do so, not sure how else to spend the majority of their time. Golf or boating is certainly fun but hardly offers the substantive experience they require to remain happy and fulfilled individuals. Travel also is great, they add, but a life constantly on the go lacks the literal grounding that most of us need. Making more money to bestow upon children and grandchildren seems to be the primary motive in these people's lives, a noble pursuit but with limited opportunity for personal growth and lacking any kind of spiritual component.

While considering myself fortunate to have a mission in life at this point in the game, reconciling the distancing of one's body from one's mind as one ages is, to say the least, a tricky business. I believe that physical decline and psychic evolution typically follow a parallel track as one ages, much in part due to a gradual gaining of wisdom as well as an increasing awareness that it is inevitable one will eventually die. Resolving this inverse, two-ships-passing-in-the-night relationship between one's physical being and one's psyche (barring the onset of a debilitating cognitive disease, of course) seems to me to be one of life's most daunting challenges, but certainly one worth taking on. Ideally, the yin of the mind should connect with the yang of the body, making them complementary, dynamic forces that create a kind of synergy for an individual. I hope to do that with whatever time I have left, and by doing so become a more complete human being.

The commonality of this existential crisis is one of the primary reasons for my taking on the researching and writing of this book. In order to help lay a conceptual groundwork for the book, my working definition of aging revolves around the social, political, and economic issues surrounding the process of getting older in America, particularly after the age of fifty. A book about aging in America can be easily justified given its cultural significance and the demographic dynamics of our time and place, but I believe that any project has to speak to readers in a special way at some level. From the conversations I've had with individuals of all stripes and from my more formal research, it is clear that aging is one of those subjects that nearly everyone can relate to in some way. My story is hardly unique, with its themes well documented in many studies of older people. More than anything else, perhaps, this book is a resource that adds valuable context to the thorny issue of aging by tracing its history over the past half century. My modest goal is to shed some additional light on the subject, and in doing so perhaps help some readers come to terms with this most fundamental and fascinating part of life.

# Introduction

*Aging in America: A Cultural History* is, as the title makes clear, a cultural history of aging in the United States. No such book has been recently published, something surprising given the centrality of the subject in contemporary life. Much interest currently revolves around aging in America, as the tens of millions of baby boomers head into their sixties and seventies. While I spend considerable time following the trajectory of the generation born between 1946 and 1964, all Americans are somehow and necessarily involved in the story. Everyone is aging, after all, making the subject something with which we all can identify. Aging goes to the heart of individual identity, a good reason why its cultural history is a worthy venture. On a deeper level, aging goes to the essence of humanity; it is one of our very few common or even universal experiences. I am interested in stories that bring us closer together rather than push us apart, and from this perspective it is difficult to imagine a more pertinent topic, as each of us gets older every day regardless of our race, gender, or other socially defined division.

Focusing on the past half century of American history makes sense for a number of reasons when thinking about aging, the most obvious being the demographics. Never before has there been a generation so large and so influential, making its evolution over time an attractive topic for any historian. Ten thousand Americans will turn sixty-five years old every day for the next twenty years, an astounding figure. More remarkably, perhaps, eighty-five to ninety-four-year-olds represent the fastest-growing age group in America, according to the most recent census, with that segment of the population increasing almost 30 percent between 2000 and 2010. Although much has been understandably made of American youth culture, the nation's past fifty years have in many ways been heavily defined by the idea of aging, with key

moments ranging from politics (the passage of Medicare) to science (the genetic revolution) to medicine (the rise of "antiaging" medicine) to education
(the creation of gerontology as a field of study).

Given its significance, tracing the story of aging in the United States over
the course of this era reveals key insights that add to our understanding of
American culture. One of the key points here is that the idea and reality of
aging have contradicted prevailing social values, attitudes, and beliefs, a phenomenon that has largely disenfranchised and marginalized older people
from the rest of the population. One could reasonably conclude that the
aging of the largest generation in U.S. history would have significantly altered
American values over the past half century, but this simply hasn't happened.
Our ageist society has deep roots, going back decades to produce what is
perhaps the most youth-oriented culture in history. On the cusp of old age,
baby boomers like myself are now increasingly the target of ageism (thinking
or believing in a negative manner about the process of becoming old or about
old people), a likely byproduct of a culture in which getting older has little or
no positive value.[1]

More than that, I suggest, there is currently no useful narrative of aging in
American culture, leaving a large social vacuum as our population becomes
older. Older people "find themselves with no mythology to support their
presence, no place—figurative or otherwise—for themselves in the culture,"
the spiritual teacher Ram Dass wrote in his 2000 book *Still Here*.[2] The absence of a clear definition of aging is reflected by our difficulty in arriving at
an acceptable label for those whom I call older (versus old) people. The once
popular term "elderly" is no longer considered appropriate for many in their
seventies and eighties today, and even "seniors" and "senior citizens" (the latter coined during LBJ's Great Society programs that promoted the first Older
Americans Act) carry connotations of dependence and cantankerousness.
Both "older adults" and "mature adults" have recently increased in usage, especially among academics, but to me each sounds more like a movie rating
than a group of people. "Geezers" (a term coined in the 1880s) has also gained
some currency in recent years, but some are pushing for more politically correct terms, such as "seasoned citizens," "wellderly," and "superadults."

Many of the problems associated with aging can be seen as rooted in a
lack of knowledge about the experience. It is fair to say that we simply do not
know how to age, as we are never provided with the informational tools to
gain any kind of fluency in the process. There are now many books devoted
to aging "gracefully," but that body of work is overwhelmed by the plethora of

resources advising individuals on how to stop or slow the process. Without any real "story" to aging, except as something to be delayed as long as possible, all kinds of antiaging therapies have flourished, further denaturalizing the perfectly natural act of getting older. Much of this is the boomer generation's own fault, as this cohort has largely failed to turn the idea of aging into a relevant and meaningful part of life. Rather, boomers have clung desperately onto their youth, an ultimately futile pursuit that does not bode well as they rush headlong into their senior years.

Marketers and the media have each encouraged the idea that aging does not and should not have to happen, further entrenching the peculiar idea that getting older should be avoided at all costs. My local PBS station frequently airs antiaging shows such as *Aging Backwards*, for example, whose producers promise viewers they can "reverse the aging process and look nineteen years younger in thirty minutes a day." Olay, the maker of skin care products, urges consumers to look "ageless," an appeal that reflects our general antipathy toward getting older. Despite their popular appeal, "aging backwards" and "agelessness" are, of course, absurd concepts that have absolutely no foundation in how the human body or any other living organism works. Those who yearn to reverse the aging process are attempting to negate a fundamental part of life that every human in history has experienced. "Antiaging" is, quite simply, antihuman, making any and all efforts to achieve such a thing contrary to the basic mechanism of life as we know it. More people should embrace the idea that aging is a natural part of life, versus trying to turn the clock back. Even if it were possible, achieving antiaging would result in myriad truly horrific scenarios, one more reason we should not just accept but welcome the fact that our bodies get older.

Women especially have been urged to try to evade aging, a reflection of our youth-obsessed society that places so much emphasis on appearance. "Such evasion comes at considerable social, material, and existential cost," argues bioethicist Martha Holstein in her 2015 book *Women in Late Life* as she considers the all-too-common sight of old (and usually wealthy) women in young-looking bodies. A leading force in the field of aging for decades, Holstein can understand why many women pursue such strategies, however. "Women face particular difficulties that derive from the intersection of age and gender across their life spans," she writes, with a host of economic, physical, caregiving, and health-related inequalities in play.[3]

For both women and men, the problematic subject of aging can be seen as a natural result of our devaluation of older people and our inability or refusal to confront the reality of disappearing youth. The first two acts of our lives are sharply defined (growing up and getting educated in the first act, working and raising a family in the second), but what should we do in the third act of our lives? Continue to work as long as we can? Play as much as possible as a reward for our hard work? Spend time with grandkids or travel? Give back to society in some way or leave some kind of legacy? The answer is not at all clear, and, what is worse, few people are even asking the question. Some have argued that boomers will pursue a path of "unretirement" in their senior years, but there is little evidence to suggest such an option is realistic.

The need or desire for baby boomers to work into their senior years is further complicated by blatant, although hardly ever mentioned or acknowledged, ageism in many, if not most, American companies. If anything, one would expect people of different ages to be eagerly welcomed into organizations as an expression of diversity—a prime initiative of human resource departments. Discrimination against older people in the workplace is commonplace (and illegal), however, a product of our deeply embedded aversion to people considered past their prime. "It would be awkward and embarrassing to have an older person work for me," younger friends of mine have explained in my attempt to understand the underlying reasons for ageism in the workplace. True, perhaps, but white people got used to working alongside black people and men alongside women, making age the only remaining demographic criterion in which it is acceptable to discriminate (often in the name of something like "overqualification"). Imagine the legal and social consequences if millions of American employees casually mentioned their discomfort in having to supervise or work for an African American, woman, Latino, or gay or disabled person! A huge class action suit would result if the same kind of bias being shown by corporate America toward older people was based on a job applicant's gender, race, or other biological attribute, something a clever lawyer might want to think about.

All expressions of ageism are the natural result of aging being seen in American culture as a state of decline, the downward side of the curve of life. Despite laudable attempts by AARP and some "pro-aging" advocates, the years following the age of fifty or perhaps sixty are commonly considered a kind of existential purgatory between the end of one's active life and death. Older people are generally deemed weaker, less attractive versions of their younger selves, a terrible and simply untrue expression of identity. It is easy to see how seniors are often viewed as little more than slow-walking, bad-driving, hard-of-hearing, *Matlock*-watching citizens. (Studies show that ageism and negative attitudes toward older people are present in young children, and these feelings are difficult to change by the time they become tweens.)[4] Hollywood has been especially unfriendly toward older people, either portraying them as comic foils or ignoring them completely. This attitude has reinforced cultural stereotypes related to aging and has lowered older people's own sense of self-worth. Without a clear appreciation for what aging is and how it could be something to embrace rather than deny or ridicule, we may be headed toward a social crisis during the next few decades. Aging should be viewed in positive terms, and older people should be considered valuable parts of society. I urge fellow baby boomers to start telling that story while we still have the chance.

There is a rich and abundant literature devoted to aging in the United States, of which space here allows only a cursory review. While leading figures in the field of gerontology may have tended to ignore its cultural dimensions, they were instrumental in forging a body of work that helps to theoretically frame this study. The legacy of Matilda White Riley is an especially important one, as she perhaps more than anyone else understood the value of bringing an interdisciplinary perspective to the field. From the late 1960s until her death in 2004, Riley, often in conjunction with her colleague and husband, Jack Riley, "presented a compelling vision of the need for other disciplines to consider the role of social forces in shaping both aging as an individual, lifelong process and age as a feature of culture and social systems," as Dale Dannefer, Peter Uhlenberg, Anne Foner, and Ronald P. Abeles expressed it soon after her death. Gerontologists from many disciplinary backgrounds were influenced by her work, something all the more remarkable given the fact that she did not begin to study aging until her mid-fifties.[5]

It is also difficult to overestimate the contribution of physician and gerontologist Robert Butler to our understanding of aging in America. Butler, who began his career in the 1950s and died in 2013, was the founding director of the National Institute on Aging (NIA), where he made Alzheimer's disease a primary area of research. He was also the first chair of a geriatrics department at an American teaching hospital (Mount Sinai in New York City). He coined the term "ageism" after observing the lack of respect shown to the elderly and their conditions in medical schools, a theme that heavily informed his 1975 book *Why Survive? Being Old in America.* In 1963, he published a paper entitled "The Life Review: An Interpretation of Reminiscence in the Aged," which, without exaggeration, redirected the trajectory of gerontology in this country. Via a "life review," elderly people were offered the rare opportunity to look back on their personal past and see their "life course" in a larger context. Gerontologists found that such "memory work" proved to be a beneficial psychological process offering significant therapeutic value, so much so that mental health experts and social workers adopted the approach in their own practices. It is easy to see how conceiving of one's life in narrative terms with a beginning, middle, and end rather than as a more or less random series of events can help an older person make sense of his or her time on the planet, something that Butler keenly recognized. He was a "visionary of healthy aging," wrote historian W. Andrew Achenbaum in his fine biography of the man, devoting his own life to improving those of older adults.[6]

Peter Laslett, an English historian, also contributed greatly to the field after he retired from teaching in the early 1980s. Although he devoted much of his career to British political history, Laslett turned his attention to aging later in his own life. His concept of the Third Age and the Fourth Age, as outlined in his 1989 book *A Fresh Map of Life*, is as relevant and useful as ever. As his model makes clear, it is important to make a distinction between older people, as there is great variation within the population based on individuals' respective mental and physical health. Laslett posited that the Third Age is typically one of activity and fulfillment, while the Fourth Age is one of dependency and frailty, a major difference in terms of viewing the concept of aging.[7]

Laslett's supposition speaks directly to the cultural dynamics of aging in the United States today. Americans are inclined to lump all older people together into one group, just one example of how aging is often overgeneralized, misunderstood, and misinterpreted in contemporary society. As Laslett's theory implies, it is important to distinguish Fourth Agers from baby boomers, as the latter have substantially different health care and economic needs than the former. Likewise, psychologist Bernice Neugarten (a "giant" in the field in her own right) believed there was a pyramid of aging composed of the "young-old, old-old, and oldest old" that also offers a constructive way to segment the population.[8] Finally, in their *Rethinking Old Age*, British sociologists Paul Higgs and Chris Gilleard echoed Laslett's idea of a Fourth Age while emphasizing its serious social consequences, something the present book also attempts to achieve.[9]

While this work is a cultural history of aging in the United States, it is impossible to ignore the universality and timelessness of the subject. Many of the great minds of their day offered key insights regarding aging that are still relevant, ranging from Cicero's view of getting older as a natural part of life to Francis Bacon's dream of eliminating disease and perhaps even death. In his *Aging in World History*, David G. Troyansky offered a whirlwind tour of aging through time and space, beginning with how hunters and gatherers understood getting older, then moving to the concept of old age in classical civilizations and to the role of later life in the Middle Ages and during the Renaissance. Troyansky traces how the modern concept of aging emerged in Europe and North America, leading to its creation as a social problem in the nineteenth and early twentieth centuries. Learning how a cross-section of civilizations over thousands of years have interpreted getting older, not to mention the wisdom of the likes of Aristotle, Socrates, Plato, and Shakespeare, is not only fascinating but has the unexpected effect of making those encroaching physical signs of aging a bit less vexing for a middle-aged reader.[10]

A brief overview of aging in the United States from the beginnings of the country through the post–World War II era does much to show how we got to what today is arguably a troubling situation. We now take our youth-oriented culture as a given, but this was not always the case. From the seventeenth through the early nineteenth centuries in America, people who lived a long life were venerated, their advanced age seen as divinely ordained. "Old age was highly respected in early America, perhaps in part because it was comparatively rare," wrote David Hackett Fischer in his *Getting Old in America*, with just 20 percent of the population living to be seventy years old in 1790. This began to change soon after the American Revolution, however, as the first Americans to be born in the new country distinguished themselves from those who had immigrated to the colonies. By the turn of the nineteenth century Americans no longer exalted old people as their parents and grandparents had, a major shift in the social dynamics of age. "The authority of age began to be undermined, and at the same time the direction of age bias began to be reversed," Fischer continued. The nation's core values of democracy and independence had much to do with this leveling of a social hierarchy based on age, with economic class now the primary means of differentiation among Americans.[11]

Through the nineteenth century, older Americans continued to lose social status as the cult of youth gained traction. "After the Civil War, new scientific and economic data and theories gradually undermined the comparatively favorable assessments of the aged's worth," wrote Achenbaum in *Old Age in the New Land*. Oldness in all forms was condemned in an increasingly modern society, and old people were considered a drag on the noble pursuit of progress. More people were living longer, making old age less special than it had been a century earlier. The heroes of the nineteenth century also tended to be young men filled with determination and energy, whether they were conquering the frontier, herding cattle, discovering gold, or fighting wars. Against this backdrop, it is not surprising that old age homes became popular, a way to segregate people believed to be no longer capable of contributing to society. Forced retirement also became common in many occupations in the late part of the century, a reflection of Americans' negative attitudes toward older people.[12]

The "demotion" of older Americans became institutionalized in the twentieth century through a number of powerful forces that led to viewing older people these past hundred years or so primarily as a social problem. Gerontology emerged as a professional field about the time of World War I, with those involved in it dedicated to help solve the perceived challenges of the elderly.[13] With older people generally no longer welcome in the workplace, the idea of providing pensions for them gained acceptance. At the same time, the average life span continued to increase, meaning there would be more years of retirement and more money required to pay old folks' living expenses. The notion of saving for one's later years had not yet caught on, and pension plans for both company employees and government workers remained rare. This changed between the world wars, however, as labor leaders and politicians led the way to provide support for older Americans, culminating in the Social Security Act of 1935.[14]

In his 1991 book *The New Aging*, Fernando Torres-Gil of UCLA located the 1930s as the time in which attitudes toward older people began to become more negative than positive. Wisdom, and the simple act of exceeding longevity expectations, lost considerable worth during this decade, he argued, with a new kind of appreciation for values associated with youth. The 1920s had been a golden era for youth culture, of course, and the economic pressures of the Depression may have served to reward those exhibiting vitality and forward thinking. At the same time, older people were becoming increasingly defined as a segment of the population who were economically dependent on the government, a natural result of FDR's New Deal policies, particularly the Social Security Act. Federally subsidized benefits were wonderful for many retirees, but they no doubt played a key role in creating the image of older Americans as unproductive people and a costly drain on society.[15]

Aging became increasingly defined within the context of science and medicine after World War II, deepening the perception that getting old was not unlike contracting a disease, or at least warranting a well-deserved rest after one's vital and productive years. The founding of AARP in 1958 was an important milestone in the history of aging in America, a result of the emergence of what was then considered a new life stage. "Retirement" was a reaction to what was commonly seen as the major social problem of older people in mid-century America, transforming what A. Barry Rand, current CEO of the organization, describes as a "'life in purgatory' to a much desired destination."[16] While the creation of AARP was certainly a positive development from many respects, it could be argued that it also helped to brand older people as less than fully contributing members of society and more of a liability than an asset to the country.

During the postwar era, Americans who were aged sixty-five or more increasingly became seen as a kind of special interest group separate from the rest of the population because of their "idleness" and dependence on government support. In his address to the White House Conference on Aging in 1961 (the first of a handful of such events held once a decade), Rabbi Abraham Joshua Heschel astutely captured the dilemma facing older Americans. In a society singing the praises of capitalism, he argued, the lives of those who were no longer working were considered meaningless, the reason why older people were often trivialized and belittled. "The moment the machine [for the making and spending of money] is out of order and beyond repair, one begins to feel like a ghost without a sense of reality," he told the gathered audience, with retirement encouraging people to live "a pickled existence, preserved in brine with spices." Despite the pleasures to be had in retirement, a life of leisure was seen as a wasted one in postwar America, contrary to the principles of free enterprise and upward mobility that so defined the times.[17] That same year, Elaine Cumming and William E. Henry published *Growing Old*, which reinforced the idea that older people were no longer relevant. In fact, separating the elderly from the rest of society was mutually beneficial, according to their "disengagement theory," making retirement a convenient mechanism to make them out of sight and mind.[18] Some scholars, notably Robert Havighurst and Bernice Neugarten at the University of Chicago, strongly argued otherwise, however, maintaining that personality was a significantly more important variable in relative life satisfaction than level of engagement was.[19]

Following the conference hosted by JFK, organizations dedicated to the interests of older people lobbied for more federal funding, leading to the Older Americans Act of 1965 under LBJ. Medicare and Medicaid programs began that same year, expanding the field of geriatric medicine and formalizing the aging "industry" that we have today. While the rise of gerontology and the various social policies put into place over the past one hundred years have unquestionably benefited older people financially and in terms of longevity, the deal that was made can be seen as a devil's bargain. Both geriatric medicine (the treatment and prevention of disease in older persons) and gerontology (the study of the process of aging) helped to instill a negative view of older Americans by focusing on the problems of aging, transforming them into a group seen as requiring special care.[20] "In our [twentieth] century, vastly improved medical and economic conditions for older people have been accompanied by cultural disenfranchisement," wrote Thomas R. Cole in *The Journey of Life*, defining this marginalization as "a loss of meaning and vital social roles." Since World War I, the later years of many if not most Americans have been "impoverished," Cole believed, with an inverse relationship between the quantity and quality of the final third of life. Over time, old age became detached from the former, purposeful part of life, an epilogue to the main story.[21]

Today, society generally views aging as a looming, sinister presence, threatening to bankrupt the national economy due to the anticipated health care costs of elderly baby boomers, and/or it spawns a generational war over how tax money should be spent. Their money, power, and influence notwithstanding, boomers are beginning to be considered unwanted guests as younger generations squeeze them out of the workplace and view them as socially over the hill. On an individual level, aging is typically ignored, with the prospect of physical and cognitive decline too painful to consider in our youth-obsessed culture. This book attempts to show how and why we got to this place, picking up the story in the mid-1960s when our current narrative of aging can be said to have begun.

# 1

## Old in the Country of the Young

America today faces a great paradox: It is an aging
nation which worships the culture, values, and
appearance of youth.
                              —American Catholic Bishops, 1976

I
n August 1976, just a month or so after the nation celebrated its bicentennial, the American Catholic bishops released a statement that revealed a
key insight into one of the country's most important issues. Rather than
view aging as "an achievement and a natural stage of life with its own merits,
wisdom, and beauty," the religious organization's statement read, Americans
preferred to look to the carefree lifestyle and rebellious ways of young people
as inspiration. "Our culture appears to be unhappy and uncomfortable with
old age," said Patrick Cardinal O'Boyle, a retired bishop from Washington,
D.C., noting that negative attitudes toward anyone who was not young had
intensified over the past decade.[1]

This sentiment, perhaps best captured by the popular counterculture
phrase "Don't trust anyone over thirty," was reflective of the country's rather
recent aversion to aging. To be "old in the country of the young," as *Time*
magazine expressed it in 1970, was to feel like an outsider in one's own home,
an ironic state of affairs given that older citizens had of course been Americans longer than younger ones. Born around the turn of the twentieth century, the nation's current crop of seniors had served on the front lines of the
Depression and World War II, even more reason why their treatment could
be considered unfair and even immoral. From a social sense, at least, the so-
called generation gap was decidedly in favor of those on the younger side of

the fence; those on the older side were typically cast as not in tune with where the country was and was heading. People over sixty-five (the mandatory retirement age at the time) were deemed as having little or nothing to contribute, making many Americans loathe the very idea of aging. (The famous line "Hope I die before I get old" from the 1965 song "My Generation" by the Who could be considered an anthem of the times.) Over the course of the late 1960s and 1970s, aging began to be seen as nothing less than an enemy, something that should be kept at bay or, if at all possible, be wiped out entirely.

Against this backdrop, it was not surprising that science launched a full-scale attack on aging, with some of the country's best and brightest dedicating themselves to making old age a thing of the past. Defenders of America's increasing older population pointed out, however, that aging was a social problem rather than a biological one, and they urged seniors to fight for equal rights just as other marginalized groups had recently done with considerable success. Politicians of the time, including President Nixon, recognized the clout older citizens held and appealed to them as an important voting bloc. While legislation to help seniors live better lives would certainly be helpful, it was proving to be difficult or impossible to change Americans' feelings toward aging in general. Only the gradual recognition that a large older population would in the future become a major economic problem seemed to capture people's attention during this era, as aging in America took a historic turn for the worse.

## The Curious Property

Consistent with the thinking in the mid-1960s that social ills could be eliminated if Americans set their collective mind to it, many concluded that the best way to solve the problem of aging was simply to make it go away. Scientists enlisted in the cause of aging in considerable numbers, seeing it as a frontier that could first be discovered and then conquered. In 1966, for example, the president of the American Chemical Society challenged fellow scientists to join him in what promised to be one of humankind's greatest pursuits. A "fountain of youth" was just waiting to be discovered, William J. Sparks announced at the annual meeting of the society, with chemistry the means by which to realize this long-sought dream. More specifically, he explained, it was the kind of chemistry that created plastics and synthetic rubber, firmly convinced that human aging was caused by molecules not unlike those manipulated to produce these scientific wonders. While admittedly a controversial idea, Sparks's molecular theory was representative of the sort of bold approach that needed to be taken if science was to achieve the very real possibility of humans living much longer and much healthier lives. The study of aging as a whole was vastly underfunded and underresearched, he and others at the conference agreed, urging the federal government to devote much more money and effort to solve what was perhaps our most enigmatic puzzle.[2]

Unless or until the United States Government launched a full-scale war against aging, however, it was up to individual scientists, most of them industry personnel or university professors, to try to crack the code of how and why humans became older. Extending the human life span was tricky enough, but some researchers in the field were interested only in lengthening the period of life that preceded old age, a view the fountain of youth had engrained in the popular imagination. The Human Genome Project was decades in the future, but already a few scientists theorized that more knowledge about the structure of DNA could lead to the ability to manipulate cellular processes, including those having to do with aging. Others were focused on environmental factors that perhaps caused the body to eventually become, in layman's terms, allergic to itself. What we interpret as the signs of old age were actually the physical wreckage left by antibodies that had attacked their host, researchers such as Roy L. Walford of the UCLA Medical School suggested. Preventing, reducing the number of, or repairing these mutations was the means by which to prolong the prime of life, Walford held, one of a growing number of scientists investing a good deal of time in unraveling this especially complex riddle.[3]

With Cold War rhetoric lingering in the mid-1960s, it was not surprising to hear antiaging efforts expressed in aggressive, sometimes militaristic language. Also in 1966, Bernard L. Strehler of the National Institutes of Health (NIH) gave a talk at the New York Academy of Sciences called "The New Medical and Scientific Attack Against Aging and Death"—a fair representation of the kind of approach that was seen as needed to achieve victory. "An understanding of the biology of aging is within reach of this generation," Strehler told the scientists, quite typical of the self-assured, rather audacious thinking of the time, where anything seemed possible. Breaking the current life span barrier of seventy to eighty years could be seen as analogous to other contemporary great scientific and technological feats like landing on the moon or harnessing atomic energy, with two things—good brains and loads of money—required to get it done.[4] At the very least, many scientists agreed, the human life span could and should be extended by a few decades. Scientists at the California Medical Association, for instance, believed that we all should be living a hundred to 120 years, barring the onset of a rare disease or an accident that prematurely cut life short.[5]

Even if it was almost entirely speculation at this point, such theories seemed feasible and promising to journalists covering the scientific beat. "It is not inconceivable that scientists someday may be able to control human life to the extent that old age and senility are all but eliminated," wrote Harry Nelson, medical editor of the *Los Angeles Times* in 1966. Nelson envisioned a normal period of childhood followed by "a 60- to 70-year-long plateau of maturity, health, and high performance," cutting out the two decades or so of old age. (He did not explain how and why death would suddenly occur after so many years of wellness.)[6] Other scientists were meanwhile focusing on a single aspect of physical aging, hoping that it would lead to an understanding of the overall process. Arthur Veis of Northwestern University's medical school was intent on discovering the cause of skin wrinkles, for example, thinking that wrinkles could possibly point the way to why the human body chose to get older in general.[7] Scientists were frankly perplexed by the whole notion of aging because it contradicted what was widely recognized as nature's most powerful instinct: to survive.

While individual scientists at corporations and universities pursued their particular line of research, the NIH, an agency of the federal government, stepped up its efforts to combat aging. In 1968 (nearly three decades after Nathan Shock, a pioneering gerontologist, began his intramural lab in the Baltimore City Hospitals), the NIH swung open the doors of its brand new Gerontology Research Center in Baltimore, the largest federal facility for aging research in the United States. The goal of the center, which had been founded by Shock and others in 1941, was to uncover "the mysteries and problems of aging that have perplexed our philosophers and scientists over the years," said William J. Cohen, secretary of the Department of Health, Education, and Welfare (HEW), who dedicated the new building.[8] Millions of dollars of taxpayers' money were going toward winning the war against aging, locating the initiative within the public arena. Indeed, the dream of solving the aging problem went far beyond the halls of science, crossing over into popular culture in the late 1960s. A 1968 episode of *The 21st Century*, a television series hosted by Walter Cronkite, for example, explored the phenomenon of aging and the possibilities of prolonging human life. "Can we live to be one hundred?" Cronkite asked, visiting the NIH and the Institute of

Gerontology in Kiev in the Soviet Union, to try to determine the likelihood of most of us reaching the century mark. (Cronkite himself would make it to ninety-two.) Organ banks would be one way to keep people alive longer, the scientists told Cronkite, as would germ-free "life islands." By enclosing hospital beds in plastic packages, patients would be protected from infection, a not uncommon cause of death.[9]

Saving lives through such interventions would of course extend longevity but did not directly address the actual aging process. Slowing or stopping the body from getting older in a biological sense required something truly miraculous, but that did not prevent scientists and physicians from trying to make such an amazing discovery. Like today, many medications designed to treat a particular condition were considered to also possibly have antiaging properties, each one (briefly) entertained as perhaps the much sought after wonder drug. One such drug was sodium warfarin, which was commonly used to keep blood from clotting in veins and arteries. After prescribing that medication to a number of older people, a physician, Arthur G. Walsh, noticed that his patients' mental and physical conditions improved, cause enough for him to report his findings in a 1969 issue of the *Journal of the American Geriatrics Society*. The narrowing and hardening of arteries in the brain played a significant part in the aging process, Walsh proposed, meaning anticlotting drugs like sodium warfarin might be a way to dramatically extend the human life span.[10] Although in hindsight this could be seen as much too big of a leap to make based on the limited evidence, it was a prime example of the race to find a cure for aging muddying scientists' normally clear thinking.

With aging now a highly visible issue, notable scientists from around the world made their voices heard on the subject. One of the leading advocates of antiaging in the late 1960s and early 1970s was the British scientist and physician Alex Comfort. Just a year before he published his hugely successful *Joy of Sex*, in fact, Comfort was considered in academic circles quite the expert on aging. While he often served as a much needed voice of reason, Comfort did firmly believe that scientists would soon figure out a way to extend the human life span by another fifteen years. (He had actually been researching and writing about aging since the early 1950s and was the author of a pair of books on the subject, *Aging: The Biology of Senescence* and *The Process of Aging*.) Over the past century, he explained in a 1971 issue of the scientific journal *Impact of Science on Society*, great strides had been made in preventing premature death. Little or no progress had been made in getting already old people to live longer; this was the next logical frontier. The "clock" of aging needed to be first found and then adjusted, Comfort proposed, with scientists' determination to do just that increasing over the previous few decades. Extending the lives of mice through calorie reduction had already been achieved, he pointed out, making this approach the sensible one to explore with humans. Science would solve the aging problem before it found a cure for cancer, he felt, although preventing aging could very well lead to preventing cancer.[11]

While as knowledgeable as anyone about aging, Comfort freely admitted how little scientists like him really knew about the process. Aging was "the curious property that makes us more likely to die the older we become," he wrote in 1972, as vague a definition as one could put forth. Eliminating some causes of premature death was a piece of cake compared to extending the human life span beyond a hundred years old, he explained; it was becoming increasingly apparent that science had hit a kind of biological wall that prevented this next leap. But space travel too had until recently been just a farfetched dream, a good way of justifying all the effort that was going into what seemed like the stuff of science fiction. The most challenging piece of the puzzle would be to increase the average human life span without lengthening the period of old age, something that even the most ardent of antiagers admitted would test the limits of science. Modern medicine (and, even more so, public health measures) had already added a few decades of old age to the human life span, and the consensus was that tacking on a few more decades was a very unpalatable prospect indeed.[12]

## A Bad Press

The aggressive effort to discover the cause of aging and then try to delay it as much as possible was directly correlated with the rise of youth culture in the late 1960s. Younger people in America gained social status at the expense of older people during the counterculture years, a fact that did not go unnoticed by leading gerontologists of the time. "How much youth fixation can a culture allow?" asked Bernard Coughlin in 1969, his question perhaps influenced by the media frenzy surrounding the recent Woodstock Festival. Coughlin, dean of the St. Louis University School of Social Services, was attending the International Congress of Gerontology, a group of researchers from forty nations who studied some aspect of aging. (Practicing gerontologists had little interest in the scientific effort to extend the human life span; rather, they focused on improving the lives of people in their later years.) Some kind of "generation gap" could be expected in any society, Coughlin noted, but the current one in the United States was excessive. Youth was being overvalued and age undervalued, he felt, keenly recognizing the historic shift that was taking place. Another attendee at the conference, Walter Walker of the University of Chicago, argued that older people in the country now made up a "minority group," their social status analogous to that of people of color and other oppressed groups. Unlike African Americans, women, and even farmworkers, however, seniors had no movement to support their civil rights, reason enough for Walker to urge them to organize in order to gain political and economic power.[13]

Walker's wishes were answered the following year in Philadelphia with the formation of the Gray Panthers. The mission of the organization (whose name was inspired by the militant Black Panthers) was to dispel stereotypes about older people and to influence legislature affecting them. There were about eight thousand Gray Panthers in the United States by the nation's Bicentennial, each member committed to fighting prejudice against older people and to bringing attention to their cause. Activism centered around the "three H's"—health, hunger, and housing—with much of it directed at the Ford administration's budget cutting as it dismantled a good part of LBJ's Great Society programs.[14] The so-called medi-gap in health insurance was a particular problem, with Medicare covering fewer medical expenses than when the program began a decade earlier.

The marginalization of older Americans could be seen as the result of many different factors. One was the medical approach of treating aging as if it were a disease, popularizing the idea that all older people were somehow chronically ill. Such a view helped to turn age into a social problem, and served as a wellspring of negative attitudes toward anyone who was not categorized as young (again, typically less than thirty years old). Carl Eisdorfer, a psychiatrist at Duke University, which had a major gerontology center as part of its medical school, believed older people were generally seen as an ecological problem, like no deposit, no return bottles, accounting for why they were considered disposable. Instead, he proposed in 1971, the twenty million Americans over sixty-five could and should be "recycled" rather than simply be discarded. Eisdorfer went further, arguing that the nation's universities should reinvent themselves from being degree-granting institutions for young people into resources offering lifelong education for all (still a good idea, I believe). Contrary to popular belief, research showed that older people were capable of learning new things, and did not deserve to be thrown onto a kind of trash heap as soon as they reached retirement age.[15]

Some textbooks included charts indicating how intelligence declined with age, however—which was completely wrong information given recent studies showing otherwise.[16]

Indeed, a study published in *Psychology Today* that same year did suggest that older folks could be recycled. Two collaborating psychologists, Robert Kastenbaum of Wayne State and Bernice Neugarten, now at the University of Southern California, studied two thousand people between seventy and seventy-nine years old and found that many of the widely held beliefs about this age group were untrue. The majority of these septuagenarians were mentally competent, adaptable, and active, Kastenbaum and Neugarten reported, not at all the senile oldsters living lives of quiet desperation that many would have expected. Most surprising, perhaps, many of those in the study were sexually active, even more so than when they were younger. (Retirement communities and nursing homes were and remain ideal settings for residents to hook up. It was not unusual, however, for residents in nursing homes to be scolded for making sexual advances toward someone of a similar age; the younger employees considered it unnatural or, perhaps, potentially harmful.) Kastenbaum and Neugarten's group also tended to be quite liberal in their views, dispelling the myth about the crotchety, prudish senior firmly set in his or her ways. Besides offering valuable, counterintuitive insights into an underresearched segment of the population, the study helped to illustrate the cultural bias against aging in this country. Americans in general "[have] an irrational fear of aging and, as a result, maintain a psychological distance from older persons," the coauthors perceptively wrote; their findings showed that seventysomethings were a lot more like the rest of us than we liked to believe.[17]

Aging as a whole was often viewed in the United States as something that happened to other people when, of course, it was, like birth and death, a universal experience. The aversion to, even hatred of, older persons was all the more peculiar given that everyone would become one of them if he or she lived long enough. (The same could not be true of racism or sexism, as people did not change color or, with few exceptions, gender.)[18] Other ways in which Americans distanced themselves from aging was to think that individuals turned into different people when they got older, or that the process took place quite suddenly. A person was young and then boom! he or she was old, this notion went, a completely inaccurate reading of how humans actually (that is, gradually) age. (Also, from a biological standpoint, each body part aged at a different rate, depending on the individual, meaning there was no single physical process of aging.) Grouping people into an anonymous mass of "old people" was equally silly but not uncommon; seventy-year-olds were just as individualistic as thirty-year-olds (if not more so given they had had more time to develop their unique personalities). Finally, older people did not remain in a constant state of "oldness" but continually changed, another fact that anyone younger than middle-aged might find hard to believe or accept.[19]

No one agreed more with such thinking than Sharon R. Curtin, who was downright angry about the way older people were treated in America. In her 1972 book *Nobody Ever Died of Old Age*, which was based on an article she had written for the *Atlantic*, Curtin looked at how seniors were deliberately separated from the rest of the "productive" population. Whether placed in nursing homes, retirement communities, or what were called at the time "geriatric wards," she argued, those in the third act of their lives were now regarded as outsiders. Things were not much better for those simply left on their own to collect their meager Social Security checks and to fend for themselves as best they could. "We live in a culture that worships youth and denigrates the aged, no matter how honorable their past contributions," Curtin wrote, like others labeling this a shameful aspect of American society. As she pointed out, however, this was a relatively recent phenomenon, with grandparents much more likely to be welcomed into an extended family setting up to the 1950s. Even spinster aunts could often be found living with their families before the Second World War, a situation that would be viewed as quite odd in the 1970s, when households had shrunk considerably. With no responsibilities assigned to them or expectations of them, older relatives were now often seen as burdens to their families, a sad situation for all parties. Although things were rapidly changing in Europe and Asia, grandparents were still typically welcomed into the homes of younger relatives in foreign countries, a reflection of the greater recognition and respect given to older generations.[20]

Although the discarding of a large segment of the population was very real, older Americans could be said to have had, in public relations terms, an image problem. Eric Pfeiffer, another Duke psychiatrist, believed aging in the United States had received a bad press, meaning the media had been unfairly critical of older people. Aging was popularly perceived as a "hopeless, unremitting downward drift, an image of despair, deprivation, disease, poverty, and social isolation," he claimed, not at all reflective of reality. Instead, he suggested, Americans should look to the many "successful agers" for inspiration, people like comedian Jack Benny (aged eighty in 1974), Supreme Court Justice William O. Douglas (aged seventy-five), and Senator Strom Thurmond (aged seventy-one). Thousands of ordinary people were living similarly active and productive lives, he maintained, not at all the impression one would get from reading newspapers and magazines or watching television.[21]

Arthur Flemming no doubt thought similarly when he told a congressional subcommittee a few years later that forcing people sixty-five years old to retire was a clear act of discrimination. "We should never deny anyone the opportunity for employment simply because of age," the seventy-one-year-old head of the U.S. Commission on the Aging declared, comparing mandatory retirement to illegal biases of sexism and racism. (Despite new legal statutes, it should be noted, there are more litigations today based on the Age Discrimination in Employment Act of 1967 than on women's charges of employment inequities.) Making people stop working when they reached a certain age was reflective of America's attitude that older folks should be placed "on the shelf," Flemming stated, a view that often resulted in real psychological damage to new retirees. (A full quarter of suicides in the nation were among those sixty-five and older, in fact.) Flemming, who had served as the secretary of HEW from 1958 to 1961 during the Eisenhower administration, linked this high number to the "traumatic experience" of mandatory retirement. Almost one-third of retired people over sixty-five would indeed prefer to be working, according to a 1974 Harris poll, more evidence that current labor policies were out of sync with the wishes of a sizable percentage of older Americans.[22]

Flemming's vigorous appeal appeared to work. Following the passage of the Age Discrimination in Employment Act, Congress lifted the mandatory retirement age to seventy in 1978. (Congress's decision to bump up the age by five years was not completely altruistic, as the move lessened Social Security payouts, at least in the short term.) Moving back the mandatory retirement age made even more sense given that many older people had to continue working beyond age sixty-five whether they wanted to or not. By the late 1970s, galloping inflation had effectively shrunk the value of savings and pensions, forcing those who had planned to retire to keep their jobs for a few more years. Inflation was also making older people rely more on Social Security as their personal nest egg lost value, increasing the burden on younger people to support them. Experts were forecasting that the number of Americans aged sixty-five or older would balloon from 18 percent to 30 percent of the nation's adult population by 2025, early signs that the baby boomer age wave could perhaps crash the economic system. Older people continuing to work was one of the best things that could happen to the economy, in fact, making federal policies encouraging early retirement contrary to the nation's long-term interests.[23]

## A Revolution in Our Thinking

Lessening discrimination against older people in the workplace through legislation can be seen as one outcome from a process that had begun in earnest about a decade and half earlier. History was made on April 1, 1965, when, by a vote of 394 to 1, the House passed a bill to create an administration on aging within HEW. The bill still had to go to the Senate for approval, but with the nearly unanimous vote (the sole nay was from Representative Dave Martin, a Republican from Nebraska) it seemed clear that Washington intended to improve life for those sixty-five years or older (10 percent of the population). An initial $17.5 million over two years would go toward providing retirement income, health care, housing, and job opportunities for this group of Americans; the agency would coordinate current such efforts that were scattered across many departments.[24]

With the election of Richard Nixon in 1968, however, much of the enthusiasm behind LBJ's Great Society began to seriously fade. As part of his ambitious tax-cutting measures, Nixon pared back some of the domestic programs created during the Johnson administration, including those earmarked for older citizens. Over the course of his first term, however, he frequently mentioned in speeches his commitment to improving the lives of older Americans, giving seniors hope that the federal government would direct much needed funding their way. Much excitement thus revolved round the third White House Conference on Aging as it approached in late 1971. The first such conference, initiated by President Truman, was held in 1950; the second was hosted by President Eisenhower in 1961, out of which ultimately came Medicare, Medicaid, and the Older Americans Act of 1965. The Nixon administration had previously held official conferences on hunger (1969), children (1970), and youth (1971), and it realized that much work still needed to be done regarding the nation's large and growing aging population. This conference was considered important enough for the U.S. Postal Service to issue an eight-cent stamped envelope to commemorate the event.[25]

Although critics correctly noted at the time that the administration's three previous conferences were much more talk than action, the expectations for this one were high. The goal of the conference was, in President Nixon's words, to work out a "comprehensive national policy" for older Americans, something that did not come of the first summit.[26] Some thirty-four hundred delegates would converge on Washington, D.C., in November 1971, each of them committed to pressuring the president to pass measures that would help older Americans. More than twenty million citizens were now aged sixty-five or older, obviously a large contingent whom any politician wanted to have on his or her side. Older people also consistently voted in great numbers, even more reason to try to win them over.[27] Skeptics noted that it was not a coincidence that the conference was held just as the 1972 presidential election was heating up, however, and warned seniors thinking their ship would soon come in to curb their enthusiasm.

Democrats, especially Frank Church from Idaho, were cautiously optimistic that the president's call for this conference was more than just about getting reelected. Church was chairman of the Senate Special Committee on Aging, which was an outcome of the second White House Conference on Aging. Church was a staunch defender of the rights of older Americans, and he made it clear that this third conference was an ideal opportunity to make real progress. "I think there is no country, that has the means that we do, that has done as badly in providing for the elderly as we have here in the United States," he said on the eve of the conference, calling our performance in this area "one of the greatest travesties of the contemporary American way" and "one of the most conspicuous of our failures." Church and his colleagues on the Senate Special Committee were fully aware that getting the president to agree to all their demands would be an uphill battle given his record (especially as there was at least as much interest among politicians in capturing the youth vote), reason enough for them to turn up the heat as the meeting approached.[28]

Another politician friendly to the cause of aging was Representative James A. Burke (D-MA), a member of the House Ways and Means Committee. In one speech leading up to the conference, Burke proclaimed that there was a need for "a revolution in our thinking about the elderly," just the kind of thing the delegates and seniors themselves wanted to hear. Some kind of national policy on aging was expected to result from the conference, although both the president and Congress would have to agree to whatever was presented to them. Hopes were high that a bill creating a heavily funded federal department of aging with a cabinet-level secretary would ultimately result from the conference—only this was likely to lead to the revolution Burke had in mind. If affordable health care had been the biggest outcome of the second conference, however, financial assistance was clearly the goal of the third. Many retirees lived in poverty or close to it, making money the central issue for older Americans.[29] The high inflation rate of the early 1970s was hitting anyone living on a fixed income hard, with those subsisting solely on Social Security especially vulnerable to rising prices.[30]

The president was well aware that this third White House Conference on Aging was an opportunity to repair his image when it came to federal policies related to aging. Over the course of his first term of office, Nixon had not only cut programs related to aging but also vetoed a host of bills that if passed would undoubtedly have made life better for older Americans. Making comprehensive amendments to the Older Americans Act, giving more power to Flemming within the administration, and awarding big grants to states were just a few proposals that the president had killed, earning him a much deserved reputation as no friend to seniors. This was clearly his greatest chance to remedy his standing with seniors, a smart thing to do, if only for political reasons.[31]

In words at least, Nixon acted quickly after the White House Conference on Aging, an obvious move to silence his many critics. The biggest news was that he would multiply the budget of the Administration on Aging by almost five times to $100 million, vastly improving services for the elderly should the Democrat-led Congress approve. Making Social Security benefits inflation proof was another promise he made, something that would be hugely beneficial if it too became a reality. Conference delegates were elated by the president's intentions, with virtually everything they had wished for included in Nixon's plan.[32] During the 1972 campaign, Nixon understandably continued to appeal to older voters whenever he had the opportunity to do so. In a speech to Congress in March of that year, for example, he offered a five-point strategy to bridge what he called "the generation gap between those who are over 65 and those who are younger." It was clear from his speech that he had relied heavily on Flemming to form the strategy, which focused on income and living conditions for older Americans. What was not clear was how such measures, while certainly helpful if enacted, would bring older and younger people together, making his message more campaign rhetoric than anything else.[33]

Nixon continued to mention the "generation gap" in speeches during his second term, however, seeing it as a highly charged term that made him appear to be a uniting rather than a divisive political force. "We cannot afford a generation gap which shuts out the young in this country but neither can we afford a generation gap that shuts out the old," he said in an October 1972 radio address, calling on all Americans to develop a new attitude toward aging. He was especially proud to announce that Program Find, a program his administration had launched, had so far been a success. Some three hundred thousand "isolated" older people had been "found" and were now receiving the help they were entitled to but otherwise would not get, the president claimed, an example of his commitment to those over sixty-five. Riffing on "black power"—a bit ironically given his often contentious relationship with leaders of the African American community—he proclaimed that "senior power" was a valuable resource for the country, a prime example of his efforts to hold together an increasingly fragmented nation.[34]

## The Walking Wounded

While Washington moved slowly toward passing measures designed to better the lives of older Americans after the historic White House conference in 1971, experts in some aspect of aging continued to get together to discuss what else could and should be done. The Annual Conference on Aging, which had been sponsored by the University of Michigan since 1948, was a central gathering place for gerontologists and others interested in the social and cultural dynamics of aging in America. Susan Sontag, the author and critic, made an appearance at the 1974 conference, for example, quite fitting given that this meeting was devoted to issues faced by older women. In her speech, entitled "The Double Standard of Aging," Sontag discussed the inequalities that existed between older men and older women, an expression of the vast gender bias of the time. While aging men simply met their natural fate as they got older, she argued, women were seen as facing a losing battle and were socially chastised for showing the physical signs of age. Given this view, she asked, was it surprising that many women lied about their age and did everything they could to preserve their youthful looks?[35] To Sontag's point, an increasing number of fiftyish women reaching menopause were seeking estrogen therapy in the hope that it would keep them looking and feeling young. The body stops producing estrogen during menopause, making many women (and some physicians) think that continuous, large doses would delay the effects of what was commonly called the "change of life." The research was unclear, but most doctors hesitantly provided the hormone to their patients when pressured to do so.[36]

The limits some women and men would go to try to slow the aging process were sometimes extreme. Visitors returning from Romania (and some other countries) in the late seventies were bringing in a drug called Gerovital H3 that purportedly had antiaging properties. The drug was not approved in the United States, and for good reason: controlled trials showed that it did absolutely nothing to improve the physical or mental health of patients.[37] This was not the first time Romania was believed to the source of some magical potion created for modern-day Ponce de Leóns. A dozen years earlier, a biochemist from that country cooked up a "youth cocktail" said to reverse some of the effects of aging. (The key ingredient was cysteine, an amino acid commonly used in food, pharmaceutical, and personal-care products.) A decade or so before that, another Romanian scientist was injecting people with some kind of "rejuvenation treatment," which also turned out to be a complete hoax.[38]

Of course, one did not have to smuggle in a drug from a foreign country to antiage, at least cosmetically. Plastic surgery boomed in the United States in the 1970s as Americans sought all sorts of ways to look not just more beautiful but specifically younger. Middle-aged workers, many of them men, were feeling pressure from younger employees as they rose up the corporate ladder, one more dimension of pervasive youth culture. Some men, worried about their jobs in certain hard-hit industries such as aerospace, were especially keen on smoothing out wrinkles. Wives suspecting their husbands were cheating on them with other women (and legitimately so, given the sky-rocketing divorce rate) were, meanwhile, getting tummy and bottom tucks. Plastic surgery had long been just for the wealthy, but now ordinary folks, thinking a facelift was just the thing to maintain a youthful appearance, were going under the knife. As with the prescribing of estrogen, some doctors were refusing to perform surgery because a patient only wanted to retain his or her youth, but the genie was already out of the bottle.[39]

As Sontag suggested, the seeking of medical intervention by ordinary women in order to appear younger revealed the complex relationship between aging and gender. It made perfect sense that some feminists of the 1970s, most of them older women, vigorously addressed issues of "ageism." (Robert Butler had coined the term in 1969 to describe individuals who faced discrimination and prejudice because they were considered old.) Separate from the obvious matter of injustices based on gender, women usually lived longer than men, extending the amount of time that they would be older people. The odds that a wife would eventually become a widow made getting older a different and often more difficult experience for women. Henrietta Quatrocchi, an anthropologist and gerontologist, considered many older women in America to be "the walking wounded," with no clear purpose in life after completing their primary role of domesticity. For every Eleanor Roosevelt or Golda Meir, she felt, there were millions of older women who, because of social pressure to do so, assumed an image not unlike that portrayed in the famous painting colloquially known as *Whistler's Mother.* It was up to older women themselves to stay active and defy cultural stereotypes, Quatrocchi insisted, suggesting they do things like take karate lessons rather than "do things with egg cartons."[40]

Social critics from a variety of backgrounds took a long hard look at aging in America as the subject reached a kind of critical mass in the mid-1970s. Butler's *Why Survive?* was a scathing indictment of ageism in America, detailing how older people were consistently socially excluded and routinely taken advantage of. In the spirit of the famous line from the movie *Network*, which was released the following year—"I'm mad as hell, and I'm not going to take this anymore"—Butler argued that it was up to older Americans themselves to adopt the kind of militancy that other oppressed groups had. Voter registration drives, marches, and whistle blowing were all things seniors could do to strike back against the virulent form of discrimination that was ingrained in American society.[41] A number of experts on the subject wrote chapters for the 1978 anthology *The New Old: Struggling for Decent Aging*, which served as a sort of manifesto for older Americans. Seniors were treated shamefully, the book argued; its contributors made a compelling case that ageism was the last form of segregation in the nation. As with *Why Survive?* the book also included an agenda for action, urging that older people stand up for their rights.[42]

Not surprisingly, gerontologists were working the hardest to try to dispel the myths and misconceptions that surrounded aging. "Ageism is an attitude no less destructive than racism or sexism," said Sue Smolski, a registered nurse in Connecticut who was educating other gerontologists on what was and what was not true regarding older people. First and foremost on her list was that, again, aging was not a disease, something many, including a fair share of physicians, did not understand. In fact, seniors themselves did not so much mind growing older as dreaded getting sick, illustrating the distinction.[43] It was a serious illness or injury that often triggered what was commonly considered "old age" and its various problems, many older people clarified, this too not very well understood by those considerably younger. And contrary to popular belief, most seniors did not spend their days preparing themselves for death; they were as directed toward living as anyone else.[44]

Nurses like Smolski seemed to have keen insight into the dynamics of aging, no doubt because they spent so much time with older people. Another Connecticut nurse serving as a consultant on aging felt that the scientific efforts to solve its mystery were, more than anything, a diversion from having to think about the fact that we were all getting older. The real problem with aging was our inability to accept its reality, Nancy Gustafson told a group of women in Hartford in 1977, explaining that it was more of a social than a bio-logical issue. As Curtin had described in her *Nobody Died of Old Age*, older people no longer had a recognizable role in family life, Gustafson added, a byproduct of our more disposable and mobile society. (No need for grandma to mend those pants now that a new pair could be easily and cheaply bought, especially if she lived miles away.) If productivity was the main currency of the times, which it certainly appeared to be, Gustafson observed, things did not look good for older people given the physical changes that typically took place at a certain point. This was unfortunate, since most seniors remained as psychologically fit as ever and had much to offer if given the opportunity. "Aging is life," Gustafson wisely concluded, "the integration of all our experi-ences here on Earth and with other humans."[45]

As Gustafson suggested, the mythologies surrounding seniors were not limited to physical abilities; the mental aptitude of older people was often called into question. The majority of older Americans were not institution-alized as some thought (just 5 percent, most of them over eighty years old, were in institutions in 1977, with a mere 1 percent in psychiatric hospitals), and they did not spend an inordinate time just lying in bed. Depression was fairly common among the elderly, however, a result perhaps of the losses (of friends, family, jobs, and homes) that many endured as they outlived oth-ers.[46] Oddly, however, relatively few psychiatrists took on older people as pa-tients, viewing them as "unfixable" because of their advanced age. Less than 2 percent of the psychiatrists in the Washington, D.C., area offered therapy to people more than sixty-five years old, for example, and even these were unlikely to prescribe any of the antidepressants available at the time.[47] Older people *should* be depressed, the thinking was; it was a natural state given their reduced position in life and proximity to death.

While few psychiatrists were interested in treating older people, it made perfect sense for those dabbling in the brand of pop psychology so prevalent at the time to address issues of aging. "The September of your years can be exactly what you make of it," counseled Tom Greening and Dick Hobson in their 1979 book *Instant Relief: The Encyclopedia of Self-Help*; the pair sug-gested that seniors counter their negative portrayal in the media through "positive thinking." Bombarded with representations of people like them-selves as having little value or worth, it was up to older folks to avoid seeing aging in a negative light. "With the right attitude, attention, and preparation," the two wrote, "aging can be experienced as a full and meaningful matura-tion process, like the ripening of a fine wine or a musical instrument." No longer having to raise children, climb one's way to success, or move up the social ladder offered a kind of freedom younger people did not have, they argued, making "the golden years" the ideal opportunity to develop deep self-awareness and wisdom. Most important, perhaps, older people should take responsibility for their own sense of well-being and not see themselves as victims—classic 1970s self-help talk that actually made perfect sense given the profound stereotyping of the times.[48]

While obviously not a good thing, the dismissal of older people by psychiatrists was in part a function of their training or, more accurately, lack thereof. Medical schools did not at the time provide their students with an adequate education in aging, which accounted also for some physicians' equation of old age with disease. Few if any courses in geriatrics were required at the nation's 114 medical schools, with just thirty-one of them offering elective courses in the subject. Also, older people's tendency to get sick and die was a frustrating fact of life to future physicians being taught to keep patients alive and well at all costs; this was a contributing factor to physicians often displaying a glaring insensitivity to seniors after receiving their degree. Practicing doctors were known to say to a no longer young patient with a particular health complaint things like "Well, what did you expect, you're old," not exactly what one would consider good medicine or a good bedside manner. In fact, the acquaintance many medical students had with an old person was as a corpse, hardly a good model by which to offer good health care to a very much alive septuagenarian or octogenarian.[49]

## One of Nature's Best-Kept Secrets

While medical schools did not do an adequate job teaching students about the bodies and minds of older patients, some in medicine and the sciences continued to target aging as an exciting area of inquiry and research. Corporate and academic funding committees clearly recognized that unlocking "one of nature's best-kept secrets," as the *Atlanta Constitution* described it, would be quite a feather in their organization's hat. (The financial payoff for achieving such a feat would also likely be enormous.) In 1972, for example, Morton Rothstein, a biologist at SUNY Buffalo, won a million-dollar, five-year grant from the National Institute of Child and Human Development (NICHD) to try to learn the causes of aging and, it was hoped, how to control the process. Rothstein was eager to find a cure for aging should there be one, admitting that his getting close to the age of fifty played a role in his ambitious project.

The biologist was very much in the cellular theoretical camp, and he planned to study how nematodes (small worms) aged over their brief (twenty- to forty-day) lives. Unlike humans, nematodes retain the same cells throughout life, offering a comparative analysis of aging at the molecular level that could perhaps reveal the precise reason for why all organisms get older. Rothstein's initial thinking was that "ineffective enzymes" were the culprit, these faulty molecules triggering a chemical reaction throughout the body, which led to the aging process.[50]

The startling array of theories regarding aging was in part a result of the limitations placed on scientists. Besides the ethics involved, experiments on aging in humans were less than practical because of our long life spans. An eighty-year study was obviously not feasible, as subjects could very well outlive the researchers. (Alex Comfort quipped that mice were preferable to Ph.D. students as subjects because they died much more quickly.) With studies limited to laboratory animals, little persuasive data had yet to be collected on precisely why organisms aged, making researchers look in unusual places. One promising area was progeria, the rare and tragic disease that prematurely aged infants and usually caused death in the early teenage years. Scientists investigating the process of aging believed they could learn much from children with progeria, although thankfully there were precious few cases reported. (Fewer than sixty could be found in the medical literature up to the early 1970s.) A bit more common was Werner's syndrome, which was similar in some ways to progeria, but it too did not offer many cases to study.[51]

There was a busy parade of supposed causes of aging through the 1970s, each one briefly taken quite seriously. Almost as a rule, scientists were over-eager to conclude that their particular line of research was the pot of gold everyone was searching for, perhaps in order to receive additional funding to pursue their work. Glands were often suspected of being at the heart, so to speak, of aging. In 1973, for example, a team at the University of Texas claimed that thymosin, a hormone produced by the thymus gland, was a major factor in the aging process. Blood levels of the hormone decreased dramatically as a person got older, the biochemists reported, hindering the body's immune system's ability to combat disease.[52] At the very same time, other scientists down the road in San Antonio pinpointed the prostate gland as the thing that explained the mechanics of the aging of the human body. It was the eventual inability of that gland to maintain its normal growth and development that served as the first evidence toward understanding the molecular basis of aging, a pair of researchers from the Southwest Foundation for Research and

Education crowed, not addressing how this applied to women, who do not have a prostate.[53] Meanwhile, Alexander Leaf, a Harvard internist, claimed that it was the protein amyloid that accounted for some people living so long. As some other researchers had done, Leaf traveled to remote parts of Ecuador, the Soviet Union, and Pakistan to study the relatively numerous centenarians that lived in these areas. High concentrations of amyloid were found in the century-plus locals, making him think that the mysterious substance was the main ingredient of longevity.[54]

Virtually any and every part of the human body was responsible for aging, according to scientists in the 1970s. Some said that the hypothalamus at the base of the brain contained a central "pacemaker" that instructed the body to get older, one version of the popular "clock" theory of aging.[55] That timer in the brain told the pituitary gland to release "death hormones," an extension of this idea went, killing the body when it was automatically programmed to die.[56] Linking specific body parts to aging was not only silly but reminiscent of ancient medical theories such Hippocrates's belief that certain bodily fluids affected human personality. That any of them were judged to be real possibilities demonstrates how little was actually known about physical aging in the late twentieth century. In his 1976 book *Prolongevity*, Albert Rosenfield compiled many of the theories about aging and extending life that had surfaced over the preceding decade. (The book's subtitle—A *Report on the Scientific Discoveries Now Being Made About Aging and Dying, and Their Promise of an Extended Human Life Span—Without Old Age*—hardly needed extending.) Theories ranged from the sublime to the ridiculous, making anyone with anything close to an objective viewpoint conclude that this field of research was not one of science's better moments.[57]

With concern over air pollution (often called "smog" at the time) and other ecological threats a significant part of the national conversation, it was not surprising that scientists included them on their list of potential causes of aging. It was, more specifically, heavy oxidant stresses on cells that led to premature aging and disease, scientists theorized, justification for identifying agents that could protect against such damage. One of them was vitamin E, which was discovered in 1923 but whose precise function remained uncertain. Most experts agreed, however, that the nutrient did serve as a cellular defense against oxidants such as nitrogen dioxide and ozone, atmospheric gases known to be elevated in areas with high air pollution. Studies done at Berkeley in 1974 confirmed as much, bringing more attention to vitamin E as a potential antiaging agent. (Vitamin C was also believed to help delay the aging process.) Scientists stopped short of recommending that individuals gobble up large quantities of vitamin E to combat oxidants and thus slow down the aging process, but there was a consensus that the substance might very well play a major role in halting the decay of human cells. If nothing else, this line of research proved that cells did not self-destruct because of some kind of predetermined biological mechanism, an important revelation.[58]

Although a minority of scientists was interested only in lessening the effects of old age during a normal lifetime, most equated the battle of aging with extending life expectancy. Over the course of the first three-quarters of the twentieth century, life expectancy in the United States jumped by about twenty-five years, from about forty-seven (46.3 for men and 48.3 for women) to roughly seventy-two (68.8 for men and 76.6 for women), an amazing phenomenon by any measure.[59] By the 1970s, however, this dramatic extension of Americans' average life span was slowing down considerably, a source of frustration to scientists who saw no reason it should not continue at a rapid rate. (The biggest factor contributing to the increased life expectancy was the much higher survival rate of infants and children.) Only a greater understanding of the basic processes of aging could lead to another exponential leap in life expectancy, making what was seen as the "deterioration" of the human body one of the central questions of science. The best genes, nutrition, and environment could not prevent aging, and the finest health care in the world would not prevent death—each a biological annoyance that kept many a scientist up at night. The problem of aging was a main topic of conversation at the 1974 annual meeting of the American Association for the Advancement of Science, with both physicians and academics offering their respective takes on what to do about the disturbing situation. Even a cure for cancer or heart disease would yield just a few more years of life expectancy, one of the attendees pointed out, not nearly enough for what was believed to be very much achievable: a society full of centenarians.[60]

Like many scientists working in the area at the time, Alan Richardson, a professor of chemistry and biology at Illinois State University, was fairly confident that the average human life span could be extended by a decade or two, or possibly much longer. The key question, he told colleagues at the 1976 meeting of the American Aging Association, was whether aging was genetically programmed, something his own research with rats suggested. Should our genes be responsible for making us get older (specifically by a decline in protein synthesis, Richardson theorized), it would be "fairly straightforward" to slow aging down. "If aging turns out to be a regulatory process at the cellular level, it should be possible to extend the human life span 200 or 300 years or indefinitely," he claimed, more concerned about the moral implications of a nation of Methuselahs than the obstacles to achieving such a thing.[61] Scientists at the National Institute on Aging in Baltimore also pegged two hundred years as a reachable goal, possibly via a vaccination much like the vaccinations used to prevent diseases. "Doubling the lifespan potential is a reasonable objective from what we know now," said Richard G. Cutler of the institute in 1978, envisioning injecting people with an "aging cocktail" to fool the body into repairing damage to cells' genetic material.[62]

For Richardson and others, the symptoms of getting older had been addressed through medicine, but science had yet to confront aging itself; this was the much bigger opportunity and challenge.[63] Although no breakthrough had yet come to pass, journalists consistently presented scientists as being hot on the trail of aging, with something big expected soon. "Aging Reversal Is Called Near," declared a headline in the *Atlanta Constitution* in 1976 based on some findings reported by Johan Bjorksten. Bjorksten was positively brash in describing his research, calling a news conference at the American Chemical Society to announce what he had found so far. "I'm not interested in gaining five years here and five years there," he puffed, proud to say that he was "shooting for the whole pot." For Bjorksten, the "whole pot" was nothing less than an average life expectancy of eight hundred years, with a yet to be discovered enzyme to be the ace up his sleeve. Other chemists were confident the enzyme would soon be identified. With intensive research, "I think we could have the thing done in 5 to 10 years," agreed Rolf Martin of City University of New York, quite assured that science was on the brink of realizing what many would consider its greatest achievement.[64]

## A Quietly Ticking Social Time Bomb

Lost in the scientific pursuit to add many years to human life was the fact that those intimately involved in the lives of older people already had their hands quite full. Gerontology, a field that had been around in some form since the turn of the century, was booming in the late 1970s as America's population became noticeably older due to both demographics and life extension. It was the future, however, that presented abundant opportunities for those considering careers in gerontology. There were about 32.7 million Americans older than sixty in 1977 (15 percent of the population), while demographers were forecasting that 41.9 million citizens would fall into that age category in the year 2000 (16 percent of the population). (Their forecast turned out to be spot on, although that number represented about 17 percent of the population.) Many social workers were already switching their emphasis from children to seniors, taking courses in gerontology to take advantage of the expanding field. Hospital administrators, registered nurses, and government employees were also equipping themselves with the educational tools to work with older people, fully aware that both social and economic factors were on their side. At the New School in New York City, for example, about one hundred students were pursuing a master's degree in gerontological services, a program that covered virtually every aspect of aging. Duke University, the University of Michigan, and Columbia University also offered programs in gerontology, with many other colleges planning to do so soon.[65]

The leading school in gerontology, however, was arguably the University of Southern California. Since 1973, the university's Ethel Percy Andrus Gerontology Center had focused on the problems of the elderly and was serving as the prototype for other institutions interested in starting up their own research facilities. (Andrus, a retired school principal, founded AARP in Los Angeles.) For James E. Birren, founding director of the center, the work completed to date in aging was just the tip of the proverbial iceberg, with much more research to be done as additional problems were identified. Given how older Americans were viewed and treated, it made perfect sense that the nation's top institution in gerontology subscribed to the idea that aging represented a "problem." All kinds of professionals—sociologists, biologists, psychologists, urban planners, social workers, nurses, hospital and nursing home administrators, and even architects—were required to take care of older members of society, Birren rather condescendingly pointed out, with many more to be needed in the next few decades. "Gerontology is an embryonic field," agreed Ruth Weg, associate director of training at the center, calling on the federal government to support institutions like hers as the nation's population aged.[66]

One need not have been an expert to know that the nation would likely have some kind of crisis in half a century or so when baby boomers entered their senior years en masse. Carl Eisdorfer, the Duke psychiatrist who had become the president of the General Services Administration by the nation's Bicentennial, called aging "a time bomb" as he looked ahead to the not-too-distant future. Just the next decade and a half was cause for considerable concern given the expected numbers: the sixty-five-plus demographic was forecast to almost double over the next fourteen years, from twenty million in

1976 to 38 million in 1990. With this many older people in America, Eisdorfer saw two major problems—mandatory retirement at age sixty-five and stereotyping of seniors—that would make this bomb explode if was not defused. Allowing seniors to remain productive by working would be a big help, his research showed, and not separating them from the rest of the population would be of considerable psychological benefit. More generally, treating older people like "old people" actually accelerated the aging process, good reason for him to encourage the rest of the population to try to resist categorizing them into some special group.[67]

The metaphor of a looming demographic explosion gained traction in the late seventies. "A quietly ticking social time bomb—America's rapidly aging population—is due to explode in 20 years or so with potentially revolutionary impact on the nation's economy," warned Philip Shabecoff in the *New York Times* in 1978. Little had been done to prepare the country for this "future shock," Shabecoff reported, although the Senate Special Committee on Aging was beginning to consider what, if anything, the federal government could do about it. The slower economic growth of the past decade, as well as other factors, such as inflation, a jump in early retirement, and a greater demand for health care, only added to the foreseeable problem. Science had yet to lengthen the human life span to a century plus, despite all the efforts to do so, but biomedical advances were dramatically increasing the number of Americans living to be eighty years old or more. Some fifty-five million people, almost one-fifth of the nation's population, would be sixty-five years old or older by 2030, Joseph A. Califano Jr., secretary of HEW, told the Senate committee, the baby boom gradually turning into the "senior boom." Where would the money to take care of all these older people come from? Califano asked the senators, the fact that all this doom and gloom was still a half century away not offering much consolation.[68] As America entered the 1980s, the subject of aging intensified, as did the conversation that, whether we liked it or not, we were all constantly getting older.

# 2

## The De-Aging of America

Chronological age is not a reliable indicator of the
ability of a person to function.
We need to find measures that predict aging better than
a person's birth certificate.
— John W. Rowe, Harvard University, 1985

On the morning of June 26, 1983, the Clinique consultants at Rich's department store in Atlanta were delighted to find the new line of products that had just come in. Clinique, the high-end skin care marketer, was launching a program called "Daily De-Aging at Any Age," which the store's wealthier customers were bound to find very appealing. Clinique's dermatologists had reportedly determined that "older skin needs more aggressive exfoliation," good news for the company given the number of products that were said to be required to remove the dead skin cells. Consumers likely to subscribe to Clinique's "Daily De-Aging at Any Age" regimen—most of them middle-aged women—would start with a "scrub cream" to soften wrinkles and rekindle glow, after which would follow a twice-a-day application of various soaps, lotions, and moisturizers. Included in the program was a computer for Clinique's consultants to analyze customers' skin type, quite an innovation at the time and supposed evidence that the products had been scientifically formulated.[1]

Clinique's new line of products focused on aging was very much in sync with the cultural zeitgeist in America. The largest and most influential segment of the population, baby boomers, were beginning to head into their forties in the 1980s, quite a shock for the generation said to be perpetually youthful. The nation as a whole was getting older as longevity increased, making aging a central issue, both personally and socially. Many Americans, however, were simply not ready to accept the fact that their youth was becoming or already was something of the past. The 1980s were the beginnings of what *Prevention* magazine called in 1984 "the de-aging of America," as a good number of baby boomers as well as seniors actively sought ways to stall or reverse the physical process of getting older.

Efforts to delay the natural aging of the human body were largely a reaction to the negative attitudes toward oldness that were still very much in play after the youth-oriented counterculture era. Although some progress was being made as American society generally became more tolerant, discrimination against older people remained pervasive, a means perhaps to publicly display the aversion and antipathy to aging that was a defining element of Western culture. The pure reality of getting older was, however, reason enough for individuals to arm themselves with whatever resources were available to manage the aging process as well as possible. Not surprisingly, gerontology flourished in this decade, as the field was perfectly aligned with the demographic surge that was taking place. "De-aging" was a nice idea, perhaps, but there was no getting around the fact that Americans and America would get older in the years ahead.

## A Phenomenon Peculiar to American Society

No one was more aware of the realities of aging than senior citizens themselves. As their numbers grew, older people were becoming a more powerful political constituency, something the no. 1 senior citizen of the United States, President Ronald Reagan, well knew. Because of the landmark legislation that came out of the second and third White House conferences on aging, much anticipation surrounded the fourth as it approached. (Little had resulted from the first such conference held by President Truman—so little in fact that many people were not even aware that it had taken place. The White House had not officially sponsored that conference, another reason for its being largely forgotten.) "A phenomenon peculiar to American society which occurs every 10 years is now taking shape again," announced Matthew Tayback, Maryland's director on aging, a good year and a half before President Reagan's 1981 conference would commence.[2]

Despite (or, as it turned out, because of) all the planning that had begun during the Carter administration, this conference turned out to be a chaotic one, making it seem more like a particularly contentious political convention. Unlike the three previous White House conferences, which were largely free of politics, the fourth was clearly partisan in nature. Reagan fired those appointed by Carter, setting the tone for the 1981 conference. Social Security, health care, and other programs had become hot political issues since the third conference; these issues also made Reagan's conference far more divisive than the one President Nixon had held a decade earlier.[3] (Reagan had proposed in May 1981 to reduce Social Security deficits by cutting early retirement, disability, and other benefits for future retirees by almost 23 percent. He withdrew that plan in September but called for a bipartisan task force to study the issue, leaving things rather uncertain.)[4] Also, a contributing factor to the antagonistic nature of the conference was the decline of trust in the government that had originated during the Nixon administration. "I fear that we are being and have been manipulated and are limited in what we can do," said one conference delegate from California, not optimistic that any of the proposals that came out of the meeting would be taken seriously by the budget-conscious president.[5]

Fearing that liberals would react strongly to the administration's proposed cuts to Social Security benefits and cause some embarrassment to the president (most delegates did indeed lean left), Republican leaders went to extraordinary measures before and during the conference to try to prevent that from happening. "From all indications, the White House was in no mood to risk criticism of its policies," the editor of *Newsday* later wrote as the dust settled.[6] First, the Republican National Committee carefully screened potential members of the conference advisory board prior to the meeting, selecting only those people who were open to the idea of making cuts to Social Security benefits. Second, Richard S. Schweiker, the health and human services secretary whose department was responsible for the conference, oversaw the adding of hundreds of "mystery" delegates pooled from the president's campaign donor lists in order to stack the deck of important committees.[7] Third, key conference administrators were removed and proposals introduced to minimize debate and dissenting opinions, significant enough "irregularities" for the House Select Committee on Aging to launch an investigation even before the event began.[8]

Even more draconian steps were taken at the conference itself either to sabotage potential divisiveness or to encourage a positive outcome for the president, a report by the General Accounting Office subsequently found. There was abundant evidence that Reagan's people employed techniques evocative of old-school political machines or borrowed a page from Nixon's manipulation of the press. Efforts were made to silence certain elected delegates and speakers, for example, notably eighty-one-year-old Representative Claude Pepper, the Democrat from Florida, who served as honorary cochairman of the conference. The administration also apparently made up fake credentials to crash committees and sessions, and it went so far as to raise the temperature in the auditorium in order to encourage people to leave the room.[9] Rumors even circulated that meeting rooms were bugged, not that far-fetched an idea given a recent president's habit of taping conversations for political purposes.

Happily, the Republicans' shameful ploys backfired; not one of them was in the least bit effective. The conference thus turned out to be an embarrassing episode for the president after all, reinforcing his image as not especially responsive to the interests of senior citizens despite being one himself. Some were even calling the administration's failed attempts to get an unfair edge "a mini-Watergate" or "Graygate," the last thing Reagan wanted to get out of his own conference. Despite the overt infusion of partisan politics, however, many agreed that the 1981 conference was for the most part a success given the consensus that was reached. Some six hundred resolutions were passed, including greater opportunities for older workers, more income support, improvements to Medicare and Medicaid, increased publicly financed housing for seniors, and, most important, the maintenance of Social Security benefits. "Social Security can and will be saved," Reagan told the anxious delegates at the convention, although it was agreed that general tax revenue would not be used to pay for the benefits.[10] While all of these resolutions were just goals at this point, most delegates were happy with what they saw as a solid blueprint for action through the 1980s.[11]

## Maximum Life Span

Some Americans were no doubt surprised that Reagan was not an avid supporter of seniors. The man was, after all, the oldest elected president in the nation's history, although it was easy to forget that. During his first term, Reagan was a prime role model for "positive" or "productive" aging in both body and mind. Images of the seventy-year-old man riding horses or chopping wood only reinforced the idea that forced retirement at any age was a silly law. "The graceful aging of President Reagan's body has become a matter of record," wrote Sandy Rovner of the *Los Angeles Times* a few months after

Reagan took office. The fact that the president had recovered quickly from his March 1981 shooting further proved wrong the many skeptics who had said that he was too old for the job. More than any other American, perhaps, Reagan defied stereotypes about aging, something gerontologists were quite pleased about. Having a septuagenarian in the White House was a powerful vote of confidence in and respect for older people—an all-too-rare commodity in our ageist society.[12]

In addition to the public recognition of a senior citizen showing few if any signs of advanced age, there was good news on the scientific front of aging. Thankfully, many of the more specious attempts to slow or stop the aging process had by the early 1980s disappeared as it became increasingly clear that no fountain was youth was just waiting to be discovered. Experimentation of all kinds was tolerated if not encouraged during the counterculture years, but now there was more scrutiny of scientists' claims that they could potentially solve the mystery of aging. Work in the field continued, of course, with much of it centered around the not very sensational role of genetics and cellular processes.

Still, there was the occasional report of an alleged breakthrough in an off-the-beaten-track area of aging research. In 1980, for example, an East German scientist, one Baron Manfred von Ardenne, told the media that his "multistep oxygen therapy" was making elderly people quite peppy and dramatically lessened their age-related ailments. Another scientist making such a claim might have been quickly dismissed, but the seventy-three-year-old baron had an impressive background, including pioneering the development of television and the Soviet atom bomb. He also reportedly held more than six hundred patents, making him appear to be more than just a mad scientist with a lab in Dresden. "It returns the [oxygen] supply to levels normally found in the young," he explained, with clinics across Europe adopting the treatment for wealthier patients searching for a way to maintain their youth.[13]

While pumping high levels of oxygen into the bloodstream was no doubt an effective pick-me-up (the therapy is still done today), most scientists saw no miracle cures for aging on the horizon. "No simple therapy for arresting the aging process has been discovered and few scientists expect one," Caleb E. Finch of the University of Southern California conceded at a 1981 symposium on aging. The phenomenon of aging remained mysterious, much to scientists' chagrin, but two principal theories, each having something to do with the cellular workings of the body, had emerged. The first was that aging was the result of a number of "errors" that gradually occurred in an individual's

DNA, while the second was that humans got older due to an erosion of the body's immune system.[14] The idea of there being some kind of genetic clock that programmed a person's life span was beginning to fall out of favor, but in some scientific circles it was still vigorously debated. (Some, along these lines, likened aging to the turning of leaves, with the human body experiencing changes analogous to the triggered breakdown of chlorophyll in certain trees.)[15] The consensus, however, was that aging was a lot more complicated than previously believed, making the acceptance of any single theory (or solution) highly unlikely.[16]

In place of identifying a single, master theory of aging, which no longer seemed viable, scientists drifted toward finding a cause of or contributor to the decline of a particular part of the human body. More scrutiny was being paid to the effects of smoking marijuana, for example, as researchers linked the active agent in the weed to a loss of brain cells in rats. Tetrahydrocannabinol (THC) appeared to affect these cells in the same way as aging, Philip W. Landfield of Wake Forest University had found, although it was too early to say that the chemical compound caused humans' brains to age prematurely.[17]

Likewise, most serious scientists were now largely abandoning the formation of a grand plan to add many decades to the average human life span. Instead, they were focusing on a specific condition that could perhaps slow the aging process. One of these was space travel, oddly enough, as research by NASA scientists showed that being weightless required less oxygen and food—each something that demanded the body to expend a considerable amount of energy in order to use. Simply fighting the effects of gravity used up about a third of a human's calorie intake, and so eliminating that factor would theoretically allow an individual to maintain a lower level of metabolism. Reducing the wear and tear on bodily organs via weightlessness would go a long way toward decelerating aging, the NASA researchers believed, conceding that the practicality of gravity would be with us for some time.[18]

Paradoxically, while scientists were retreating somewhat in the area of dramatic life extension, authors exploring the topic were moving full steam ahead. Americans appeared to remain quite interested in adding many years to their lives despite recent research indicating that achieving such a thing was a long shot at best. Durk Pearson and Sandy Shaw's *Life Extension: A Practical Scientific Approach*, for example, was on the *New York Times* bestseller list for months in the early 1980s. The book suggested that readers should, like the coauthors, gobble up huge quantities of vitamins and supplements to radically extend their lives. A host of other books about how readers could possibly live significantly longer were being published, including Roy L. Walford's *Maximum Life Span*, Saul Kent's *The Life-Extension Revolution*, John A. Mann's *Secrets of Life Extension*, Kenneth R. Pelletier's *Longevity: Fulfilling Our Biological Potential*, and Osborn Segerberg Jr.'s *Living to Be 100.*[19] Despite the popularity of such books, the promises contained within them were definitely more sizzle than steak. With the possible exception of severe calorie reduction, there was precious little evidence at this point that an individual could extend his or her life at all except by the tried-and-true methods of eating a balanced diet, doing regular exercise, and avoiding unhealthy activities like smoking.

Not everyone was even sure that achieving a "maximum life span" for humanity was such a good idea. The science fiction trope of a society whose members lived half of their very long lives as old people lingered over the efforts of scientists still intent on pushing the limits of our biology. Walford, who was also the author of *The 120-Year Diet*, was a strong advocate for life extension via "undernutrition," the only path that so far appeared to potentially offer a big leap in longevity. Some gerontologists, however, were cautioning his vision of people living twice as long as they currently did by dramatically restricting calories. Leonard Hayflick of the Center for Gerontological Studies at the University of Florida, for example, imagined such a society not unlike that depicted in Jonathan Swift's *Gulliver's Travels*, where citizens (the Struldbrugs) never died but became increasingly disabled. Be careful what you wish for, he and others of a similar bent warned those scientists continuing to maintain that the average human life span could and should be one hundred years or more.[20]

Of course, a fair number of individuals were reaching the century mark without nearly starving themselves or popping dozens of pills a day. (Doing so famously earned some a mention on NBC's *Today* show by the ebullient weatherman Willard Scott.) About twenty-five thousand Americans were aged one hundred or older in 1986, according to the NIA, with more than a hundred thousand centenarians forecast by the year 2000. Roughly half lived in households by themselves or with others, with the other half residing in group-care situations. Interestingly, the percentage of centenarians varied widely in different parts of the United States. The percentage of 100+ers in Hawaii was almost twice that of Washington, D.C., for example, suggesting that lifestyle or climate played a role in longevity. (Simple genetics was likely much more responsible.) Whatever the factors for living to an extraordinarily long age, it was clear that there would be many more centenarians in the future. "If the trend continues, we need to rethink our definitions of young-old, old, and old-old," the UCLA/USC Long Term Care Gerontology Center noted—exactly what would indeed take place over the next few decades.[21]

More than anyone else, perhaps, gerontologists understood that aging did not need an aggressive push by science, at least from a social sense. Simple demography was already dramatically extending the mean age of Americans, in the process triggering a host of challenges that would only intensify in the years ahead. Quality of life was more important than quantity, they believed, making the thought of a few decades more of old age for the average person something to be terrified of more than to wish for. By the mid-1980s, the long quest for discovering a scientific fountain of youth in order to indefinitely postpone mortality had been largely eclipsed by the rather pedestrian but much more realistic effort to have more Americans live longer and healthier lives. Developing a stronger immune system in older people was key, they agreed, as it was typically the ability to fight off disease and infections that allowed an individual to reach a ripe old age.[22]

This did not, however, stop marketers from offering consumers a wide range of products said to have some kind of antiaging properties. Many anti-aging products had hit the marketplace over the years despite there being no evidence that any of these skin creams, vitamins, nutritional supplements, minerals, and "power" foods did anything to slow the aging process.[23] Not surprisingly, the Food and Drug Administration (FDA) was not pleased with how companies were marketing products with "anti-aging" or "skin rejuvena-tion" promises, as such claims would classify them more as drugs than cos-metics. "Each Niosome sphere mimics the support structure of younger skin and carries active anti-age agents into the skin's inter-cellular structure," con-sumers were told on one Lancôme product label, scientific double-talk that sounded good but had little or no basis in fact. Through the eighties, more marketers such as Clinique jumped on the antiaging bandwagon, forcing the FDA to take more aggressive action. In 1987, the agency issued twenty-three regulatory letters to firms including Revlon, Estée Lauder, and Avon, warning them that they better have hard evidence to make the claims they were mak-ing in advertising and on labeling.[24]

The fact was, however, that consumers were eager to purchase anything that offered even a remote possibility of antiaging. Simply accepting the phys-ical signs of aging was commonly viewed in the competitive 1980s as a kind of defeat, especially among women of a certain age. "'Growing old gracefully' is apparently out of fashion," noted Ellen Goodman in her syndicated column in 1988 after surveying a stack of women's magazines. A product called Retin-A with alleged wrinkle-smoothing properties was seen as something of a magical potion among women over forty, just one of various elixirs that those averse to aging naturally kept in their medicine cabinets. Unlike the FDA, women couldn't care less whether Retin-A and similar products were considered to be a cosmetic or a drug; all they cared about was whether the stuff could make them look five or, even better, ten years younger.[25]

## A Different Species

One did not have to be a marketing genius to know that demographics were on the side of companies trying to sell antiaging products. In 1950 the average age of Americans was around twenty, while in 1980 it had risen to about thirty. In another fifty years, the average age in the United States would be around forty, demographers were predicting, a bubble that would undoubtedly impact not just the marketplace but also education, health care, and even the way homes and cities were built. Given that the very makeup of the United States would be fundamentally altered, many sensibly argued, it was time for our perception of older people to be modified in an equivalent manner. Americans had to "integrate the aging into the full life of society," remarked Robert C. Benedict, the U.S. commissioner on aging, in 1980, calling for the end of the widespread stereotyping and discrimination of older citizens.[26] Carroll L. Estes, a professor of sociology and director of UC Berkeley's Aging Policy Center, felt similarly. "Our perceptions and policies define old people as a major societal problem but, in fact, it is society's treatment of old people that is the primary problem," Estes wrote the following year; she saw Americans' equation of aging with decline and dependence as the root of the issue. Research showed that chronological aging caused no major changes in personality or behavior, meaning there was little or no basis for our common practice of distancing ourselves from older people.[27]

Other experts chimed in on what they justifiably believed was a distorted view of aging in America. Rose Dobrof, a pioneer in social work and director of Hunter College's Brookdale Center on Aging, argued that our muddled perspective had a ripple effect that compounded the problem. Young people naturally became fearful about getting older because of the way we characterized aging, she astutely held, thinking that our discomfort with the subject also served as an unhealthy divisive force. It "widens the sense of difference and distance between the generations," she said in 1982, leaving older people in a kind of no-man's-land within society. Aging was one of the most basic and obvious facts of life, yet it was clear that major misconceptions surrounded it. For example, it was safe to say that a good number of people considered aging to be a state when it was really a process, a basic misunderstanding that likely led to many others. No one woke up "old" one day, Dobrof explained, although this would come as news to young folks conditioned to regard aging as a peculiar condition limited to a particular segment of the population.[28]

Because children and teens often had little contact with older people (and due to the simple fact that becoming old was further into the future), aging was generally an alien concept for the former. In one's youth, the elderly "seem like a different species," Walter Goodman of the *Chicago Tribune* posited, a good way of describing not just how young people viewed seniors but also the loss of humanity that aging brought on.[29] Some authors of children's books, such as Richard Worth, apparently agreed. His 1986 book *You'll Be Old Someday, Too* introduced the subject of human aging to students between grades 6 through 9 in a valiant attempt to make older people seem not so foreign to them. In half a century or so, Worth explained, young readers would be old themselves, a nice way of personalizing the rather abstract idea of aging.[30]

Interviews with real children confirmed their unfamiliarity with and reservations about aging and the aged. "To think that one day all my friends and I would walk real slow and say things we don't really mean scares me," said one eleven-year-old girl when Minnesota educators asked her and twenty-seven hundred other students to describe their thoughts about becoming old. Not surprisingly, kids had the same trepidations about aging that many adults did: being dependent on others, having major health problems, living alone or without family, and dying. Visiting grandparents in nursing homes often reinforced such fears, as even if grandma or grandpa was in relatively good shape there was bound to be at least one senior who was not. (Young children are also known to overestimate the age of grandparents. Barbara Cartland, the famous romance novelist, for example, remembered thinking at the age of six that her grandmother was ancient, when she was in fact just fifty-two at the time.)[31] Most old people were just plain mean, some kids thought, based on their experiences at nursing homes or interaction with neighbors, their nastiness a natural function of their dire straits. Some kids believed that being old had its benefits, however, such as not having to go to school or work, not having anyone to tell them what to do, and getting free money from the government. The freedom to sleep late and eat anything one wanted seemed like a pretty good deal to children continually ordered around, even if it did mean walking slower and occasionally not making much sense.[32]

To young people's credit, not every one of them viewed aging negatively save the lack of responsibilities. "You're the same person you were before you became old," wrote an especially wise nine-year-old girl from Minneapolis in a school essay in 1987. She and her fellow students at Andersen Open School were part of an innovative intergenerational writing class that put kids and older people together to address the hardly easy subject of age. Senior citizens wrote about their life experiences and what it was like to become older, after which students created their own stories about what they had learned about aging. Growing old was not as frightening an experience as they had thought, the kids explained in their essays after hearing that seniors' lives were not all that different from when they were young.[33]

This was not the only intergenerational class in Minneapolis helping to blur the usually sharp lines between young and old. At the Kenny School, seniors were bringing in objects from their past to share with second-graders, another way to defuse fears about aging by making it real and tangible. The kids, meanwhile, showed "new" things of which they believed older people might not have been aware. (Nintendo, perhaps?) Seventh-graders at Northeast Junior High School were meanwhile comparing their journal entries to seniors' descriptions of their childhood during the Depression, while third-graders at the North Star School were matched up with seniors in a "computer pen pal" program (an early use of what would become e-mail). Such classes were precisely what was needed to help reverse over the long term the deeply entrenched stereotypes of aging in America and lessen the dread of getting older oneself.[34]

The Gray Panthers, the best-known elderly-rights social movement, also found more in common with young people than one might have thought. The organization was still very much alive and well at the end of the 1980s, first and foremost fighting age discrimination but also engaged in a variety of other social activist issues. In opposing the Vietnam War and domestic economic and social disparities, its mission differed from other members of the Gray Lobby. After twenty years, the organization had become more intergenerational, with members of all ages committed to helping Americans develop a better understanding of aging. The Gray Panthers used its primary platform of promoting a positive attitude toward aging to address other relevant causes such as national health care insurance, one reason why the group had attracted a more diverse membership. Leaders of the organization were especially interested in dispelling stereotypes related to age among young people; they were fully aware that many adolescents were empathic to all kinds of social injustice. Teenagers faced their own form of age discrimination, after all, something that was likely to make them understand and appreciate the pervasive negative portrayal of older adults. Framing ageism within the larger context of biases based on race, gender, and class made a lot of sense, making the Gray Panthers much more than a collection of grumpy old men and women.[35]

The common misunderstanding of aging among children and adults alike could perhaps be expected given that it was a young field. Aging itself had been around forever, of course, but the medical study of it was relatively new. Between 1975 and 1985, in fact, the entire body of medical literature dedicated to the subject had doubled. Much of the recent material focused on redefining aging by challenging existing stereotypes and debunking myths that surrounded it. While not at all sanguine about how older people were currently (mis)perceived, many gerontologists envisioned a day when the latter years of life were not seen as a separate and sad epilogue to the main part of the story. All agreed that much more study of aging was needed for older people to be fully integrated into society, a process that would undoubtedly take decades.

Those in gerontology and geriatrics were especially excited about the Baltimore Longitudinal Study that was in its twenty-eighth year in 1985. (The study had been in process since 1958 for men and 1978 for women.) Researchers were studying the normal aging process of some 650 healthy men and four hundred women (all volunteers), with preliminary findings showing that humans were extremely adaptable as they got older. An old dog could learn new tricks, so to speak, something that would come as a surprise to many people. Aging was not a disease, the study also made clear, the first step in a long process that it was hoped would change the way older people were seen and treated in America.[36] Another long-term aging research project was the Seattle Longitudinal Study, which was in its thirty-third year in 1989. Findings from this study suggested that aging took place in a start-and-stop manner, with abrupt changes (such as forced retirement or a heart attack) accelerating the process.[37]

Scientific studies could go a long way toward debunking the many myths surrounding aging in America, but pictures, as it is said, are worth a thousand words. In 1986, the Smithsonian Institution organized a traveling exhibit called "Images of Old Age in America" that consisted of about one hundred photographs of older people. The show, which began in Ann Arbor and ended at the Smithsonian in Washington, offered a historical perspective of how aging was viewed in this country over the preceding hundred years, and it addressed the many contradictions pertaining to the subject. Most compelling, perhaps, was the series of questions curators of the exhibit asked visitors to consider: "Why do we have such conflicting feelings about growing old? Why do so many dread what they cannot avoid? Was it invariably true that in other times and places old age was exalted? What changed, if anything?" There were no easy answers to such questions, of course, but the Smithsonian show was a rare opportunity for Americans to even address the touchy topic of aging. Some museums that hosted the photography exhibit complemented it with other entertainment related to aging. At the Science Museum of Minnesota in St. Paul, for example, visitors could attend a "Seniorfest" weekend and an original, locally produced play called *If You Live, You Get Old*. Audience members were asked to decide the fate of the lead character (an eighty-year-old widower with weakening sight and hearing), an interesting twist that put people of all ages in the shoes of an octogenarian.[38]

On Broadway, meanwhile, two plays in the mid-eighties that centered on aging, Herb Gardner's *I'm Not Rappaport* and Samuel Beckett's *Krapp's Last Tape*, were doing brisk business with their respective existential takes on getting old. Hollywood too appeared to be more interested in the subject of aging, which historically had not been a particularly popular one in films. Both Henry Fonda and Katharine Hepburn had won Academy Awards a few years earlier for 1981's *On Golden Pond*, and *Cocoon* with an all-star cast of older actors (including Hume Cronyn, Jessica Tandy, Maureen Stapleton, and Don Ameche, the latter also winning an Oscar), had recently been a box-office hit. Movies such as *That's Life* starring Julie Andrews and Jack Lemmon and *Tough Guys* with Burt Lancaster and Kirk Douglas took a more realistic (though still Hollywoodesque) look at being old than the ubersentimental *On Golden Pond* and far-fetched *Cocoon*, a reflection perhaps of the changing winds of aging.[39]

## Our Aging Society

Hollywood screenwriters were not the only ones using creative license when it came to aging. In their 1986 book *Our Aging Society*, coeditors Lydia Bronte and Alan Pifer of the Carnegie Foundation's Aging Society Project imagined a future America where, because of their numbers, older citizens led society. Youth, meanwhile, would be cherished because of its relative unusualness in

Bronte and Pifer's envisioned tomorrowland, a cultural turning of the tables that may not be as sci-fi as it sounds.[40] A central theme of *Our Aging Society* was the increasing diversity of America, specifically that dualisms based on race (black/white) and gender (male/female) were no longer sufficiently representative of the nation's population. Importantly, the book made a distinction between individual aging and population aging. Population aging is "an enormous social force comparable in scale to any of the great social movements in past years," Pifer told the *Los Angeles Times*, likening it to "the Westward movement, the civil rights movement, and the women's movement." Individual aging, meanwhile, took place at a micro and personal level, making the getting older of both people and society as a whole a double whammy in cultural terms.[41]

A number of other books, meanwhile, were being published on how people could cope with the realities of aging. Leslie Kenton's *Ageless Aging: The Natural Way to Stay Young* was a throwback of sorts; its very title suggested that there was a miraculous formula to avoid getting old. Through "natural healing," Kenton contended, one could achieve "ageless aging" (whatever that meant), although there was little or no medical evidence to make such a claim.[42] The (rather silly) notion of "successful aging" also remained in circulation. (Clearly there were better ways to describe aging as either "successful" or "unsuccessful.") But that did not stop Anne C. Averyt from offering more than five hundred pages of practical information to navigate the often rocky terrain of getting old in America in her book *Successful Aging*, or Isadore Rossman to do much the same in her *Looking Forward: The Complete Guide to Successful Aging*.[43]

One age in particular—fifty years—seemed to most capture people's attention in the 1980s, perhaps because it was just around the corner for the first wave of baby boomers. Rather than being simply another milestone, that number carried hefty personal freight, some experts suggested. In his *Fifty: Midlife in Perspective*, for example, Herant Katchadourian argued that the half-century mark was the time to "come to terms with yourself," meaning that one should finally accept who one was and not try to be anybody else. David Karp, a sociologist at Boston College, agreed. "The 50s is a kind of fulcrum decade, a turning point in the aging process during which people, more sharply than before, are made to feel their age," he wrote in the journal the *Gerontologist*.[44] (E. B. White, the famous essayist, quipped that one feels as if one had "about twenty minutes to live" after reaching age fifty.) Leo Buscaglia, the popular motivational speaker, also saw fifty as the age at which many realized their true identities. "After 50, it seems easier to be ourselves," he wrote in 1984, believing that it took that long to develop a certain kind of wisdom.[45] That a fiftysomething individual often found himself or herself having to care in some way for elderly parents only added to the challenges of that time of life.[46]

Although some were saying "fifty is the new forty," there did appear to be some truth to the idea that youthfulness at that age was just not possible. "At fifty you can no longer claim that you are young, the way you might, say, at forty-five, and get away with it," a writer going by the name Aristides suggested in the *American Scholar* in 1986. The age of fifty or thereabouts was also commonly viewed as the time at which one accepted what one had achieved thus far in life and recognized that some act of true greatness was unlikely at this point. "Fifty is an age old enough for one to have suffered serious disappointments," Aristides added, "yet young enough not to be completely out of hope."[47] The age of fifty was enough of a turning point in life to occasionally show up as a principal theme in fiction. In Avery Corman's 1987 novel entitled simply *50*, the protagonist reaches that age as both physical and emotional challenges intensify. The man, divorced with joint custody of his two children, also loses his job and suffers the loss of his father, things that some real-life fifty-year-olds were no doubt experiencing.[48] Others, however, saw reaching not fifty but sixty years old as the pivot point of "oldness." Bill Case's *Life Begins at Sixty*, for example, defined the third act of life as beginning in one's seventh decade; that was the time to be "living," he told readers, the two previous acts being mostly about "learning" and then "earning."[49]

Books focusing on women and aging represented a literary subcategory all of its own in the late 1980s. Most notably, sixteen years after publishing its landmark *Our Bodies, Ourselves*, the Boston Women's Health Book Collective (along with the Midlife and Older Women Book Project) produced the mammoth *Ourselves, Growing Older: Women Aging with Knowledge and Power*. No fewer than forty-five women contributed chapters to the book for those in midlife and beyond, covering everything from health issues, to social concerns and psychological matters. Quotes from more than three hundred women sharing their thoughts on getting older personalized the important but rather dry subject matter.[50]

Less practical but much more interesting was Erica Jong's 1987 novel *Serenissima*. Jong had made quite a sensation with her erotic novel *Fear of Flying*, but now, fourteen years later, her interests had turned to aging. The protagonist in her new book was a forty-three-year-old woman who often lied about her age, something many real-life forty- and fiftysomethings were frequently doing to avoid being seen as over the hill. (Jong was forty-five when the book was published). "Aging is very cruel," she said at the time, although she felt some notable women, such as Elizabeth Taylor and Joan Collins, each in her fifties, were successfully defying stereotypes. "Forty is not old, it's young," Jong added, thinking the definitions of age were beginning to change in a positive way.[51]

The particular circumstances relating to women and aging reached a critical mass in the 1980s as older women gained greater political clout and a louder voice in social policy. Leaders of the women's movement and those of aging organizations believed a collaboration of sorts could help each other's cause. The majority of older Americans (including three-fourths of nursing home residents) were women, after all, although research in the field was heavily stacked toward men. (Older women were also far more likely than older men to be poor.) Betty Friedan was serving as the most visible bridge between the two groups, often paired with notable aging advocates (such as Claude Pepper) at gerontology conferences. Friedan, who was in her sixties, had testified before Congress about the problems of older women who lived alone, leveraging her platform as one of the country's most well-known feminists. As she entered her own senior years, the author of the 1963 classic *The Feminine Mystique* recognized strong parallels between feminism and aging, coining the phrase the "mystique of aging" to describe older people's narrowly defined roles in society. Her efforts were clearly paying off; AARP had recently turned its attention to issues faced by older women, and the National Organization of Women was spending more time on issues related to aging. Better long-term health care was the logical common denominator between women's and aging organizations, not too surprisingly, as that initiative was central to each organization.[52]

The attention being given to aging in the 1980s reflected the greater realization of how central the subject was in American life, and how much about it had changed in people's lifetimes. There was no doubt that the parameters of age in America had significantly shifted over the past few decades. A 1950s article about aging in the *Reader's Digest* defined "young" as being under thirty-five years old, "middle age" as being between thirty-five and fifty-five years old, and anything older as "old." While many agreed in the 1980s that one's mid-fifties were a period of transition, few would now suggest that a person of that age was truly old. Some in their sixties, seventies, and eighties were taking part in marathons, then all the rage, hardly an activity one would place alongside bingo and shuffleboard. Others around the typical retirement age of sixty-five were literally ready for the rocking chair, however, something that made aging a highly complicated issue for everyone. Geriatricians were not at all sure what condition a new seventy-year-old patient would be in when he or she walked through the door: it could be anything from perfectly healthy and fit to frail and infirm. Most Americans tended to err on the side of the latter, however, when meeting an older person for the first time. People would often shout at a septuagenarian-plus, for example, assuming he or she was nearly deaf, when usually that was not the case at all.[53]

As is typical with many subjects, the more that was known about aging, the more there was that was considered unknown. For decades, aging had been seen in relatively simple terms, but that was no longer the case. "The older you got," as Carol Tavris at the *Sun Sentinel* wrote of the previous model, "the more you lost—sex drive, memory, brain cells, energy, and intelligence." Now, however, almost everything about aging was being questioned, even the definition of "old." Longer average longevity had pushed back the boundaries of "oldness," making aging something to be understood as much more than a process of loss or decline. The age of sixty had long been considered the entry point to being old, but, as many people reached eighty or beyond without major physical or mental incapacities, chronological years were increasingly viewed as a not very reliable indicator of health or well-being. It was not aging but some medical factor, usually poor nutrition, lack of exercise, or disease, that led to "oldness," researchers had come to believe. (Poorly conducted research had in the past equated adverse medical conditions with aging.) The psychology of aging had been separated from the biology of aging, in other words—a huge step in the development of the field.[54]

The new views about and questions being asked about aging could be detected across society. "Something strange is happening in America," wrote Marj Jackson Levin for the *St. Louis Post-Dispatch* in 1988, finding that what she called "the former boundaries of age" were being expanded or relaxed in many arenas. Whether it was fortysomething baseball players, midlife women having babies, or the oldest president in the nation's history, it did indeed appear that the preconceptions surrounding aging were eroding. As baby boomers entered midlife, the idea of oldness was being pushed back, and the expectations for what people should or should not be doing at a particular age broadened. Turning fifty had only recently been commonly viewed as the unofficial turning of the corner into one's senior years, for example, but now that number did not automatically mean one could not start a new career or family. In a good number of cases, at least, age was becoming less significant, a clear victory for those lobbying for a less age-centric society. Some experts in the field, such as Neugarten at Northwestern University, were going much further with this observation by arguing that age had become "irrelevant," a historic achievement if at all true.[55]

## A Pig in a Python

While the concepts of aging and "oldness" were in flux in the 1980s, one thing remained certain: America was getting grayer, posing major social and economic consequences for the future. There just were not enough "baby busters" to pay for their parents' generation's retirement benefits, policy makers fretted, with the rapidly escalating cost of health care only compounding the potential problem. In his *Born to Pay: The New Politics of Aging*, Phillip Longman defended boomers' right to strain the nation's social and economic systems when they reach retirement age, seeing the generation as a kind of special-interest group. Boomers deserved what was coming to them, he argued, and the government should do everything it could to not let numbers get in the way of their promised Social Security benefits and Medicare. Impoverishing future generations to make that happen was not the answer, Longman made clear, seeing changes in public policy as the only real solution.[56]

While baby boomers were no doubt the elephant in the room from both a social and an economic point of view, there was another demographic megatrend that could not be overlooked. "When demographers look into the future, they see American life profoundly altered by two trends now taking shape," wrote Fernando Torres Gil, then a professor of gerontology at USC, for the *Los Angeles Times* in 1987, those being "the rapid growth of the Latino population and the aging of the so-called baby-boomer generation." The Latino population was growing three times faster than the population of the country as a whole, making some sociologists examine the relationship between that development and the boomer phenomenon. The Latino population was relatively young, while the white population was getting decidedly older, suggesting that it would be the former who would be footing much of the bill to pay for the latter's retirement benefits. Latinos did not earn as much as whites, however, meaning the tax base in a few decades might simply not be large enough to maintain the current system.[57]

While policy makers fretted over such a scenario, the age wave kept rolling. Demographic history was made on July 21, 1988, when, for the first time since the 1950s, Americans aged thirty-five to fifty-nine outnumbered those eighteen to thirty-four years old. As the now seventy million or so baby boomers (about a third of the nation's population) moved through the demographic pipeline, the metaphor of a "pig in a python" quickly caught hold. With the bulge came significant social changes; the beginning of middle age for the leading edge of boomers was having a profound effect on the national scene. Neotraditional values that centered around the home and family had taken hold, for example, buttressed by the Reaganesque conservatism of the 1980s. Crime was down significantly in the early part of the decade, much in part to the aging of the population.[58]

It was within consumerism, however, where the effects of the boomer bulge could most easily be detected. Marketers in many industries were naturally ecstatic about having this many people with increasing disposable income to whom they could target their products and services. Cable television, microwave ovens, and home computers were especially hot in the late eighties primarily because of boomers' spending, as were co-ops and condominiums in big cities like New York.[59] Many companies planned to cling closely to boomers as they aged, knowing that continuing to appeal to this relatively affluent, sophisticated, and well-educated group was the key to their success. "When baby-boomers start turning 65, the maturing and aging of this demographic phenomenon will be the major driving force in the U.S. marketplace," the *Wall Street Journal* reported in 1989, with experts predicting the arrival in about thirty years of a host of products specifically designed for older people.[60] The Marriott Corporation was already in the process of opening up six "catered living" communities aimed at elderly people who wanted to keep independent living arrangements but required medical supervision. With their "Brighton Gardens" communities offering assisted-living services, a licensed nursing facility, and "personal-care suites," Marriott execs believed they would be in the right place at the right time as the age wave became a tsunami.[61]

More than anyone else at the time, Ken Dychtwald recognized the commercial implications of America's passing from a young to a middle-aged society. Dychtwald's 1989 *Age Wave*, co-written with Joe Flower, was a decidedly upbeat take on baby boomers' aging trajectory, so much so that some reviewers saw it as a quasi-motivational or self-help book. As he was a corporate consultant specializing in the boomer market, however, it was not surprising that Dychtwald saw a rosy future for the largest generation in history and for companies that effectively targeted products and services to them. The wave would alter the culture of aging in America, he and Flower maintained, creating a much more friendly social climate for older people. Deeply ingrained stereotypes about seniors would fade away, they predicted, and the workplace would one day welcome employees of any age. Rather than spelling economic disaster for America, as policy experts were foretelling, the age wave was in Dychtwald's estimation a positive force and an unprecedented opportunity for those who were prepared for it.[62]

Until such a happy picture took shape, however, the unique set of demographic circumstances that were in play deeply affected baby boomers' everyday lives. As they entered midlife, boomers had become what was popularly known as the "sandwich generation," responsible both for children and for aging parents. On the brink of becoming empty nesters, many in middle age found themselves having to care for their mom and/or dad, often hardly an easy task.[63] Although boomers were obviously getting older, it was thus more their parents' aging that presented the larger concern for many of them in the 1980s and into the 1990s. Whether or not to "institutionalize" an elderly parent often became a critical choice, although that was just one of various causes of stress for adult children. What sociologists called "role reversal" was another source of anxiety, as, for example, the younger generation gradually took over the caregiving of an older one. Things got even more problematic if the relationship between the generations was not especially good. "Middle-aged children may have difficulty in handling the reversal of roles with an aging parent who they previously experienced as rejecting, unloving, and uncaring," wrote Dorothy A. Miller in the journal Social Work, an all too frequent occurrence.[64]

Further complicating things was the fact that it was often not clear if the parent was able to live independently. Again, one simply didn't wake up old one day, making the situation much more likely to be gray than black and white. Maintaining independence was understandably a priority among many seniors, putting their children in a tough spot if they believed otherwise. "Older people who cannot manage alone, but who think they can, tend to worry their children," wrote Judith E. Dobson and Russell L. Dobson in the Journal of Counseling and Development, with health, money, and socialization just a few of the factors to consider. If and when it was agreed that the parent would be better off with some outside help, another difficult decision then had to be made among three basic options: moving to a nursing home, hiring a live-in companion, or bringing mom or dad to the child's home. Each of these choices had its own complexities—a good nursing home could be difficult to find in some communities, a live-in companion might be quite an adjustment, and bringing a parent home might very well alter the dynamic of the family—adding to the pressures of the sandwich generation.[65]

Thankfully, there were a number of valuable resources to help boomers through this difficult process. Local chapters of an organization called Children of Aging Parents (CAP) were popping up in various places around the country, for example, offering training, education, and counseling for individuals having to care for an older person. The most interesting dimension of the organization, however, took place at its support group meetings that often resembled emotional therapy sessions. Members told their personal stories about an aging parent, such as when they had to move their mother or father to a nursing home. Feelings of guilt were a common theme at such sessions, as were frustration and resentment about being put in the tough position. "I feel guilty if I don't visit my mother every day," a Los Angeleno admitted at a CAP meeting in 1988, with another angrily saying, "My brother and sister are no help." As safe, warm, and caring environments where members did not judge others, CAP support groups were one of the few places where adult children could share what their experiences with an aging parent were.[66] Also helpful was Barbara Silverstone's and Helen Kandel Hyman's book *You and Your Aging Parent*, which offered good advice for those members of the sandwich generation experiencing emotional, physical, or financial problems related to the aging of a parent.[67]

Legal issues also were not uncommon when aging parents were involved. "Elder law" as a whole was becoming a fast-growing field, as more lawyers decided to specialize in legal matters specific to older people. Not only were there simply more older people in America, government programs designed to assist them were getting more complex, another reason for the emergence of what was a new discipline of law. Issues related to home ownership, discrimination in the workplace, or just establishing eligibility for Social Security or Medicaid were a few areas in which an attorney well versed in elder law could be particularly helpful.[68]

## "One of the Most Pertinent of the Late Twentieth-Century Questions"

The visceral metaphor of a pig working its way through the nation's demographic python attracted people wanting to be part of the historic phenomenon. Colleges were quickly responding to the need for more workers with some education in gerontology. "Tomorrow's professionals are flocking to the field of gerontology," declared the *Sun Sentinel* in 1987, as many students embarked on the study of the aging process. Classes in gerontology could be found in departments of psychology, sociology, education, and health, and many colleges were beginning to offer bachelor's and master's degrees in the field.[69] University after university started up gerontology centers over the course of the 1980s as educators recognized the potential for drawing more students and more money. In 1957, there were only fifty-seven schools nationwide offering classes in gerontology; thirty years later, twenty-two hundred of the thirty-two hundred accredited institutions of higher learning had at least one class in aging.[70]

Obviously, gerontology was not for every college student, and vice versa. Those choosing to major in the field didn't mind spending time with old people, quite often to their friends' surprise; rather, they felt that doing so offered many rewards. Almost guaranteed employment for the entirety of their careers was certainly one of them. Typically graduates with a degree in social work and coursework in gerontology quickly found jobs as caseworkers whose primary mission was to keep seniors living alone out of nursing homes. (While there were many good nursing homes, some were essentially dumping grounds for elderly people without family or financial resources.) It was hardly easy dealing with sickness, depression, and death, but such work became familiar territory for these rather remarkable twentysomethings. Closeness with a grandparent was often the basis for such students' unusual career choice; these young people clearly did not subscribe to the all-old-folks-are-mean school of thought.[71]

Although many excellent gerontology centers were scattered across the United States, the Los Angeles area was quickly become the nation's capital for the study of aging. In 1986, Cal State Fullerton broke ground for a center whose mission was to help seniors lead more useful lives, such as by continuing to work as long as possible.[72] Things were certainly humming down the road at USC's Ethel Percy Andrus Gerontology Center, much in part due to the work of Caleb Finch. The professor was "intent on cracking one of the most pertinent of the late 20th Century questions," according to the *Los Angeles Times*, the question being the neurobiological process of aging. By studying the molecular biology of the brain, Finch believed he might uncover the cause or causes of Alzheimer's disease, not sure at this point whether hormones, stress, heredity, or environmental factors were at work.[73]

Gerontology itself was going through a transition in the 1980s, as professionals in the field revised their thinking about aging in general. More gerontologists were coming to believe that aging was, as Cy Brickfield, executive director of AARP, put it in 1985, "a matter of choice," meaning people decided if and when to get old. Alex Comfort, who had relocated from London to Southern California, was in this camp, arguing that most aging resulted from "a kind of self-fulfilling prophecy." ("If we insist that there is a group of people who, on a fixed calendar basis, cease to be people and become unintelligent, asexual, unemployable and crazy," he had written a few years earlier, "the people so designated will be under pressure to be unintelligent, asexual, unemployable and crazy.")[74] The theory that aging was a matter of choice warranted serious research, some felt. With a $2.1 million MacArthur Foundation grant, John W. Rowe of Harvard University and a team of scientists and sociologists were exploring why some people aged "successfully" and others did not, focusing on whether the process was indeed more mental than physical.[75]

What was most exciting was that, rather than be contained in the ivory towers of academia and research institutions, gerontology worked its way further into real-life health care as it expanded. "The growing concern of the health care profession for the elderly is unprecedented," wrote Lucia C. Grassi in *Nursing Homes/ Long Term Care Management* in 1988, believing that the problems that often came with aging should no longer be considered inevitable. Quite simply, medical science and technology had advanced to the point where many health issues could be better managed, creating an almost entirely new field that those in it called biomedical gerontology.[76]

Interestingly, while aging was no longer considered a disease, health professionals were treating it as such even more so than in the past. The principal goal of biomedical gerontology and that of the closely related field of geriatrics—extending the productive years of life—was, after all, not that different from the goal of health care as whole. Most scientists working in the area of aging now believed that each individual had a finite, unique life span heavily determined by genetic factors, with environmental factors playing some role in how well or not well a person aged. No manipulation of the latter could extend longevity much beyond its maximum capability, they also agreed; not even finding a cure for cancer or heart disease would significantly extend this maximum. (This view differed from the notion of a "genetic clock," however, as proponents of that theory argued that all humans had an automatic, predetermined "turnoff" point.) Rather than trying to discover the elusive fountain of youth, then, delaying the deterioration of the human body that took place over time was biomedical gerontologists' primary effort.[77]

In part because of the growth of and advances in gerontology, the reluctance or even refusal for therapists to treat older people had greatly faded over the preceding decade. Therapists were in fact now expressing a keen interest in seniors primarily because of the changing demographics in America. Quite simply, more potential clients were in their seventies or older, making what was referred to as gerontologic or geriatric psychiatry a hot area within the field of mental health.[78] Older people had their own, unique set of psychological issues and problems, shrinks were finally realizing, good news for seniors needing help in this area.

The most pressing issue relative to the mental health of older Americans, however, was unquestionably the sharply rising number of dementia cases, dementia being defined as a decline in mental ability significant enough to interfere in daily life. Alzheimer's accounted for roughly half of all those cases. "Dementia is emerging as a major public health concern," wrote Philip G. Weiler in the *American Journal of Public Health* in 1987 as it became clearer that there were few other diseases that impacted individuals, their families and friends, and society as a whole so profoundly. Dementia was relatively common among older people, but little was known about why it occurred or how to treat it. The medical community and ordinary people had long believed that a deterioration of cognitive functioning was a natural part of the aging process (Webster's dictionary had for years defined "senility" as "old age"), but now it was understood that dementia was a distinct and especially sinister disease.[79]

Because dementia had been considered essentially "normal," not much attention had historically been given to it, but now the age wave was making those working in public health recognize the seriousness of the disease. The number of potential dementia patients was ballooning as more Americans lived into their eighties and beyond, a function of both the rising population and longer longevity. (Some felt that the incidence of the disease was also increasing completely independent of the demographics. Improved medical care allowed more time for the disease to mutate, compounding the problem.) It was estimated that about three million people in the United States were "moderately affected" by dementia, according to Weiler (ten times the affected number in 1900), a good many of them living in nursing homes. More than half of nursing home residents were believed to have the disease; in fact, the onset of a chronic mental condition was often the reason for admission to these homes.[80]

It was, however, future potential scenarios involving Alzheimer's that were most alarming. By 2000, the number of Americans with severe dementia was forecast to jump 60 percent, an outlook that understandably made public health professionals very worried. If baby boomers could possibly crash the nation's economy in a couple of decades, some warned, so might they wreak major damage to our health care system should Alzheimer's reach epidemic proportions. The more that was learned about Alzheimer's, the more there seemed to be concerned about. There was some evidence to suggest that dementia was the third or fourth leading case of mortality in the United States, in fact, although the disease was rarely reported on death certificates.[81]

As any close relative or friend of a person with Alzheimer's could tell you, the disease carried a very high emotional and financial burden. Over the course of five to ten years, Alzheimer's typically progressed from simple forgetfulness to total dependence on others, with family members and friends frequently opting to care for the patient until it was no longer possible to do so. Witnessing the gradual deterioration of a relative or friend was an especially painful, cruel experience, as the intellectual and physical abilities of the loved one slowly faded away. Even if the sufferer was institutionalized, family and friends typically contributed to caregiving in some manner until his or her death, turning others into victims of sorts. The time, energy, and money required and the emotions involved could take over the lives of a relative or friend, making Alzheimer's a major social and economic problem that was very likely to get considerably worse in the decades ahead. What was perhaps most troubling was that there were currently few if any solutions on the horizon. "Alzheimer's Disease is not likely to be a disease eliminated by a quick 'technical fix,'" Weiler concluded, calling for a "far more concerted and long-term public health effort" to help alleviate the tremendous costs both now and in the future.[82] Concerns about Alzheimer's would only grow in the 1990s as aging in America emerged as one of the most important topics in the national conversation.

# 3

## The Aging of Aquarius

This great nation is on the brink of becoming a geriatric society full of wrinkled, frail, disease-ridden, liver-spotted economic parasites, vacantly staring at big-screen nursing-home TVs, watching *thirtysomething* reruns.

—Ronald Klatz, president of the
American Academy of Anti-Aging Medicine, 1996

Dave Barry was turning forty and, ironically, the humorous author and columnist was not amused. For the first time, Barry was thinking about the aging process after noticing various changes in his own life. He had become greatly concerned about his gums, for one thing, and noticed that people were now often calling him "Mister." Barry was also finding himself having long conversations with friends about dietary fiber and, even worse, enjoying elevator music, behaviors that he interpreted as the onset of middle age or, at least, the end of his youth. As a baby boomer, Barry recognized that he was part of what he called a "major lifestyle trend"—that is, aging—but worried that he and his cohorts were not quite ready to fully grow up. "I think the entire Baby Boom generation is having trouble letting go of the idea that it represents The Nation's Youth and has an inalienable right to be wild and carefree," he wrote in his 1990 book *Dave Barry Turns Forty*, seeing the whole idea of middle age as contrary to what its members were all about.[1]

Barry was being funny, of course, but there was a lot of truth to what he was saying. The leading edge of baby boomers, of which Barry was a part, was reaching forty in great numbers in the early 1990s, a historic development along demographic lines. It was "the aging of Aquarius," said the *Nation*, as a few gray hairs noticeably popped up on the heads of the eternally youthful generation. The embarking on midlife by boomers ran parallel with antiaging efforts, not coincidentally, as researchers, marketers, and entrepreneurs recognized that pursuit of a fountain of youth could represent a business opportunity of immense proportions. American society as a whole was showing less interest in older people, however, with ageism still a feature of everyday life in the United States despite the obvious demographic changes. Many boomers themselves were displaying considerable hostility to aging, doing whatever they could to maintain a youthful appearance and attitude even as they crossed the threshold into their fifties. Tending to elderly parents further complicated the lives of those put in this difficult position; this kind of caregiving often carried staggering emotional and financial costs. But it was the prospect of tens of millions of elderly baby boomers that was most concerning to pundits of all political stripes, all of them wondering how we could afford to support so many older people in the not so distant future.

## A Research Agenda to Make Life Worth Living

If it was up to Richard Cutler, a biogerontologist at the NIA's Gerontology Research Center in Baltimore, Dave Barry and everyone else would not have to fret about turning forty or, for that matter, fifty or sixty. Despite his modern title, Cutler was from the old school of aging research, seeing getting old as an unnatural development that could and should be rectified. "What we really need is to declare war on aging like we did on cancer," he said in 1991, viewing the doubling or tripling of human life as the appropriate "cure" for the problem. Most gerontologists, and virtually everyone in government, were truly frightened of this kind of talk; they had a better understanding of the level of social change that would result should Cutler's dream of a "gerontocracy" be realized. Cutler was hardly alone in the pursuit of world of centenarians or even bi-centenarians, however. Biologist Thomas Johnson of the Institute for Behavioral Genetics at the University of Colorado was hunting down aging with the same vigor, hoping that his discovery of how to double the life span of roundworms through genetic manipulation would one day be transferred to humans.[2]

Just one year into the Human Genome Project, it could be understood why Johnson and Cutler were so excited about making aging as we knew it a thing of the past. (The project was expected to take fifteen years, but it was completed in thirteen.) Aging was directly connected to genetics, the research of Johnson and others showed, suggesting that the mapping of the roughly one hundred thousand human genes would reveal abundant knowledge about the biochemical workings of our species—specifically, why we got physically older and eventually died. Molecular biologists like Michael Rose of the University of California were equally enthusiastic about the possibilities of radical life extension. He had figured out how to double the life spans of fruit flies, and was cautiously optimistic that what he had learned could eventually be applied to mammals.[3] While evolutionary biologists generally believed that youth could not be maintained, as animals were simply not designed to live forever, molecular biologists like Rose were not so sure; he held that only experimentation would definitively answer the question.[4]

Significantly more experimentation in such areas of research could not only result in one of the biggest breakthroughs in human history, advocates of antiaging argued, but made good fiscal sense. In 1991 the Institute of Medicine (IOM) issued a report claiming that spending an additional few hundred million dollars a year on medical research on aging could save the United States billions of dollars in future health care costs. Some $600 million was currently spent on research dedicated to health-related aspects of aging, according to the report, a small fraction of the more than $162 billion spent on treating ailments associated with the elderly. Bumping up that $600 million by 50 percent would yield major savings in health care costs for years to come, the independent and nonprofit organization (which was part of the prestigious National Academy of Sciences) estimated, as scientists uncovered new ways to prevent or delay disabling illnesses. "This is not a research agenda to keep you from dying," said Julius R. Krevans, chancellor of UC San Francisco and chairman of the panel of experts responsible for the report, but rather "a research agenda to make life worth living."[5] It was not quite clear where or how the IOM got its numbers, but such "hard" facts backed up quantitatively by respected institutions must have buoyed the spirits of researchers working in the rather outlying field of antiaging.[6]

Indeed, just about one hundred individuals were studying the basic mechanisms of aging in 1990, making this arena of gerontology a tiny slice of the total scientific research pie. (Thousands were investigating AIDS at the time.) But with such high stakes, more researchers would undoubtedly join the crusade against aging, it was believed, particularly given what the media interpreted as very promising preliminary findings. Knowing that the idea of eternal youth made good copy, journalists took the liberty of describing any sign of progress in the field in optimistic (too optimistic, in fact) terms. The fountain of youth legend (which actually dated back to the fifth century BCE) was too difficult to resist for some covering the antiaging beat. Juan Ponce de León may have looked in all the wrong places (he famously found Florida instead), but now scientists were "on the verge of finding the true fountain of youth," *Newsweek* giddily reported in 1990. "Lab-coat conquistadors" were just as determined as the sixteenth-century Spanish explorer to conquer aging, the magazine told readers, the good news being that the secret gusher resided within our own cells and genes. "A glorious scientific quest is underway," *Newsweek* announced perfectly seriously, backed up by experts like long-time gerontologist Leonard Hayflick of UC San Francisco, who viewed antiaging as "the last great biological frontier."[7]

As researchers pursued their glorious quest, the usual parade of alleged antiaging agents made the news throughout the 1990s as scientists excitedly reported promising findings. DHEA, the naturally occurring hormone, for example, was moving beyond its cult status, as further research indicated it could possibly reverse some of the physiological and psychological signs of aging.[8] Melatonin, another hormone, was also getting a lot of attention after mice that received the substance lived to the human equivalent of 115 years.[9] Melatonin had yet to show any antiaging effect in people, however, another reason to be skeptical of the growing number of radical life-extension achievements in tiny animals.[10]

Lengthening the sweet spot of humans' lives was of course a very appealing concept, but aging research also had direct and immediate applications. Most important, work to find the cause of and one hoped cure for Alzheimer's disease was picking up steam as it became increasingly seen as already an epidemic. Four million Americans were estimated to now have the disease, a number that would almost certainly accelerate rapidly over the next few decades. Research was currently focused on the idea of the disease being a natural part of the aging process that resulted when a particular gene (located on chromosome 19, to be specific) "wore out" or became defective. Everyone would ultimately get Alzheimer's if they lived long enough, this line of thought went, a scary proposition especially given the parallel efforts to increase longevity. Metabolic waste built up in brain cells and destroyed them when the gene could no longer do its job, a Duke University study showed; this research explained the scarred brain tissue that often came with the disease.[11]

Any effort to slow the cognitive or physical effects of aging was formidable, however, given that the medical community still did not really understand the root cause of bodily decline. Were the symptoms common to older people, say, a loss of sensation in the lower extremities, part of normal aging or a manifestation of a disease? Doctors simply did not know, with some even arguing that the distinction was no longer relevant. Normal biological aging was difficult if not impossible to define, they conceded, especially given the fact that people became less alike physically as they got older. Organs tended to perform less well as humans aged, it was known, but in many instances that process closely resembled or mimicked signs of disease. (Symptoms of hyperglycemia looked a lot like those of diabetes, for example.) Although in terms of treatment it may not have mattered much whether a complaint was symptomatic of a disease or just due to aging, physicians, especially those in geriatrics, had to be careful when making a diagnosis. Labeling a patient as having a disease when he or she did not could cause all kinds of problems down the road, as anything and everything on a medical chart was routinely used as the basis for prescribed care for future conditions.[12] It was becoming increasingly clear that the more scientists knew about aging, the more they realized they did not know; many believed there was no more challenging area of research in our time.

## A Startling Phenomenon

While scientists continued their quixotic quest to conquer physical aging, the very real problem of discrimination against older people remained pervasive in American society. Women in their fifties and sixties were frequent targets, especially in the workplace, as gender bias was compounded with age bias. One of the more interesting cases of job discrimination based on age was certainly the 1991 lawsuit filed by sixty-one-year-old Joyce Stratton, who had recently been fired. Who was Stratton's employer? The New York City Department of Aging, which Stratton claimed undertook "a systematic pattern and practice of firing and forcing out the older employees." Stratton, who worked for the agency for twenty-one years helping elderly people apply for food stamps and other benefits, was understandably unhappy when she was dismissed for reasons of what a spokesperson said was "retrenchment" (that is, budget cuts). When a significantly younger (and lower-salaried) person filled her position, Stratton called her son, a lawyer, who promptly filed suit in Federal District Court.[13] Four years later, Stratton was vindicated when a federal jury awarded her a million dollars in the civil suit. Stratton's age was "a determinative factor" in her firing, the eight-member jury unanimously determined (after just one hour of deliberation); the irony of it all was not overlooked. Her victory represented "a victory for other elderly people," Stratton announced after the jury's decision was made public, hoping that her case would help prevent other employers from using age as the basis for hiring and firing policies.[14]

Inequity directed toward women of a certain age occurred in less insidious ways, even among the rich and famous. Katharine Graham, chairman of the executive committee of the *Washington Post* in 1995, was thinking a lot about aging as she turned seventy-eight, due to the ways in which she found herself being treated. (She died in 2001.) When receiving the Productive Aging Award from the Jewish Council for the Aging in Rockville, Maryland, Graham first delivered her theory on why some people aged well and others did not. Genetics was the most important factor, she believed, but there were some environmental factors as well at work. "You have to read a lot and not drink," she told the group, her antiaging recipe a lot simpler than most. On a personal level, Graham realized she had become old in other people's minds when she observed certain behaviors by friends and associates. "You look wonderful," she kept hearing a few years back for the first time in her life, interpreting the compliment as coming with the unspoken caveat of her advancing age. People had also began asking if she "still" did certain things— play tennis, for example—and noticed that close friends had started to hold her arm as if she needed help getting around. "It's a startling phenomenon and, at least in my case, it happened all of a sudden," Graham revealed, surprised to find herself treated with what she considered to be condescension given her undiminished energy and vitality.[15]

Women a generation younger, meanwhile, were negotiating the often complicated process of menopause. Well-known writers going through the experience explored the subject in considerable detail, knowing that millions of other women were going through the process at the same time, or soon would be. To write her 1992 *The Silent Passage* (based on an article for *Vanity Fair*), Gail Sheehy spoke to more than a hundred women going through menopause as well as seventy-five experts in the subject. Baby boomers were not prepared for "the silent passage," she concluded, a byproduct of America's discomfort for all physical signs of aging, especially those of women.[16]

Germaine Greer's *The Change: Women, Aging and the Menopause*, which was published the same year, also focused on the difficulties many boomers were just beginning to face as they reached the early stages of menopause. Greer's book went much further than Sheehy's by locating the subject within the broader arena of ageism directed at women. Unlike their male counterparts, middle-aged women were essentially invisible in American culture, she argued, with the half-century mark generally serving as the dividing line between being perceived as young or old. Doctors were no better when it came to the treatment of women on the old side of the fence, Greer added, especially treatment given to those going through menopause. Aging was, however, an opportunity for women to grow in a way they never could when younger, she made clear, seeing the fifty-plus years as a great time in which to focus on oneself while letting go all-too-common insecurities about one's body.[17]

Another icon of feminism, Betty Friedan, was saying much the same thing every chance she could get. She had become a visible presence on the "aging circuit," speaking at many conferences to deliver her message about the issues both women and men confronted as they got older. Her new book, *The Fountain of Age,* had quickly become a best seller, and some were thinking it might launch a "liberation movement" along the lines of what her *Feminine Mystique* had done for feminism thirty years earlier. Friedan was seventy-two when her new book was finally released in 1993 (it had taken ten years for her to write), and was she more committed than ever to help free older Americans from what she now called the "age mystique." Vigorous, dynamic people like Katharine Graham were everywhere you looked, she had found in her research; there appeared to be much truth to the adage that one was old only if one thought one was. There were few positive images of older people in the media, however, making it easy to understand why so many of those over fifty years of age believed they were indeed over the hill. "We have to get beyond the age mystique and begin to see age as a new period of human life," Friedan said on one of her many book tour stops, like Greer viewing one's later years in positive terms.[18]

Given that these women were strongly committed to continue to grow intellectually and, perhaps, spiritually, it was not surprising that they each had such a positive take on getting older. It was important to remember that some older people did and some did not, this distinction perhaps being the most significant factor in the aging process, with the notable exception of genetics. Those who were "successfully" aging were apt to simply ignore their chronological age and not fall victim to cultural stereotypes about "old people." "Some people never lose their joie de vivre, their ongoing willingness to learn new things, tackle new tasks, and, perhaps most important, to hold onto the conviction that they're only as old as they feel," wrote Kathy Keeton in *Omni* in 1992. Gilbert Brim, a psychologist and director of a major MacArthur Foundation–sponsored research project whose staff was exploring virtually every dimension of aging, also believed that approaching life after age sixty, seventy, or even eighty as an opportunity for growth and development was key to a sense of well-being. Much of aging was in the mind, he and others held, with a positive attitude toward life a lot more than just self-help psychobabble. Indeed, other studies had shown a direct link between a bleak outlook and a weakened immune system, additional evidence that the brain heavily determined the relative health of the rest of the body.[19]

Rather than being limited to a relatively few enlightened seniors, a sense of well-being in fact appeared to be quite widespread among members of the age group. A survey done by *Parade* magazine in 1993 certainly suggested this, as well as supporting the idea that it was younger, versus older, people who had the bigger problems about aging. The magazine asked twenty-five hundred Americans a host of questions related to aging and found that those sixty-five years or older were quite positive about their station in life, a story much different from the rather gloomy narrative that was commonly accepted by those who were younger. (Just 14 percent of those aged sixty-five to seventy-five said they had a negative view of aging, with a significantly higher percentage expressing some unpleasantness being that age.) "The perception of aging and old age improves with age," noted Horace Deets, executive director of AARP, in explaining the results of the poll, adding: "People who actually are experiencing what it means to be older seem to find that it's not as bad as they were led to believe."[20]

Scholarly research also supported the idea that our negative views about aging should be turned upside down. A study published in the *Journal of Personality and Social Psychology* in 1998 indicated that "a heightened sense of well-being" came along with getting older, contradicting the standard American belief that one's senior years were a mostly depressing time of life. Among a sample of twenty-seven hundred adults ranging in age from twenty-five to seventy-four, older respondents more frequently reported feeling happy than younger ones, the study by a pair of Fordham University scientists showed. Some previous studies had found that happiness increased with age, making these results appear not to be an anomaly. Were older people more cheerful because they had more experience keeping their emotions on an even keel? Was it because they were perhaps more focused on the present, appreciative of whatever time they had left in life? The researchers were not sure, but it was clear that their findings supported the view that aging was typically not the sad affair many thought it to be.[21]

As with any particular group of people, however, there was significant variation in the happiness level of seniors. Anecdotal evidence strongly suggested that the most cheerful older people were those who were involved in the lives of others, an unsurprising finding given that social engagement was generally linked to contentedness in life. Keeping busy and doing things that were meaningful were also excellent ways to simply stay alive, seniors would tell you if asked; it was a much healthier alternative to "calendar counting" (keeping track of the additional years one was likely to live based on statistics). Volunteering and doing good works for others were especially therapeutic, those who did so reported, a means of feeling one was part of a community and a reason to live in the present versus dwelling on a nostalgic past or a fearful future.[22]

As further evidence that the idea of mandatory retirement should itself be retired, meaningful employment was especially conducive to a sanguine outlook on life. Fortunately, companions to the elderly were much needed in many areas of the country, offering paid jobs for retirees who could very well be octogenarians themselves.[23] Besides the income, which many seniors very much needed, those who continued to work after the age of sixty-five were most likely to retain "mental agility," researchers from UCLA and Harvard had found.[24] If continuing to work was not feasible or desirable, mental agility could also be achieved through any number of creative avenues, some seniors were discovering. Creativity was perceived by older people as helping them stay engaged and feel good about themselves, a study published in the *Journal of Aging Studies* reported, with painting, singing, gardening, cooking, or sewing a wonderful way to remain optimistic and excited about life.[25]

## Hope and Improvement but Not Miracles

While some women recognized that their third act of life could offer much happiness and fulfillment, it did not mean they had to simply accept the physical signs of aging. Many midlife or older women understandably wanted it both ways, that is, to embrace the idea of aging well while fighting the actual signs of it with whatever means necessary. The two pursuits were not mutually exclusive, after all, meaning there were significant opportunities for companies wishing to market products and services to a wide range of women.

Maybelline, the mass-marketer of cosmetics, was one such company keen on reaching the huge audience of aging boomers with products designed to help them look younger. Like most cosmetics marketers, Maybelline had long focused on younger consumers, but by the 1990s it was clear that women thirty-five and older represented potentially big business. For some time now competitors like Clinique, Estée Lauder, Elizabeth Arden, and Lancôme had been going after upscale middle-aged consumers who shopped at department stores, but the lower end of the market was wide open for a company like Maybelline, which sold its products primarily through mass merchandisers and drugstores. Maybelline's direct competitor Revlon was choosing to stay with younger consumers, not at all interested in having a middle-aged image. For such cosmetics marketers, beauty remained entirely a youthful domain despite the fast-changing demographics of the nation.[26]

The company having recently gone public, Maybelline executives were especially excited to launch its new Revitalizing line in 1993. The line included foundations, concealers, blushes, and powders that contained moisturizers, sunscreens, vitamin A, and light diffusers that allegedly counteracted or hid the signs of aging. Sensibly, the company used what it called "age-appropriate" models in its advertising for its line of "age-denying makeup"; it was quite unusual at the time, however, to see any women with crow's-feet featured in magazines and on television. While the new brand may have seemed like a no-brainer, Maybelline execs understood they had to walk a fine line when crossing the intersection of aging and beauty. "We're not pitching it as old-lady makeup," the president of the company told the *Wall Street Journal*, seeing his Revitalizing line of products as offering "hope and improvement but not miracles" to mature women.[27]

Other cosmetics manufacturers. including Mary Kay, the multilevel marketer, were entering the growing antiaging segment with wrinkle creams and lotions targeted to middle-aged women. Avon's Anew and Pond's Age Defying Complex each used alpha-hydroxy acids (AHA) as its active ingredient to smooth out crow's-feet and make skin look younger and softer; the difference with these products was that they supposedly could "repair" skin (by creating new collagen) versus simply preventing future "damage." As the miracle cure of the moment, AHA began to appear not just in wrinkle creams for the face but also in shampoos, sunscreens, nail treatments, shaving creams, soaps, and even self-tanning lotions. The cosmetics industry had lifted, so to speak, AHAs from dermatologists, who had long used them in facial chemical peels. Dermatologists used high concentrations of the acids to work their magic, however, while over-the-counter products used much lower solutions (and were loaded with moisturizers to temporarily get rid of wrinkles). Again the FDA was looking askance at what the industry had begun calling "cosmeceuticals," not sure if they were a cosmetic or a drug or, more important, did what their manufacturers claimed they did.[28]

Whether they worked or not, antiaging cosmetics targeted to women had become a business worth hundreds of millions of dollars, reason enough for the industry to begin thinking about marketing similar products to men. Men had much less need for such products than women, however, as men were not judged so severely by youthful standards of beauty. For a brief time, in fact, a couple of famous older men became somewhat of a sensation in the media. Recognizing that some of the nation's most beloved male actors were reaching the age of seventy in 1994, the editors of a few popular magazines decided to feature one on the cover of an issue. With a new movie recently out that was getting good reviews (*Nobody's Fool*), Paul Newman was chosen for the cover of no less than three magazines in December of that year: *New York* (which nominated him as "the Sexiest 70-year-old Man Alive"), *Newsweek*, and *GQ*. (*Entertainment Weekly* had also wanted to feature Newman on a cover but dropped the idea after seeing his face on the other magazines.) It was another septuagenarian, however, whom more readers saw on the cover of a popular magazine that month. Seventy-four-year-old (and presumably makeup-free) Pope John Paul II appeared on the cover of both the *New York Times Magazine* and *Time* (he was *Time*'s Man of the Year), making him a bigger superstar than even the sexiest seventy-year-old man alive.[29]

## Generations Aging Together

While scientists tried to rid the world of aging and cosmetics marketers offered ways for consumers to hide its signs, the simple truth was that America and Americans were getting older. With the first wave of baby boomers about to begin turning fifty years old in just seven months, the timing of the White House Conference on Aging held in May 1995 could not have been better. (President Bush did not choose to sponsor such an event in 1991, apparently wanting to avoid the kind of fiasco that his predecessor, President Reagan, endured during his 1981 conference.) About twenty-two hundred delegates (and three hundred others) attended the 1995 conference, which had been mandated by the prior, Democrat-controlled Congress and was run by the Clinton White House. The theme of this conference was "generations aging together," a reflection perhaps of the defensiveness delegates held toward their cause given the budget-conscious Republican-controlled Congress. Rather than a special interest group on the fringes of society that was dependent on taxpayer money, seniors were at the very heart of the fabric of America, the aging constituency wanted to emphasize. Retirees were continually fighting the common perception of themselves as "greedy geezers" sticking to their entitlements like glue, much preferring the image of "productive citizens," if only society would allow them to be such. At the conference, President Clinton capitalized on delegates' concerns for political purposes, using the event to attack the GOP and its discussed plans to cut Medicare in order to pay for tax cuts for the wealthy. (The uninvited Speaker of the House, Newt Gingrich, received boos when the president mentioned his name.)[30]

Besides playing some politics, Clinton used the 1995 White House Conference on Aging to pay homage to his hero John F. Kennedy. Kennedy had used his own White House Conference on Aging in 1961 to maintain the safety net for seniors that FDR had created in 1935, and Clinton was thus carrying on the sixty-year legacy that had begun during the New Deal and was advanced by LBJ's Great Society. Not surprisingly, the delegates at the 1995 aging conference strongly endorsed maintaining and even expanding the government's Medicare and Social Security programs. In April 1983, the Social Security Act was amended in a remarkably bipartisan effort to extend the fund's solvency for a few more decades by gradually raising the retirement age from sixty-five to sixty-seven and through other cost-saving measures. Subsequent crises in federal entitlements and political measures, filtered through a rising generation of neoconservatives, were the catalysts for Robert H. Binstock's notion of "compassionate ageism" and the infamous "Greedy Geezer" on a 1988 cover of the *New Republic*. Against this backdrop, the face of ageism changed, with the "new old" neither as poor nor as unhealthy as their parents and grandparents.[31]

Supporters of benefits for the elderly made sure to use the 1995 conference as a forum to avoid returning to the old "old" days. "The message is very clear—unequivocal reaffirmation of support across the generations for Social Security and Medicare and against drastic one-sided cuts," said Bill Ritz, spokesman for the National Committee to Preserve Social Security and Medicare, a day after the conference ended. Dozens of other political resolutions were discussed and voted on, but it was that one that delegates understood was the most vital for their constituency. (Republicans had proposed ending the status of Medicaid as an entitlement program and converting it into a block grant program to be run totally by the states. States would then have the power to exclude certain individuals currently eligible under the federal system.) Reconfirming stipulations in the Older Americans Act that provided meals, home visits, transportation services, legal assistance, and other benefits for the elderly also received many votes. Volunteerism was another key theme at this conference (an extension of one of Clinton's main initiatives), with many delegates interested in learning how they could "give something back" to younger people.[32]

Social Security, Medicare, and the benefits outlined in the Older Americans Act were crucial for the elderly, of course, but none of those offered the kind of care that was often needed for a dependent individual. The children of elderly parents had to fill that gap more frequently as members of the "Greatest Generation" reached their seventies, eighties, and nineties. By 1997, in fact, nearly one in four American households were involved in caring for an aging relative, a survey showed; that statistic represented a threefold increase from a decade earlier. Now 22.4 million American families were providing some kind of physical or emotional assistance to a relative, the National Caregiving Survey revealed, with the average caregiver devoting eighteen hours a week to that part of his or her life. About a fifth of that number devoted forty hours or more a week to caregiving, however, with the commitment typically lasting at least four years. "We're not talking about the son who calls his mother on Sundays and says, 'How are you?'" noted Gail Hunt, executive director of the National Alliance for Caregiving, which cosponsored the study along with AARP and Glaxo Wellcome, the pharmaceutical company. Caregivers were shelling out about $2 billion a month on groceries, medicine, and other expenses for their older relatives, a clear indication that boomers were not about to abandon their parents when the latter became financially dependent (as some had feared). More boomers were also turning down job promotions if it meant relocating because of elder care issues, the survey found, as well as frequently giving up personal activities, hobbies, and vacations due to the commitment they had taken on.[33] "Old is fast becoming the quintessential American experience," noted *Time* (somewhat exaggeratedly) in 1996, as two generations struggled to come to terms with the consequences of aging.[34]

Fittingly, the quintessential American experience of aging had much to do with money. The elder care issue had become significant (and costly) enough by the mid-1990s that *Money* magazine felt the need to publish an article called "How to Care for Your Aging Parents (Without Going Broke)." Moving mom or dad into your home, assuming he or she could no longer live alone, made sense not just for practical reasons but for financial ones as well, *Money* told readers who were understandably worried they might go broke as their parents aged. Extensive home care or a long stay in a nursing home was often prohibitively expensive (each could wipe out a lifetime of savings), making a familial arrangement usually the best option if it was at all feasible. Retrofitting the house, hiring in-home help, and considering adult day care were all steps *Money* advised the many middle-agers who were prepared to make what was a life-altering step for all parties involved.[35]

Corporate America too was concerned about and offering help to the increasing number of Americans providing care for aging relatives. In 1995, twenty-one of the nation's largest companies expanded a dependent care program that had begun three years earlier, a response to employees' growing needs in this area of their lives. Blue-chip corporations like AT&T, Johnson & Johnson, and Exxon were contributing a total of $100 million over six years to support projects ranging from day care providers to money-management courses for seniors. While the program obviously benefited employees, executives recognized that it was also in their company's own best interests and thus money well spent. Employees' taking time off to care for aging relatives would represent a bigger hit to their companies' bottom lines, they knew, and it was difficult for workers who were worried about a parent to stay focused while on the job. Many businesses in the United States were downsizing at this time, but some level of assistance for elder care was considered a necessary expense in order to attract and keep committed employees.[36]

Even with considerable help from outside parties, caregiving for older relatives was frequently the most challenging thing that baby boomers had ever experienced. Memory issues among parents, especially if part of dementia, were a particularly difficult problem to deal with. A parent could very well mistake a child for his or her own mother or father, or mix up the names and identities of siblings. Lengthy reminders and explanations often did not correct the situation, making midlife children unsure if they should even bother trying to set the record straight. A parent could be there physically but much less so mentally, a strange and disturbing development for everyone involved. Taking charge of a parent's life was fast becoming a rite of passage for boomers, and a very difficult one given that it was typically on-the-job training. Caregivers without siblings had to go it alone, while those with brothers or sisters sometimes found themselves in conflict about who was not doing his or her share. Whether or not mom or dad should be placed in a nursing home could be a contentious decision, so much so that family relationships never recovered from the squabble. Again, guilt was a common theme, with the feeling that one was never doing as much as one could even if a son or daughter was devoting many hours a week to the taking care of a parent.[37]

## The Virtues of Aging

As adult children struggled to do the best they could for the person or persons who had done the same for them many years before, middle-aged Americans themselves sought out ways to come to terms with the realities of aging. In addition to the many books on the topic, seminars and workshops addressing various dimensions of aging were becoming increasingly popular. Progressive views toward aging were more likely to be found in the margins than in the mainstream. At the Omega Institute in Rhinebeck, New York, for example, a rabbi was leading a five-day workshop called "From Age-ing to Sage-ing: The Practice of Spiritual Eldering." "The participants here are after a more transformative experience than that offered by the boomer model of keeping old age at arm's length with a busy program of physical and social activity," observed Karin Horgan Sullivan in *Vegetarian Times* after a visit to the off-the-beaten-track adult learning center. Learning how to embrace one's older years rather than fear and dread them was the goal of the course that drew not just from Judaism but also from Sufism, Buddhism, Native American spirituality, and humanistic psychology. "Many of us are rich without knowing it because we have not permitted ourselves to examine and take delight in the successes that we planted in the past," instructed Rabbi Zalman, seeing our older years as an opportunity to "harvest our lives." While such thinking could be considered avant-garde, it was steeped in the values of many traditional societies where tribal elders were revered for their wisdom and life experience.[38]

While John W. Rowe and Robert L. Kahn did not go nearly as far in yet another book entitled *Successful Aging*, they did present getting older as a much more fulfilling experience than it was commonly believed to be. Having had a ten-year MacArthur Foundation initiative to study individuals who had "successfully aged"—that is, maintained good health, were social active, and remained productive—the authors were able to debunk many of the usual myths associated with the lives of seniors. The majority of older Americans were not sick, idle, and isolated people, as many assumed they were, the pair's research showed, with lifestyle more important than genetics in determining their relative quality of life (contradicting the prevailing view among gerontologists). Interestingly, Rowe, president of

Mount Sinai School of Medicine, and Kahn, professor emeritus of public health at the University of Michigan, borrowed on both Freudian and Eriksonian theory in interpreting the results of their study, finding that physical and mental well-being in one's later years was, again, heavily dependent on having close personal relationships and staying active. In many ways, the authors were building on the work of Robert Butler, who, a generation earlier, championed the idea of "productive aging." Butler himself had done a lot of myth busting, arguing that the predominant model of older age—leisurely retirement—was not in the best interests of many seniors hoping to live long, happy lives.[39]

Butler, who had been studying aging since the 1950s, was still very much active in the field. Editor in chief of *Geriatrics* and director of the International Longevity Center in the late 1990s, he was now very much interested in the physiological effects of space flight upon aging. In 1997, the NIA and NASA cosponsored a conference to discuss that very subject, with scientists from each agency intrigued by the apparent changes in the human body with the loss of gravity. Variations in immune response, bone formation, muscle and motor control, spatial orientation, biological rhythms, and cardiovascular functions had all been observed on previous space flights, sufficient evidence to warrant exploration of these variations in more detail. "The best way to begin answering questions about aging and space travel would be to include older mammalian organisms on future space flights," Butler recommended in the journal he edited, thinking that this could possibly lead to the "next giant leap for mankind."[40]

Which older mammalian organism should be chosen for such an ambitious undertaking? One particular candidate stood out: John Glenn, the ex-astronaut and retired Democratic senator from Ohio. When asked to join the crew on an upcoming mission on the shuttle *Discovery*, Glenn was enthusiastic about going into space for a final time, believing that the questions being asked by the NIA and NASA were worthy ones. Given that Glenn had served in the Senate into his mid-seventies and was now going to be shot into space, many viewed him as the perfect example of "successful" or "productive" aging. The seventy-seven-year-old Glenn initially deflected remarks about his age, however, focusing instead on the experiments that he would help conduct on the mission. But while in space Glenn began to acknowledge that it was indeed his age that would most likely be remembered about the trip. The oldest astronaut in history even began to make jokes about it ("I can have my Tang mixed with either Geritol or Metamucil," he quipped), and was amenable to offering advice about aging when asked (don't "live by the calendar," he advised other seniors). If Ronald Reagan was the country's leading role model for seniority in the 1980s, John Glenn appeared to have assumed that title at the end of the twentieth century.[41]

Some, however, cautioned about using Glenn as a model of aging well, as his latest achievement (and extraordinary career, for that matter) were clearly more the exception than the rule. More realistic standards should be set for septuagenarians, they argued, as he was not really representative of the abilities of his age group. Going further, viewing one's sixties or seventies as a kind of "new middle age" could be a dangerous thing, as bodies did indeed typically deteriorate over time. Avoiding having to live in a nursing home was a much more realistic goal for the average person in his or her late seventies, such critics (including most gerontologists) argued, unhappy with how the media was using Glenn as a prime example of positive aging in action.[42] Still, some writers were going even further than espousing productive or successful aging, believing that a lifestyle like Glenn's was something other seniors in good shape should at least strive for. In her *Power Aging: Staying Young at Any Age*, for example, Gayle Olinekova, a nutritional and fitness expert, advised readers on how they could achieve peak physical, mental, and sexual performance regardless of their age, a very high setting of the bar for anyone of whatever age.[43]

Concepts like productive, successful, and power aging may have had their faults given the reality of older minds and bodies, but, to their credit, they did help to counter negative stereotypes about seniors in America. Aging in this country was seen primarily as a problem, a function of what Helen Kerschner and Jo Ann M. Pegues called a "dependency paradigm" that framed the subject. While "superseniors" like Glenn (or George Burns, who was still tap-dancing right up to his death at the age of one hundred in 1996) were obviously extraordinary, their images were certainly more beneficial and arguably more truthful than the popular notion of a largely poor and frail elderly population. Most older people were, in fact, independent and in relatively good health, despite the prevalent idea that almost all senior citizens were heavily dependent on myriad government-funded services and support programs to survive. "It is important to dispel the many negative myths and stereotypes associated with growing older," Kerschner and Pegues wrote in the *Journal of the American Dietetic Association*, even if that did involve using exceptional people as symbols for aging well.[44]

Other senior citizens were lauded for their ability to essentially ignore their age. Certainly not lying in a chaise longue around the pool of Sun City in the 1990s were Jimmy and Rosalynn Carter, who were also now in their seventies. In *The Virtues of Aging*, the ex-president told his post–White House story that was the very model for what Rowe and Kahn were talking about. Although he had held the highest position in the land and possibly the world, Jimmy Carter had gone on to achieve great things in the almost twenty years since leaving elected office at the age of fifty-six. Together, he and his wife had lived up to the ideals expressed in their 1987 book *Everything to Gain: Making the Most of the Rest of Your Life* through their involvement in a range of projects and activities dedicated to the public good (including Habitat for Humanity, the Carter Center, and the Atlanta Project). When not building houses or bringing local communities together, the Carters taught Sunday school and served as ambassadors for international peace, making what would be for many a cushy period of retirement seem like a lazy and wasteful exercise. "The virtues of aging include both the blessings that come to us as we grow older and what we have to offer that might be beneficial to others," the ex-president wrote in the new book, seeing an active third act of life as a win-win opportunity for both individuals and society.[45]

In his book about aging, the writer Theodore Roszak took a different tack, describing how a close brush with death in his late fifties was the impetus for his own reinvention. It was only after this crisis that Roszak became "serious about life," he explained in his *America the Wise: The Longevity Revolution and the True Wealth of Nations*, having previously been excessively focused on his career and making money. Based on his personal experience, Roszak (best known for his 1969 *The Making of a Counter Culture* and for actually coining the term "counterculture") proposed that baby boomers were ideally positioned to begin a progressive social movement grounded in the same spirit as the one they led in their younger years in the late 1960s. In twenty or so years, he argued, many of the architects of the counterculture would be freed from the demands of family life and work, and thus could renew their efforts to achieve a more just, peaceful, and civil society that was less reliant on the competitiveness of consumer capitalism. A "compassionate economy" could be achieved if graying boomers set their collective mind to it, Roszak believed, thinking they could make a much greater contribution to society in their later years than spending much of their time listening to oldies radio stations or playing golf.[46]

Not everyone, however, envisioned such an idealistic scenario for the age wave that lay ahead. There was a literal cost to so many people getting old at the same time, Peter G. Peterson reminded us, making notions like Roszak's purely wishful thinking. Money was at the heart of two books published by Peterson, as the chairman of the Blackstone Group investment firm sounded the alert about the "demographic iceberg" that was floating directly in the path of the nation's future. In his *Will America Grow Up Before It Grows Old?* of 1996 and *Gray Dawn* of 1999, Peterson argued that the country simply couldn't afford to support Social Security and Medicare as the tens of millions of baby boomers entered their retirement years. Peterson, who had been secretary of commerce in the Nixon administration, believed that such programs consisted of "subsidized leisure" and thus were an entitlement that had no basis in fiscal responsibility.[47]

As the end of the twentieth century drew to a close—a major historical marker in its own right—other observers of the national scene sounded alerts about the economic dangers of the age wave. Writing in the *New Republic* in April 1999, Robert J. Samuelson presented the aging of America as "one of the most profound—and possibly fearsome—social changes in our history," noting that until 1980 the United States had been essentially a country of young people. That had all changed as the tens of millions of baby boomers entered their thirties, and it was abundantly obvious that these same people would constitute a massive population of seniors by 2030. Indeed, the dawn of a new century and millennium appeared to spark a crisis mentality regarding the aging of America. Peterson and popular columnists such as Samuelson and George Will warned that nothing short of a calamity was approaching, using research by Sam Preston, a sociologist at the University of Pennsylvania, and other academics working in population studies as ammunition.[48]

One did not have to be a demographer to detect the seismic cultural shift that was in play, yet what might legitimately be considered a revolutionary transformation of the most powerful civilization in history was going largely ignored save for this relatively small group of obviously very worried people. "We have done little as a nation to prepare for it," Samuelson argued; "we have only dimly contemplated what it means for our politics, our economy, and the character of our society." The author of *The Good Life and Its Discontents: The American Dream in the Age of Entitlement* was chiefly concerned about the fate of Social Security and Medicare, particularly when the trend was for people to retire earlier than they used to. It was indeed true that older Americans were healthier and lived longer than ever but were retiring at younger ages, a potentially disastrous scenario given that seniors' later years were heavily subsidized by taxpayers' money. We were "mortgaging our future,"

Samuelson warned, worried that the baby boomers' final contribution would be to wreck the nation's economy.[49]

## The True Fountain of Youth

If antiaging scientists could deliver anything close to what they hoped to, however, the nightmare scenarios economists were predicting could just be the sky-is-falling fretting of a bunch of Chicken Littles. Extending the lives of baby boomers by a couple of decades would postpone the massive wave of people becoming seniors at roughly the same time, one might conclude, and thus push back the government's need to provide benefits for them. As always, the media were eagerly promoting antiaging research in excessively buoyant terms, with some kind of breakthrough right around the corner. "Scientists are just beginning to unlock the mysteries of aging and, more to the point, to discover how we may be able to prevent it," beamed *Time* in 1996. In addition to Rose's promising work with fruit flies, Siegfried Hekimi, a genetics professor at McGill University, was extending the life span of nematodes by more than five times. The rules of aging were "quietly being broken," the magazine told readers, as a growing community of researchers challenged the accepted laws of nature in labs around the world. If the cellular mechanisms that controlled aging were the same for all organisms, as scientists suspected they were, the proven ability to multiply the life spans of worms and insects could be applied to humans; this was the news that had people so excited.[50]

Although a skeptic would point out that decades of antiaging research had so far produced nothing of any consequence to prevent us from getting older, it was true that science had been instrumental in lengthening life expectancy during the twentieth century. In 1900 the life expectancy for a person born in the United States was forty-seven years old, and now, near the end of the century, it was nearly seventy-six. Why would an equivalent leap in longevity not be made in the next century, proponents of antiaging asked, using history as a means to justify their unapologetic enthusiasm. Besides that, scientific progress was exponential rather than linear, they suggested, meaning current research, especially that relating to DNA, would very likely lead to bigger leaps than those made in the past through antibiotics and other avenues of preventing illness and delaying death. The leading antiaging therapies of the day—melatonin, antioxidants, DHEA, and hormone-replacement therapy—were small potatoes to what lay ahead, they pronounced, as the building blocks of the human body were revealed at the cellular and genetic levels.[51]

Until doubling or tripling of the current average human life span was realistic, one age in particular—a hundred years old—was now often recognized as a reasonable goal to reach. More and more people were becoming
centenarians, of course, making that figure not the Methuselah-like number
it once was. The closing of a century also likely had something to do with the
rather sudden desirability of a one-hundred-year life span, as did the first
baby boomers' passing of the half-century mark. "When the boomers started
turning 50, it was like the start of the Oklahoma land rush," observed Dan
Perry, director of the Washington-based Alliance for Aging Research, in 1997;
research by his organization revealed that newly minted fiftysomethings were
determined to make it to a hundred and do so in relatively good health. One
out of twenty-six people were currently expected to live to that age, according
to Census Bureau projections (it was one out of five hundred a century earlier), but many believed that emerging and future antiaging therapies would
dramatically increase those odds.[52] Perry believed there was a great deal of
urgency attached to making the development of those therapies a reality. "We
have no more than 15 or 20 years to unravel the secrets of age-related disease
and to develop interventions," he had said a few years earlier, adding: "If we
don't, we'll have a huge population of infirm baby boomers to whom we can
offer nothing better than painkillers and nursing homes."[53]

Although no one yet even knew what caused aging, much less how to
stop it, a glance at the titles on the shelves of bookstores suggested otherwise.
*The Anti-Aging Hormones*, *Younger at Last*, and *Brain Longevity* were just a
few titles in the growing antiaging literary segment, each of them proposing
that there were known ways to turn back the clock or, at minimum, slow it
down. Because all of the body's organs, tissues, and cells were somehow involved, however, the aging process of the human body was, to say the least, a
complicated affair. Genes, hormones, molecules, and immune systems were
also directly connected to aging, good reason why so many theories (dozens
or perhaps even hundreds) on the subject were in circulation. The very term
"antiaging" was in fact oxymoronic or simply nonsensical, as there was no
evidence of it, with the possible exception of calorie restriction. A very large
industry had been created around something that could not be said to exist,
at least for the time being. That the federal government and major marketers
as well as leading scientists working for respected institutions and universities were the key principals involved made the antiaging phenomenon even
more remarkable.[54]

Not everyone, need it be said, was as gung-ho about antiaging as those working in or reporting on progress in the field. The lines between those who believed there was such a thing as antiaging and those who did not were becoming more firmly drawn. The NIA had recently cautioned the public about supposed antiaging therapies, and more journalists were beginning to take a critical view of those selling or promoting products and services promising youth, as these were exposed as ineffective or downright fraudulent. In a 1997 issue of the AARP's *Bulletin*, for example, freelance writer Beth Baker laid down the gauntlet by proposing that the very concept of antiaging was "humbug," meaning nobody really knew how to stop the aging process. In her research, Baker had spoken to some leading experts in gerontology, including George A. Martin, director of the Alzheimer's Disease Research Center at the University of Washington in Seattle. "There's not a single bullet, not a [pill] or magic diet that's going to solve all the problems of aging," Martin told Baker; the billions of dollars Americans spent every year on books, supplements, cosmetics, and surgery to stay young were a complete waste of money.[55]

Those with an opposing view, such as Robert Goldman, a physician and president of the National Academy of Sports Medicine, fought back. Goldman and his fellow members of the American Academy of Anti-Aging Medicine (fifteen hundred physicians, scientists, and researchers in thirty-six nations) believed that antiaging was simply ahead of the curve: the medical profession simply had yet to document the effects of agents that successfully countered the physical signs of getting older. "Aging is not inevitable, and we have the medication, diagnostic methods and tools to slow aging starting now," he barked in *Total Health* in 1997, wondering why the NIA was not spending at least some of its $500-million-plus to join the battle against aging. (*Total Health* was a partner of the American Academy of Anti-Aging Medicine, making the magazine hardly an objective voice.) A number of agents, including estrogen (or hormone replacement therapy, or HRT), human growth hormone (HGH), DHEA, and testosterone all were clinically proven to ameliorate the effects of aging, Goldman claimed, in terms both of quality of life and of life extension. (He did not mention that serious side effects from HGH had been reported.) Vitamin C and antioxidants counteracted aging as well, he added, urging that the NIA and medical community at large not wait for clinical studies to prove conclusively that antiaging was real. Otherwise "we may all be dead by then," Goldman remarked, convinced that the time to expand the use of such therapies was now.[56]

A couple of years later, a colleague of Goldman's, Ronald M. Klatz, joined him in promoting what they fully saw as "anti-aging medicine." Some progress had been made within the established sciences to combat aging at the cellular and organ levels, Klatz, the president of the American Academy of Anti-Aging Medicine, explained, but it was what lay around the corner that was really exciting. Cloning specific groups of stem cells would soon offer the ability to grow and restore organs damaged by the aging process, he envisioned, in the process promising to eradicate Alzheimer's disease, liver disease, and arthritis. Gene therapy was also waiting in the wings, he told readers of *Total Health* in 1999, with DNA transfer techniques utilized to block the damage wreaked by free radicals. Each of these technologies would dramatically expand maximum human life span, according to Klatz; he was certain that those bringing forth antiaging therapies were on the brink of sparking a true revolution in medicine.[57]

As the head of the American Academy of Anti-Aging Medicine, Klatz was naturally especially excited at the prospects of living longer via the myriad antiaging therapies in development. "I'll be disappointed if I don't see my 120th birthday," he had said a few years previously, a view entirely consistent with the organization's slogan: "Age is inevitable—Aging is not." Klatz conceded that antiagers like himself were ultimately on a "quest for immortality," making it clear that the goal was to expand one's middle, healthy years versus one's older, not very healthy years. Having a biological age of forty-five while having a chronological age of seventy-five sounded quite appealing, of course, reason enough for the like-minded to join the anti-aging cause. "I am confident that science is close to finding the true fountain of youth," he stated a few years after he along with a few colleagues founded his organization, seeing immortality as the next logical step in our species' evolution. Longevity for humans had continually increased, after all, which was perhaps the most convincing evidence to make the case that life spans would stretch indefinitely in the future.[58]

More than other member of the antiaging community, however, Klatz came off as much as a preacher as a doctor; he viewed greater longevity and, ideally, immortality to be not just a personal quest but a messianic crusade. America was in "deep trouble," he said in his introductory remarks at the annual American Academy of Anti-Aging Medicine conference in 1996; our nation was facing "the most perilous threat to our social stability since the Civil War." What was this looming catastrophe? It was the "sociological destruction from a ticking 76 million megaton age-bomb," Klatz announced, no doubt getting the attention of those gathered. The aging of baby boomers would cause a social, financial, and medical crisis over the next few decades, he warned, "destroying our economy as surely as the biblical plague of locusts in the book of Exodus that ravaged ancient Egypt's crops." Medicare, Social Security, and private health insurance would all crumble under the weight of boomers' aging, Klatz predicted; their grandchildren would have to work close to a hundred hours a week to keep boomers "in Depends." Peter G. Peterson, Robert J. Samuelson, and many others had warned about the economic consequences of the age wave, but nobody, it's safe to say, had expressed it so viscerally and with such fire and brimstone. Happily, there was a solution to this geriatric apocalypse: antiaging. "We, the leaders of the antiaging movements, will help to usher in a new modern age for humanity, The Ageless Society," he sermonized, seeing the assembled group's mission as nothing less than to "bring an end to aging as we know it."[59]

## Reversing Human Aging

Adding a quasi-spiritual dimension to antiaging might have drawn in followers, but it was good old capitalism that was more likely to get things done. As the science of aging became a hot area of interest in the late 1990s, entrepreneurs recognized that big money could potentially be made through commercial ventures offering some kind of fountain of youth. Biotech was the epicenter of these for-profit initiatives, with a host of antiaging avenues being explored, including drugs and organ cloning. Oracle founder Larry Ellison had recently set up a foundation for basic research in aging; the billionaire was pouring $20 million into that pool every year. Cataloging the genes involved in aging was a priority, with clinical trials of "longevity drugs" planned to manipulate them. "A truly potent anti-aging pill would trigger the social equivalent of the Big Bang," noted *Fortune* magazine in 1999, seeing that explosion as blowing up everything from retirement to relationships. A bevy of new companies were also chasing down aging in hopes of a big payday. Geron, based in Menlo Park, California, was the leader in this pursuit, focusing its cellular-oriented efforts on telomerase-based drugs that could perhaps prevent cancer, osteoporosis, and wrinkles. (Telomerase was and is believed to be an antiaging enzyme.) "I decided the most meaningful thing I could do with my life was tackle aging," explained Geron's founder (and medical school dropout) Michael West, viewing aging as "the most central problem of the human condition."[60]

Also determined to bring an end to aging as we knew it—and making a lot of money in the process—were the folks at the Cenegenics Clinic in

Las Vegas. Cenegenics was a private company dedicated entirely to antiaging medicine; its founders saw a major opportunity to attract baby boomers interested in staying young as long as possible. (The company is still very much around.) Although the fee for its program was hardly cheap (the company charged patients $1,300 for its initial, daylong workup), Cenegenics was less pricey than the services provided by such competitors as the Palm Springs Life Extension Institute (specializing in "optimized total hormone balancing") and the Life Extension Foundation (prescribing various supplements), which only the wealthy could afford. "We see anti-aging as a rigorous medical specialty," said Alan Mintz, cofounder and CEO of the company; he and his partner had gathered a wide range of experts to offer patients an extensive menu of tests and treatments. "Anti-aging is about having energy, being in control, and feeling good about yourself," he told *Health* magazine in 1998, all things that his enormous target audience very much desired.[61]

Antiagers of the very late twentieth century were also heading to the Life Enhancement Center at the Canyon Ranch resort in Tucson, Arizona. The center had started a new program in 1999 called Optimal Aging, also aimed at boomers wishing to defy nature by not getting older. To its credit, this program ($5,000 per week) was geared to making healthy lifestyle changes related to diet, exercise, and stress reduction rather than the usual and unproven antiaging treatments of injecting hormones or consuming supplements. Also, longevity was more about adding life to your years than adding years to your life, according to the medical staff at Canyon Ranch, a refreshingly sensible idea that was often ignored in the hot pursuit of age reversal. Santa Monica–based Pritikin, a disease-management clinic staffed by doctors, nutritionists, and physiologists, had also gotten into the longevity game, with a week at its facility (at the cushy Santa Monica Beach Hotel) costing $4,500.[62]

The upscaling of gerontology was all the more remarkable given that the field had historically been a not very glamorous one chiefly concerned with health-related and social problems of old people. The aging of baby boomers had made the field trendy, however, and some of the country's leading spas had cleverly found a way to turn what was still at its roots gerontology into a luxurious experience. The reinvention of gerontology in the late 1990s also had much to do with the new kind of science being applied. Manipulating genes in order to lengthen the human life span was a lot sexier than trying to improve the daily existence of the elderly, and it was difficult to think of another area of medical research that had larger implications for the future. Some were comparing the state of the field to that of bacteriology in the

1870s, when a series of discoveries establishing a clear connection between germs and disease pointed the way toward the antibiotic revolution. A kind of heady excitement hovered around the study of aging as the new millennium approached, with many thinking that we could indeed be on the brink of an equivalent scientific revolution.[63]

Some in the antiaging community were positively giddy about the possibility of having decades or perhaps even centuries added to normal longevity. "Within the next two decades," predicted Michael Fossel in the *Futurist* in 1997, "we will extend the healthy human lifespan indefinitely and, in doing so, alter human culture forever." Fossel, a clinical professor of medicine at Michigan State University and the author of *Reversing Human Aging,* envisioned major leaps in antiaging techniques and therapies despite there being little or no evidence that any of them currently worked to any significant degree. Now fast approaching that twenty-year mark, no such radical life extension has come close to being realized, of course, making such a forecast a good example of the Jetsonian school of futurism that is so typical of the *Futurist* and of those in the business of prediction. Social change equivalent to that of "the invention of agriculture more than 10,000 years ago" was coming, Fossel warned, good reason to prepare for the consequences of the reversing of human aging. Thinking that doubling the human life span was entirely possible by the year 2017, he outlined a larger global population, greater economic efficiency, and longer work lives as just a few of those consequences.[64]

Thankfully, not every advocate of antiaging was fanatical or relied on science fiction to make guesses about the future. Fluffy, harmless articles like "8 Steps to Age Without 'Aging'" in *Better Nutrition* were routinely popping up in many health and beauty magazines, each of them approaching aging through a self-help lens. There was little doubt that editors purposely hyped the titles of such articles to sell magazines; no real antiaging course of action was forthcoming, readers learned over and over. Rather, it was the old standby—regular exercise and a healthy diet supplemented by essential vitamins and minerals—that helped one avoid a premature death, disappointing but sensible news. Recommendations to include certain foods and beverages with some kind of positive nutritional benefits, such as garlic, red wine, and green tea, were often included in these pieces; these served as easy (and delicious!) ways for readers to believe they could slow the aging process.[65] Much ado was being made about recent research demonstrating the ability of certain "superfoods" (notably blueberries, strawberries, and spinach) to subdue free radicals, which were known to harm cell membranes and DNA.[66] Such foods with high antioxidant activity could possibly slow the aging process of both body and brain, researchers at Tufts University believed, although there was still much work to be done on the topic.[67]

While researchers decoded the chemical makeup of every food imaginable to determine if the fountain of youth resided within it, serious science into anti-aging was being pursued by people like Steven Austad, an evolutionary biologist at the University of Idaho (who later moved to the University of Texas). "To me, there's no obvious reason why we should fall apart," he said in 1998, wondering why human cells did not repair themselves or split in two in order to keep their host organism continually alive, as they were capable of doing. Aging research was gaining more respectability in scientific circles due to such legitimate questions that had little to do with attempts to extend the human life span by a century or two. Allowing seniors to live more active lives by suspending the onset of heart disease, cancer, and Alzheimer's disease was a much more realistic and achievable goal, Austad recognized; his research focused on the workings of DNA, brain chemistry, and chromosomes to understand "why we age" (the title of his new book). Importantly, Austad viewed aging as a function of Darwinian strategy rather than a biological mistake caused by either a decline of hormonal production or by oxygen-free radicals (in which a molecule with an extra electron creates an extra negative charge, causing havoc in the body). More scientists interested in gerontology were beginning to agree with Austad, however, as it became increasingly clear that a coherent, evolution-based theory was much needed for the field to advance.[68]

It could be seen how evolution versus biology was more likely to answer the question why humans or any other organism aged. There were no "aging genes" or "death genes," after all, or any kind of predetermined program that told the body to decline. In addition, no organ system aged at a set rate, and no particular organ was designed to wear out before another, making the "planned obsolescence" theory not very useful. More broadly, there was no consistent pattern of aging among living things; this was the thing that most frustrated scientists attempting to figure out why people or other animals got older. Humans did a host of things throughout their lives to damage their bodies—smoke cigarettes, breathe pollution, drink alcohol, lie in the sun, eat unhealthy foods—but even this wear-and-tear theory did not really explain why we aged. (People who were not exposed to such environmental factors still aged, of course.)[69] As America entered a new century and millennium, the questions surrounding aging would continue to puzzle scientists and lay people alike, and new, more aggressive efforts were begun to delay or stop the process completely.

# 4

## The Perpetual Adolescent

Aging is becoming so yesterday.
—*Business Week,* October 11, 2004

In May 2004, residents of Manhattan's Upper East Side got news of which tenant was going to occupy the prime retail space at the corner of Madison Avenue and East 67th Street. "Celebrity dermatologist" Dr. Nicholas Perricone, whose antiaging products were already being sold in upscale department and specialty stores, had handpicked the spot to locate his new flagship boutique. In certain circles of New York City, the news that Dr. Perricone was coming to town was nothing short of thrilling. "The dapper doctor, who dresses in designer suits and silk ties and treats clients like supermodel Heidi Klum, will open his doors to aging baby-boomers this fall in a two-level store that will sell his skincare products, nutritional supplements and even food items," the gossipy *New York Daily News* excitedly reported. Soon Manhattanites would be lining up at Perricone's store to buy "cosmeceuticals" like his Neuropeptide Facial Prep; a six-ounce bottle of the stuff went for $175. "New Yorkers on the crowded quest for the fountain of youth will have one more stop this fall," the newspaper told its readers, many of whom would no doubt be headed to Perricone's boutique in search of magic formulas to look and feel young.[1]

The celebrated arrival of Dr. Perricone in New York City was a reflection of the war against aging that was still being waged in the very early years of the 21st century. Aging had been a concern in the United States for the past few decades, but now the topic had exploded as more baby boomers crossed into their fifties. Many boomers had no intention to look or act their age, however, as values related to youth continued to be seen as perhaps the only social currency that really mattered. Was it any surprise that the *Weekly Standard* called the United States a nation of "perpetual adolescents" in 2004, many of us not prepared to appear or behave outside the parameters defined as "young"? Antiaging treatments and therapies were more popular than ever, but scientists would not be satisfied until they solved the riddle of getting older and created a remedy for it.

While youth remained the holy grail, the middle-aging of baby boomers brought a host of social, economic, medical, and psychological issues to the forefront of the national conversation. American popular culture was at long last acknowledging that the country was getting older, and marketers were reluctantly coming around to the fact that it was in their best interests to proactively target aging consumers. Most important, perhaps, a number of research studies were showing that those actually in their advanced years were for the most part happy and contented people, contradicting the deeply ingrained belief that aging was, as University of Cambridge gerontologist Aubrey de Grey had put it, a "barbaric phenomenon that shouldn't be tolerated in polite society." A full-fledged backlash against "antiaging medicine" was in play as well, as legitimate scientists warned consumers that no fountain of youth could be purchased, at least yet. Would America and Americans finally accept aging as being a natural stage of life that could be as rewarding and fulfilling as any other?

## A Thousand Little Massages

Until then, aging remained an enemy to be conquered. Scientists interested in aging had made advances over the past few decades, but major questions about how and why humans got older remained. Turtles, of all things, lived longer than humans, a fact that some biologists in the longevity field seemed almost perturbed by. Many otherwise ordinary Americans continued to see aging as a treatable disease, with a host of cures at one's disposal—vitamins, enzymes, B-12 shots, omega-3 oils, herbs, nutraceuticals, and bioflavonoids, or supplements. A fair number of people subscribing to an antiaging regimen were taking dozens of pills a day, some of them adding an extra shot of human growth hormone to the mix.[2]

Indeed, HGH was often the entrée on an antiaging menu, the goal being to replace one's own natural but diminishing hormone production with a manufactured version (usually through injection at the time). Users swore by HGH, attributing the stuff to better performance in everything from ten-nis to sex. Weight loss, increased muscle mass, stronger bones, and a more cheerful temperament were other commonly described benefits of hormone replacement therapy, making it understandable why antiagers were so fervent about it. Ex-dot-commers who had sold their businesses were prime candi-dates for HGH, having both the money and the time (it was quite expensive and required continued use to reap its benefits) to invest in a more youthful self. There was no evidence that hormone replacement therapy could extend one's life by a single day, but simply feeling younger was well worth the price for those who could afford it.[3]

As the success of Dr. Perricone suggested, skin care was a big part of the antiaging market. Perricone was interested in both the inside and outside of consumers' bodies, however; he had earned his fame by prescribing a high-protein, low-sugar, vitamin-enriched diet complemented by proprietary topi-cal creams to fight inflammation of the skin. He was not the only "celebrity dermatologist" in the United States; Howard Murad and Frederic Brandt had also become famous by promoting their products lines via best-selling books and frequent television appearances. (The endocrinologist Jose Comenge too had become well known as an antiaging expert.)[4] One did not have to be a superstar physician, however, to take advantage of consumers' obsession with their aging skin. The shelves of skin care counters were crowded with creams designed to make users feel as if they had a "mini-face-lift," as one woman described the effect. With just a smattering of science, millions of middle-aged women were taken in by these products that were, essentially, hope in a jar. (Gobbledygook such as Lancôme's Rénergie Lift Contour Skin Firming and Contouring Complex—"a high-tech serum fortified with a spe-cial Dermo-Cohesion Complex"—certainly sounded like the manufacturer had done its research homework.) Antiwrinkle creams alone were about a billion-dollar business and represented the fastest-growing segment of the cosmetics industry.[5]

The appearance of a new product believed to have special skin rejuve-nation properties could cause considerable excitement among the antiaging set. When La Mer introduced its Lifting Face Serum and Lifting Intensifier in 2004, for example, women crowded the counters at upscale department stores like Saks Fifth Avenue. La Mer had built up a cult-like following with its skin products over the previous decade or so, making the debut of this new product cause for celebration. Priced at just $285 (some of La Mer's other products cost as much as $1,000), the serum used blue algae that went through a special biofermentation process to allegedly restore clarity and brightness in the skin. ReVive by Bays-Brown Laboratories also was getting a lot of buzz with its bioengineered properties; each product was serving as a kind of status symbol among a certain crowd in a way a luxury automobile or large house could not. These creams could (temporarily) make one look younger, after all, offering what was perhaps the most valuable kind of social currency among the especially age conscious.[6]

Expensive skin creams might smooth out a wrinkle or two for a short while, but more drastic measures had to be taken for those wanting longer-term results. Botox (a brand of botulinum toxin, a neurotoxic protein produced by a bacterium) was fast becoming the cosmetic therapy du jour for its ability to prevent the development of wrinkles by paralyzing facial muscles. Plastic surgery remained popular among people thinking a face-lift was needed to those get rid of those lines for good, especially among those concerned about having a toxic substance injected into their body. The neck and, increasingly, the hands were also becoming progressively more common targets for plastic surgery.[7]

For those seeking a less severe approach to facial rejuvenation, there was an alternative: acupuncture. Americans subscribing to the benefits of alternative medicine were increasingly drawn to the ancient Chinese technique for facial toning and beautifying based on its apparent ability to work wonders in everything from drug addiction to weight loss to migraines. Acupuncturists at places like the Tao of Wellness in Santa Monica used the tiny needles to supposedly adjust imbalances and free blocked energy in the face, thereby eliminating crow's-feet and adding luster to one's complexion. "I feel like my face is alive and breathing," said a fifty-one-year-old satisfied customer after a thirty-minute treatment, finding the experience to be like "1,000 little massages."[8]

Not every middle-aged woman, of course, was literally buying into the attempt to make older skin look younger than it really was. "I call upon my sisters, the dyed and lifted and Botoxed as well as the earth-mother naturals, to join me in affirming ourselves the way we are now, just as we affirmed ourselves in the 1970s," urged journalist and freelance writer Joanne Omang in the *Pittsburgh Post-Gazette* in 2003. "We forged a revolution for women's lives then, and we can do it again." Omang was not happy with the ways in which sixty-year-old women like her were being treated, even by those of her own gender who were the same age. Her friends were shocked when she told them she was planning to throw a birthday party for herself for turning sixty, assuming she would keep the number secret or, if not, ask people to come wearing black. For Omang, the issues surrounding aging women went far beyond skin care. "We must demand attention for aging women—not just on magazine covers but on the job, in clothing design, product packaging, movies, music, housing arrangements, furniture, typeface sizes and all other areas now expressing contempt for our failure to stay 35," she passionately wrote. The title of her piece "Older and So Much Better" said it all, but most Americans had not yet accepted what they saw as a rather radical idea.[9]

The mad rush for aging adults to do whatever it took to try to maintain their youthful appearance could be seen as all the more absurd given the ways in which children tended to view older people. Donna Shalala, former secretary of the Department of Health and Human Services and now president of the University of Miami, was very much interested in aging, particularly kids' take on the subject. Shalala actually collected young children's essays on aging, which she used in talks at conferences to illustrate grownups' comparatively unhealthy attitudes toward getting older. "When people get old they get wrinkles on their face but their brain gets smarter," went one such essay; another said: "Growing old can be fun if you let it be." In just a few years, however, kids' positive and accurate descriptions of aging changed, a result of encroaching, deeply seated cultural stereotypes regarding older people. Aging was soon seen as a period of decline, a perspective that was more than likely to become firmly entrenched as they reached adulthood.[10]

Older children's learned repulsion toward aging was made very much apparent at a traveling exhibit organized by Boston's Museum of Science called "Secrets of Aging" which opened in April 2000. In one part of the exhibit called "Face Aging," tweens were given the chance through a computer simulation to see how their own faces might change over time. Individual portraits were taken and then, through the magic of digital technology, "aged" year by year over the course of five decades. As a rule, the kids were horrified by what they saw; the prospect of themselves getting wrinkles, blotchy skin, gray hair, and the typical other signs of age was truly disturbing. A few years earlier these same children would likely have found the trick more amusing than upsetting, but now they had clearly adopted the standard narrative of aging rooted in physical or biological deterioration. Once considered a time of growth and joy, older age had morphed into one of ugliness and self-hatred.[11]

Another museum show, "The Art of Aging," was concurrently presenting aging as a natural and inevitable part of life. Visitors to the Jewish Institute of Religion Museum at Hebrew Union College in New York City could see oils, sketches, photography, sculptures, fiber, cartoons, and video by eighty-three artists investigating the emotional and physical aspects of aging. The show explored a host of themes related to aging (and life in general), including family, creativity, friendship, wisdom, humor, optimism, and loss. The exhibition was curated by Laura Kruger, who in her sixties became acutely aware of the aging process, an experience magnified by the recent death of her mother. "Nobody wants to see a show about old people," was the response from several committee members at the museum, but Kruger won the day by convincing them that aging could be presented as a celebration of maturity rather than as a depressing period of decline. A year and a half later, "The Art of Aging" was on display at the museum, and, after a nine-month run, an edited version hit the road to Atlanta, Boca Raton, Phoenix, Portland (Oregon), and Miami.[12]

## Nothing More Than a Scary Bedtime Story

While there was a growing interest in the positive aspects of aging in the early 2000s, it was antiaging that represented a true cultural phenomenon. The irony of the success of antiaging products and services was that the vast majority of Americans did not truly believe that they could do anything to stop their bodies from getting older. Some 90 percent of those surveyed in a 2002 Harris Interactive poll said that antiaging products did not really keep people young, as ads for them suggested. Still, a fair portion of those same people bought the products anyway, according to the survey, a classic case of how advertising was more about selling an idea than a reality.[13] Those concerned about synthetic and powerful agents like DHEA and HGH but were still interested in proactively antiaging were purchasing the growing number of herbal teas being sold as a form of naturopathic medicine. One marketer, Flora USA, for example, distributed a product line called Flor-Essence that was purportedly high in antioxidant, anti-inflammatory, and antibacterial properties. Consumers could choose from teas made from burdock root, sheep sorrel, slippery elm bark, Turkish rhubarb, red clover herb, blessed thistle, kelp, and watercress; each one was said to have been drunk by the Ojibway Indians of Ontario, Canada, for their restorative powers.[14] Meditation and yoga were also being used as natural antiaging therapies; each was believed by those subscribing to Eastern or New Age philosophy to be capable of activating the body's own healing forces by rejuvenating endocrine glands.[15]

Those interested in using such products despite any real evidence that they did anything to stop their bodies from getting older were intent on reducing or maintaining what was sometimes called one's "biological age." That term referred to the rate at which your body "wore out," while chronological age was how many years you had actually lived. You couldn't do anything about the latter, of course, but many obviously felt there were active steps that could be taken regarding the former. Antiaging physicians employed a wide range of tests to identify signs of relative wellness or what researcher William Evans called "biomarkers": skin thickness and oxygen consumption while exercising. The doctors used biomarkers to determine whether a patient's body was aging faster than experts believed it should be, in which case a portfolio of therapies was typically prescribed. Commonly used procedures to detect biomarkers included an EBT scan (to measure the level of calcium buildup in the arteries), a C-reactive protein test (to detect early heart disease), and a genetic test (to discover predispositions to any number of diseases).[16]

More for-profit clinics dedicated to antiaging medicine and employing such testing procedures were popping up across the country. In addition to Cenegenics in Las Vegas, places like the Kronos Optimal Health Centre in Scottsdale, Arizona, and the Princeton Longevity Center in Princeton, New Jersey, ran a battery of biomarker tests on patients, with treatments to follow based on the results. (The Princeton center sweetened the deal with hot stone massages and champagne for lunch.) Pricey clinics were not the only antiaging game in town, however. Many doctors not specializing in antiaging were adding components from the field to their practices due to the demand, and a fair number of chiropractors and acupuncturists were claiming they could help patients stop or reverse their biological clock. A thriving antiaging business could be found on the Internet, not surprisingly, with oxygen chambers, magnets, and all kinds of potions available for those willing to believe they would work.[17]

The kind of aging research being done at the very beginning of the twenty-first century was nothing short of extraordinary. Scientists at the Scripps Research Institute in La Jolla, California, along with gene chip experts from the Novartis Research Foundation in San Diego, for example, were using microchips loaded with DNA to track the activity of tens of thousands of genes individually over time in a remarkable joint venture between biotechnology and information technology. Sixty-one genes changed their behavior as people got older, preliminary research showed, offering hope that drugs could be developed that would discourage those genes to tell the body to develop signs of aging.[18] Even if that never became a reality, the findings of this study were cause for celebration in scientific circles. At some point during midlife, the researchers concluded, cells lost their ability to reproduce, resulting in genetic mistakes and the physical signs of age. Although this was hardly startling news, scientists were excited about the findings as they offered a single, sensible explanation for why the body developed degenerative maladies over time. Whether it was bothersome but bearable conditions like arthritis or gum problems, major diseases such as cancer and heart failure, or the tragedy of Alzheimer's, it appeared to be the gradual failure of cells to replace themselves that caused what we called aging.[19]

Pinpointing precisely where in the DNA sequence aging likely took place was thus understandably the objective of a team of Harvard physicians and molecular biologists in 2001. Being fortunate enough to have a certain kind of gene or genes on chromosome 4 was the key to a long life, they announced; just one in ten thousand people were thus blessed, allowing the lucky individual to become a centenarian even if he or she did not subscribe to a particularly healthy lifestyle (barring an accidental demise, of course).[20] A few years later, a different team of researchers at Harvard Medical School had found a way to boost what they had identified as an antiaging enzyme in living cells. Here too the scientists foresaw the development of drugs to prevent myriad geriatric diseases and possibly extend the human life span. It was cellular enzymes called sirtuins that the researchers believed served as universal regulators of aging in almost all living organisms, they reported in their study published in *Nature,* making them the future target for new kinds of antiaging drugs. The next step was to find the most powerful sirtuin stimulators or to create synthetic ones and then determine their ability to extend the lives of flies and worms and, if that was successful, those of mice, monkeys, and humans.[21]

The for-profit sector of the antiaging market was not waiting for that to happen, however. About a dozen biotechnology companies, including Elixir Pharmaceuticals, LifeGen Technologies, Longenity, Chronogen, GeroTech, Juvenon, and Rejuvenon, were currently trying to develop antiaging drugs, with big money at stake in the race to provide the fountain of youth in a pill.[22] A Denver company, Lifeline Nutraceuticals, already had such a pill, called Protandim, in the works and was planning to put the amino-acid-based supplement on shelves in 2004.[23]

Skeptics, naturally, were suspect about any magic pill promising to slow the aging process. It was theoretically feasible, perhaps, but it was highly doubtful that any single formula could achieve such a thing; there were many biochemical processes that eventually caused destruction of the human body, they pointed out.[24] The brain, eyes, ears, skin, bone, muscles, lungs, heart, and bladder all deteriorated over time, a response to genetic signals and the normal wear and tear of daily life.[25]

The possibility that aging could be "treated" through pharmacology was, however, too tempting for some dabbling in forecasting the future to predict the end of humans getting older and, perhaps, dying. Writing in the *Futurist* in 2003, Joao Pedro de Magalhaes envisioned grandparents acting and looking like teenagers one day as new genetic interventions continued to advance. "Aging may soon become nothing more than a scary bedtime story," wrote de Magalhaes, a microbiologist, foreseeing the development of more powerful and efficient antiaging therapies over time. Slowing down human aging by half would yield thirty or forty more years of longevity, he somehow estimated, with more discoveries made over that time to lead to even longer life spans. Eventually a "cure" for aging would be found, de Magalhaes mused, suggesting that, "with a bit of luck, we may be around for centuries to come."[26]

## Middle-Aging

The ongoing, concerted scientific effort to help solve what was still perceived as the problem of aging was in part a function of the growing concern about an older global population. The United States was hardly the only country that was graying, of course, as European and Asian nations confronted the future implications of fewer younger people and more older people. The United Nations had declared 1999 the International Year of Older Persons, in fact, a reflection of the aging that was taking place around the world. The year was being "celebrated in recognition of humanity's demographic coming of age and the promise it holds for maturing attitudes and capabilities in social, economic, cultural and spiritual undertakings, not least for global peace and development in the next century."[27]

Much as in other countries, government officials in the United States were primarily concerned about how a rapidly aging population would affect policy decisions that would have to be made in the decades ahead. Federal entitlements remained the heart of the matter, with no consensus as to how (or even if) they would be distributed when great numbers of baby boomers retired. Some, however, made the interesting case that predicting that aging boomers would bankrupt Medicare was, in a sense, anachronistic; major scientific breakthroughs would be realized before the majority of them were entitled to such benefits, this argument went, eliminating the need for costly care due to long illnesses.[28] The debate over government entitlements aside, there was a consensus that boomers would require many more health care services than currently available. The U.S. Department of Labor was forecasting major growth for a variety of workers in occupations related to aging, including nurses, physical therapists, social workers, personal and home care attendants, and home health aides.[29]

The Department of Labor and baby boomers themselves were not on the same page, however. Aging in the present was hardly on their radar, much less that it would take place in twenty or thirty years. Some boomers did not even think the word "aging" applied to them; they preferred the term "middle-aging," as it did not have the negative connotations that "aging" did.[30] "This generation of ours refuses to believe it's getting older," said Betsy Carter, the editor in chief of *My Generation*, a new magazine from AARP aimed at fifty- to fifty-five-year-olds. The age of fifty was traditionally considered the end of middle age (and therefore the beginning of old age), but boomers were having none of that. Rather, the seventy-six million Americans born between 1946 and 1964 were adding years to middle age, to create what aging guru Ken Dychtwald called "middlescence." "As they reluctantly migrate out of youth, boomers have already begun to engineer a new and vastly extended middle period of life," wrote Dychtwald in his 2001 book *Age Power: How the 21st Century Will Be Ruled by the New Old*, seeing middlescence as a means of delaying oldness.[31] "Boomers don't do anything that is not cool," remarked Helen Dennis, an aging and retirement expert from USC's Andrus Gerontology Center, thinking that they would "redefine this new chapter so that it is cool."[32]

A slew of other books related to aging were appearing as publishers recognized a hot literary segment. Zorba Paster's *Longevity Code: Your Personal Prescription for a Longer, Sweeter Life* and Deepak Chopra's *Grow Younger, Live Longer: Ten Steps to Reverse Aging*, for example, focused on boomers' desire to preserve their youth for as long as possible.[33] David Snowden's *Aging with Grace* was another longevity how-to, but with a twist. The book presented the findings of what was commonly referred to as the "nun study"— a long-term research project involving 678 Catholic sisters who ranged in age between seventy-four and 106. The women's long lives had much to do with their commitment to serve others, Snowden suggested, an interesting premise that had major implications for the rest of us.[34] Ram Dass's *Still Here: Embracing Aging, Changing, and Dying* (a reference to Dass's earlier classic

*Be Here Now*) had a more spiritual component and was steeped in a kind of elderly wisdom. By "aging consciously, we will naturally begin to manifest those qualities that our society needs in order to survive," he wrote, those qualities being "sustainability, justice, patience and reflection."[35]

For many baby boomers, middlescence involved not just staying cool or contributing to society but also the need to take care of one or both parents. Some had been doing this since the 1980s, with more middle-aged men and women joining the ranks of caregivers over the ensuing thirty years. Gen Xers—the generation of Americans born between the mid-1960s and early 1980s—were also now finding themselves put in the position of being responsible for the welfare of a parent. Many Americans would personally experience some form of elder care, yet most were woefully unprepared for it. A national survey conducted by the *Los Angeles Times* in 2000 found that 81 percent of Americans who were not currently providing care for older relatives had made no such plans to do so, rather alarmingly. Even more concerning, perhaps, three out of five said they had not even discussed with their parents what to do if the parents became unable to care for themselves.[36]

Because of the strong emotions involved, the subject of parental caregiving could be said to have been one of our few remaining cultural taboos. Children were often in the dark about a parent's estate, insurance, or wishes regarding medical intervention—very useful information should something catastrophic suddenly take place.[37] Those who were providing care often found it to be a difficult process, especially if a parent was angry or frustrated because of his or her dependence on others. The problem was significant enough for Bernard H. Shulman, a geriatric psychiatrist, to write a book called *How to Survive Your Aging Parents*. The book, cowritten by Raenn Berman, helped adult children deal with the situation and their feelings by outlining ways for them to create a new kind of relationship with their parents given the different circumstances.[38]

The decision regarding where to locate an aging parent should he or she not be able to take care of himself or herself remained a difficult one. Senior citizen complexes were a relatively affordable option in situations where the parent did not require much assistance. If he or she did, a nursing home was usually the only option for long-term care for those who had the money. With baby boomers or Gen Xers now in charge, managers of nursing homes were finding themselves having to make improvements to their institutions along many fronts. Each generation was made up of sophisticated, demanding consumers who were not about to accept less than quality care for their loved ones. Nursing homes had long had a bad reputation, made only worse by the common perception that residents were forced to give up all independence until they died. The places were seen as a dumping ground for only the sickest and most frail patients who had been forced out of hospitals because they could not afford the care provided there.[39]

A new breed of nursing homes, rebranded as assisted-living facilities, however, was appearing on the scene, due much in part to the efforts of consumers who would not settle for less. Assisted-living facilities typically had a more caring staff, provided better food, and allowed residents more freedom than traditional nursing homes, offering an attractive alternative for residents not requiring a great deal of care. About half of such facilities were private pay only, meaning only the upper-middle class or the wealthy could afford them. But for those who could, assisted-living facilities were helping to change the mostly deserved image of nursing homes as the last resort for elderly people.[40]

Due in part because of the improvements being made to nursing homes, more Hispanic Americans and Asian Americans were considering them for their elder care needs. These cultures traditionally believed it was a violation of family responsibility to place an older relative in such a place, but that was slowing and changing as younger generations adopted more mainstream American practices. While moving a parent to an assisted-living facility was becoming more common, it was by no means an easy decision given that Hispanic American and Asian American children were often brought up with the understanding that they would care for elderly family members in their own homes. Like anyone having to move a parent into an outside facility, however, these adult children were finding it just too difficult to take care of their loved one themselves. (The decision was sometimes made based on the advice of social workers who had experience in knowing what would be best for all parties.) The cultural shift could be detected by the multiculturalization of assisted-living facilities across the country: bilingual staffs (and rice and beans at mealtime) were becoming more common at the facilities as more Spanish-speaking residents moved in.[41]

### Prime Time

The middle-aging of baby boomers could be felt in virtually all aspects of society in the early 2000s. The economic recession of those years, caused in large part by the popping of the dot-com bubble, was further impetus for boomers to try to remain active and relevant. Boomers had essentially created youth culture in midcentury America, so it was ironic that now it was they who were feeling the social pressures of having to think and act young. "Transition counseling" firms with names like New Directions were springing up to help boomers reinvent or rediscover themselves as they headed into the third act of their lives. Another extended run in Corporate America was unlikely for displaced business executives in their fifties or even forties, so forging a personally rewarding form of self-employment was usually the best option.[42]

While the idea of middlescence was an attractive proposition to a generation determined not to grow old, the physical signs of aging could not go wholly ignored. As hordes of baby boomers entered their fifties in the early 2000s, more women were going through menopause, a subject that a few leading feminists had addressed in detail a decade earlier. But now some research was showing that there was such a thing as male menopause, or what was more scientifically termed androgen deficiency syndrome. ("Andropause" was another term for the condition.) Decreased libido was one early sign of the condition, noted Phillip C. Ginsberg, director of the Male Menopause Center at the Albert Einstein Medical Center in Philadelphia, with decreased bone and muscle mass, increased body fat, lowered strength and energy, and a host of mental issues also common to those supposedly suffering from it.[43]

While male menopause was now getting some attention from the medical community, it was considered largely undiagnosed because of the difficulty for doctors to discuss sexuality with their patients (and due to men's reluctance to talk about anything with anyone related to their health). Doctors believed that androgen deficiency syndrome was treatable, primarily via testosterone replacement therapy, and advised men between the ages of forty-five and fifty to take note of troubling physical and emotional changes as they aged.[44] Within a few years, however, some physicians were casting doubt on the entire concept of male menopause; they saw those same symptoms as simply a normal, natural decline in testosterone levels. In 2003, the Institute of Medicine of the National Academies issued a warning against the rising popularity of testosterone replacement therapy, stating that more research needed to be done before it was widely used to improve older men's strength, sexual function, and cognitive abilities.[45]

Baby boomers may have not wanted to admit they were now in their fifties or were fast headed that way based on their changing bodies, but marketers were gradually becoming more aware of that fact. Americans aged fifty-five and older held 58 percent of the nation's disposable income, making them too valuable a market to ignore even in our youth-driven consumer culture.[46] Consultants were urging their clients to pay more attention to older consumers, something that required an approach different from the one many marketers were used to taking. In his consulting work for his company Age Wave, Dychtwald was advising businesses to develop products that would enhance the functions of both the mind and body—unfamiliar territory for most marketers selling sex appeal or some kind of hedonistic pleasure to younger consumers.[47] The television networks too remained largely fixated on the youth market, this despite the fact that it was older people who watched television the most.[48]

Some more farsighted experts like Marc Freedman, author of *Prime Time: How Baby Boomers Will Revolutionize Retirement and Transform America*, could imagine a new paradigm for baby boomers as they entered their later years. Freedman envisioned the development of new kinds of community centers that eschewed games like bingo and checkers; instead, such centers would be part café, part fitness club, part tech lab, and part employment agency, the latter offering resources for those interested in finding volunteering opportunities.[49] Such a place—the North Shore Senior Center in Northfield, Illinois—already existed, in fact, a prototype of perhaps many more to come to serve aging boomers.[50] Freedman, president of the nonprofit Civic Ventures, viewed retirees as "an untapped natural resource" who could serve the common good by redefining themselves as agents of positive social change.[51] Freedman had founded Civic Ventures in 2000 with the goal of finding caring, committed adults to help young people growing up in poverty as mentors, teachers, and youth workers. That organization was in many ways an extension of his work with HEW secretary John Gardner, who was widely considered the architect of LBJ's Great Society domestic programs.

Whether through volunteering or paid employment, many boomers did not see themselves embracing the traditional model of retirement. Rather than the deserved payoff for a life of hard work—a time to travel, play golf or tennis, or finally get around to cleaning out the basement—retirement would be recast as an opportunity to be productive in new and different ways. Some experts were even predicting a "retirement revolution," thinking that most people in a financial position to relax would choose instead to go back to school or become entrepreneurs if not electing to give back to society in some way. Many boomers were confessed workaholics and fretted about not getting up in the morning and going somewhere to do something they considered important. With Americans now living longer, healthier lives, the third act of life could consist of three decades—a long time to rest and relax after one's retirement party.[52] A change in the cultural geography of retirement already appeared to be in play: more new retirees were moving to northern tourist destinations like Cape Cod, the Dells, and the Poconos rather than fleeing to the Sunbelt.[53] Others were choosing to stay put by adding pools to their homes or moving next door to local golf courses.[54]

Retirement communities too were retooling to prepare for what might be massive waves of baby boomers wanting to do more than play shuffleboard in their later years. Springfield Lakes outside Phoenix was one such "active adult" community being constructed; with the oldest boomers having just turned fifty-five, its developers expected considerable numbers of recently retired boomers to come knocking at its newly built doors. (Fifty-five was the minimum age restriction at many retirement communities.) Springfield Lakes was a place to "exercise your mind as well as your body," its sales brochure read, much as Dychtwald had recommended, positioning itself as a cross between a high-end spa and a small college. Del Webb Corporation, the developer of the gigantic Sun City retirement community in Arizona, had begun referring to boomers as "Zoomers," a reference to the pace the group was expected to maintain even after they stopped working full-time.[55]

## A Celebration of Aging

Other industries were slowly adapting to the age wave as it increased in intensity. Hollywood and the media had traditionally leaned toward reinforcing versus dispelling negative stereotypes related to older people; there are many possible examples to cite as evidence of this. When making the 1985 release *Cocoon*, for example, director Ron Howard reportedly decided that costars Don Ameche, Hume Cronyn, and Jessica Tandy (each in their seventies at the time) were not acting "old" enough when filming started. To remedy the situation, the story goes, Howard hired an acting coach to teach the actors how to act old through worse posture, a slower gait, and less clear speech.[56] And in 1992, the editors of *Vanity Fair* reportedly airbrushed Elizabeth Taylor's image for the magazine's cover (of the famous "AIDS issue"), taking a few decades off the sixty-year-old woman's still gorgeous face.

While Hollywood and the media would of course continue to traffic heavily in illusion, significant strides were made in how aging was represented in American popular culture over the course of the next decade and a half. Happily, more accurate depictions of older people had gradually worked their way into television and movies, into magazines and novels, and into advertising as America aged. On the CBS drama *Judging Amy*, for example, the character Maxine (played by Tyne Daly) was a gray-haired, sixtyish woman who had returned to work as a social worker and enjoyed an active romantic life—each plot point defying cultural stereotypes of single ladies past their childbearing years. A special aired on ABC in 2002 also brought some refreshing reality regarding aging to television. "Looking Younger, Living Longer: What Every Woman Wants to Know," featured such celebrities as Cybill Shepherd and Lauren Hutton, who exposed the pressures fiftysomething women faced to look young, especially in youth-obsessed Hollywood.[57] And in May of that year, men discovered that two of their favorite magazines, *GQ* and *Esquire*, were each devoted to the practicalities of aging rather than the more typical subject of how to live the high life.[58]

Movies too were more often featuring older characters facing issues drawn from real life. In the 2003 movie *About Schmidt*, for example, the lead character played by sixty-five-year-old Jack Nicholson acted the star's actual age, something that did not go unnoticed by critics, viewers, and Nicholson himself. "When I look in the mirror, I may feel that I'm the same person I was when I was younger, but I know I'm not," he confessed at a stop on his promotion tour for the film.[59] Some novels also examined the trials and tribulations of aging. Margaret Drabble's *A Natural Curiosity*, for example, focused on how middle-aged women dealt with getting older, a storyline that would have been more uncommon a generation earlier. And in a recent catalogue, retailer Neiman Marcus ran a fashion spread featuring a gray-haired model along with a manifesto of sorts. "When we become evolved enough to separate silver hair from the idea of personal decline," it read, "then we can see the color for what it is: symbolic, spiritual, splendid." Louise Lague, a psychotherapist who specialized in midlife issues, had written the essay; she rejected the standard narrative of older women as being less beautiful, instead perceiving them as being more interesting.[60]

Some felt, however, that the media and marketers were going a bit too far in trying to present seniors as active adults. In the rush to be seen as pro-aging, magazine editors and advertisers had taken to portraying older people as engaged in adventure sports and vacationing in exotic locales, something that no doubt did occur but not with the implied frequency. In feature articles, print ads, and television commercials, a disproportionate number of sixty- and seventysomethings were climbing mountains, riding dirt bikes, surfing, scuba diving, or skydiving—activities that anyone, including much younger people, might find challenging.[61] A commercial for Best Western hotels, for example, featured a sixty-plus woman in her swimsuit jumping off a waterfall in Maui, not a particularly representative vacation experience.[62]

It could not be denied, however, that some older folks who could very well be just taking it easy were doing extraordinary things. A fair number of the most beloved rock 'n roll stars in history were pushing sixty, and showing few signs of slowing down. Their music, which included that of musicians like Eric Clapton and Bob Dylan, was sometimes referred to as "geriatric rock." Bands like Judas Priest, Black Sabbath, Yes, AC/DC, and Deep Purple were still recording and touring, often earning bigger bucks and attracting bigger crowds than ever. Much was being made of Mick Jagger's approach to that time of life, particularly when the British senior magazine *Saga* decided to put the fifty-eight-year-old member of the Rolling Stones on the cover of an issue in 2001. Like anyone over fifty in the United Kingdom, Jagger was eligible for some of *Saga*'s AARP-like discounts (25 percent off eyeglasses and 50 percent off cruises), but he had yet to take advantage of the great deals.[63]

While Hollywood, the media, and marketers began to get more comfortable with the idea of aging because it was impossible to ignore demographics, some cutting-edge artists were pushing the boundaries of our discomfort with older bodies. In 2000, two photography shows in New York City used nude bodies of seniors as their subjects, each artist challenging our conventional concepts of beauty and art. (A few photographers had pursued a similar artistic path beginning in the 1970s.) At the Andrea Rosen Gallery in Chelsea, John Coplans used his own eighty-year-old naked body in his seventeen self-portraits, while around the corner at the Stephan Stux Gallery, Manabu Yamanaka used nudes of women between ninety and a hundred years old in his sixteen photographs. Many viewers found the images in each show disturbing (some had to turn away, in fact), as it was rare to see bodies that old. The wrinkled, saggy bodies also served as visceral reminders that we ourselves might look that way if we were lucky to live that long, another distressing truth in our culture where beauty was almost equivalent with youth. Some felt, however, that these daring shows could be an indication of something bigger coming as America aged. "Age is coming out of the closet," art critic Vicki Goldberg observed in the *New York Times,* "because the old have reversed the natural course of things and are multiplying."[64]

Age had also come out of the closet at Gallery NAGA in Boston. In her show called "A Celebration of Aging," Harriet Casdin-Silver used three-dimensional, holographic images of people seventy-five or older complemented by audiotaped oral histories by the subjects. It was a lifelike yet eerie experience, particularly for those not used to sharing an intimate conversation with an older person.[65] Personal glimpses into the lives of older people could also be found in Chicago, where the seventh annual Silver Images Film Festival had recently completed its run. The event was an opportunity for filmgoers to "reimagine aging" by viewing films and videos that demonstrated the joys and sorrows of older adults and dispelled myths associated with the aging process.[66]

In their book *Aging in America: The Years Ahead*, photographer Ed Kashi and writer Julie Winokur painted a portrait of older people different from the one usually seen. The book contained dozens of black-and-white images of Americans ranging from their late fifties to 104 who were each involved in some kind of nonprofit cause. War veterans, athletes, newlyweds, prison inmates, grandparents, great-grandparents, and others appeared in the book, all of them actively giving back to society. The authors believed this was a harbinger of a future large-scale social movement when baby boomers, having retired from their careers, would seek out volunteering opportunities to remain productive people. "There's a tremendous reservoir of energy and expertise and caring and concern that needs to be tapped into," Kashi told the *Chronicle of Philanthropy* in 2004, seeing good things ahead when the largest generation in history had the time to devote to others.[67]

Some were even more gung-ho about the future of baby boomers, picturing them as a catalyst for major social change that would benefit all Americans. Writing in the *Futurist* in 2003, Aviv Shahar predicted that our youth-centric values would be overturned when the age wave reached its peak, marking a return to a more traditional society where elders were revered. Rather than a looming generational war fought over public money, Shahar envisioned the rise of multigenerational communities working together to solve social problems, with the wisest (that is, oldest) members of the tribe to lead the way. In short, Shahar (a consultant specializing in "whole person development") foresaw a more holistic society ahead due to the aging of boomers, as greater strides in science meshed with a deeper appreciation of spiritual matters. In their golden years, he concluded, baby boomers were going to "bring the 'golden' experience back into the evolving dynamic of cultural metamorphosis."[68]

## The Aging Game

That baby boomers would be active contributors to society as seniors rested on the assumption that their cognitive abilities remained intact. The long-held view was that memory and thinking in general naturally faded when people got older, a function of dying brain cells. New research showed this was not true, however; human brains could generate new cells throughout a lifetime, especially when they were challenged by some kind of intellectual stimuli. There was apparently much truth to the expression "use it or lose it," at least when it came to the cerebral cortices of older people. Hence the greater perceived need for seniors to stay mentally, physically, and socially active, an idea that found expression in myriad ways.[69]

More evidence was being gathered to suggest that the aging process was indeed as much mental as physical. As part of the Ohio Longitudinal Study of Aging and Retirement, for example, researchers who tracked 660 residents of a small Ohio town found that those with positive attitudes toward aging lived seven and a half years longer than those with negative views. This finding, which was published in the *Journal of Personality and Social Psychology* in 2002, was a good example of how long-term studies of older people were proving what many of them already knew: aging was not as bad as it seemed.[70] A nationwide poll conducted by the National Center on Women and Aging at Brandeis University that same year confirmed as much, at least among women. A majority of women aged fifty and older said the experience of aging was better than they had expected, the survey reported; nearly 70 percent of them described their own physical health as good or excellent, and 90 percent of those older than eighty rated their emotional health as equally positive.[71] A survey conducted by the National Council on the Aging and the International Longevity Center a few years earlier supported the idea that older Americans were a generally happy lot. It found that 44 percent of those sixty-five and older said that this was the prime of their lives, something that would come as surprising news to younger people who assumed things were not likely to get better for them as they aged.[72]

The "normalizing" of older people, if one could call it that, could also be noticed at some of the nation's medical schools. As part of their training to become physicians, medical students at the University of Minnesota were playing something called "the Aging Game," in which the young men and women assumed the identity of elderly patients. About fifteen hundred students had played the game since 1994, in fact, engaging in an interactive experience intended to help them gain a greater appreciation for the health care needs of older people. Professors of geriatrics at the school had borrowed the idea from Duke University, where it had become clear that many of those in their twenties and thirties could benefit from what it might be like to be seventy or eighty. In the game, students put popcorn in their shoes to simulate osteoarthritis (a common condition that made walking painful), earplugs in their ears to replicate hearing loss, and tape over their eyes to produce blurred vision. Neck braces, arm slings, and crutches were employed to mimic what it might feel like after a fall. Students also had to act as if they were in a nursing home, finding themselves having lost much of their control over their own lives. While the elderly had older bodies and had special health needs, they were still people who deserved respect, the course taught future physicians. Elated when the game was finally over, the med students were invariably better prepared to practice their trade with older patients after they graduated.[73]

Gerontology students were also being exposed to the realities of aging. Students enrolled in a year-long symposium called "Gerontology: What Does It Really Mean to Be 'Old'?" taught at St. John's University and the College of St. Benedict in Minnesota were given the rare opportunity to spend a night in a real nursing home. Students were admitted to nearby Good Shepherd nursing home and put in beds right alongside actual residents; aides took them to the bathroom when necessary and turned them over every couple of hours to "avoid bedsores." They also received crushed "medicine" in applesauce as part of the experience designed to give students a greater understanding of the issues facing older people in such a position. Some of the students were understandably affected by the overnight stay and by the class in general. In fact, one premed student changed his major to nursing home administration after completing the class, feeling he could contribute more to the lives of seniors in a managed care setting than through medicine.[74]

## A Grand Experiment

Not coincidentally, as all spheres of American society made serious efforts to incorporate older people back into the mainstream and end their status as marginalized citizens, a strong counterattack was launched against the antiaging movement. More voices of reason could be heard that provided a welcome reality check to some of the claims antiagers were now making. Leonard Hayflick had served as a spokesperson for the more conservative school of gerontology for some time, for example, but he raised his profile

as theories of longevity went from the sublime to the ridiculous. Even doubling the average human life span was "wishful thinking," the University of
California at San Francisco professor and former president of the GSA said in
2000, seeing maximum longevity at about 125 years (about what it currently
was). Advances in medicine, nutrition, gene therapy, and genetic engineering would no doubt continue, he believed, but life span was something very
different from life expectancy. While the latter had increased dramatically,
Hayflick explained, the former had not and was unlikely to given that it was
likely set many thousands of years ago. Human cells replicated about fifty
times and then stopped, he and some colleagues had discovered (by accident)
in the 1960s, with only cancer cells showing any signs of "immortality."[75]

It was precisely this kind of research grounded in elementary biology that
began to pose a serious threat to advocates of antiaging. While consumers
were spending billions of dollars a year on products and services promising
some kind of fountain of youth, it was becoming increasingly clear that most
if not all that money was being wasted. The first real volley against antiaging was fired in 2000 with the publication of S. Jay Olshansky and Bruce A.
Carnes's book *The Quest for Immortality: Science at the Frontiers of Aging*. The
coauthors, based at the Center on Aging at the University of Chicago, had
spent almost a dozen years working in the new field of biodemography, or the
study of the dying process. The obsession with the fountain of youth at the
beginning of the twenty-first century was remarkably similar to the one that
took place a hundred years earlier, the pair learned, putting antiaging in some
useful historical perspective. (Visions of longevity go back much further, of
course, as Gerald J. Gruman showed in his classic 1966 essay, "A History of
Ideas About the Prolongation of Life").[76] While the treatments had certainly
changed ("volcanic mineral oil" was thankfully no longer being prescribed
by quacks), the same kind of hucksterism was in play. Popular and harmless antiaging remedies like ginkgo and vitamins could not stop the hands
of time, the two argued in their book, nor could potentially dangerous substances such as HGH.[77]

Over the next few years, what may called the anti-antiaging movement
led by Olshansky picked up steam. In April 2002 the International Longevity Center (ILC) in New York issued a strongly worded caution against the
increasing popularity of antiaging medicine. "There is as yet no convincing
evidence that administration of any specific compound, natural or artificial,
can globally slow aging in people, or even in mice or rats," the ILC's panel's
statement read, adding that the antiaging movement was made up of "a long

chain of quacks, snake-oil salesmen and charlatans."[78] The following month, another warning, endorsed by fifty-one scientists from around the world, appeared in *Scientific American*. Basic research on aging was one thing, but the antiaging movement was quite another, each statement made clear. "This is becoming a public health mess," said Olshansky, now at the University of Illinois School of Public Health; his accompanying article in *Scientific American* called antiaging a "myth," with those dabbling in it performing "a grand experiment on themselves."[79]

Olshansky wisely recognized, however, that he had to reach an audience broader than the scientific community if he was going to make much of an impact. In 2002, the Silver Fleece Award for Anti-Aging Quackery was born, a clever way to get the general public's attention. Olshansky awarded a product called Clustered Water™ the first Silver Fleece, earning its manufacturers a bottle of vegetable oil labeled "Snake Oil." Every year, Olshansky announced at the time, a Silver Fleece would be awarded to "the product (and its producer) with the most ridiculous, outrageous, scientifically unsupported or exaggerated assertions about aging or age-related diseases." The dubious distinction was based on an evaluation of purported health and longevity benefits, claims about scientific evidence supporting the product, the degree to which legitimate scientific research was exaggerated, and the profit potential of those selling it. (The makers of Clustered Water™ claimed that the product, which cost $39.95 for a four-ounce bottle, "truly assist[ed] our body's natural processes in counteracting the cellular malfunctions that many health practitioners and researchers believe are responsible for degenerative health."[80]

Olshansky and his fellow Silver Fleece committee members, Hayflick and Carnes, were not done, however. Right after designating Clustered Water™ as the winner of the Anti-Aging Quackery award, they bestowed the Silver Fleece Award for an Anti-Aging Organization to the Academy of Anti-Aging Medicine (AAAM); it was that organization, they deemed, that contributed the most to disseminating misinformation and/or products associated with the claim that human aging can now be stopped or reversed. "More than any other organization in the world, the American Academy of Anti-Aging Medicine is responsible for leading the lay public and some in the medical and scientific community to the mistaken belief that technologies already exist that stop or reverse human aging," said Olshansky. "It has created an alleged medical subspecialty and accreditation in anti-aging medicine, even though there are no proven anti-aging medicines in existence."[81]

Other experts in the medical and scientific communities hopped on the anti-antiaging bandwagon. Rather than being an extension of preventative health care, as the leaders of the AAAM presented their field, more critics began to view the field as a pseudo-science filled with misleading claims and fraudulent products that could do real harm to consumers. Kenneth L. Minaker, chief of the Geriatric Medicine Unit at Massachusetts General Hospital, for example, had a big problem with the very term "antiaging," seeing it as "anti-living" because getting older was a natural part of life.[82] Now legendary gerontologist Robert Butler worried in 2003 that antiaging medicine was well on the way to becoming a "scam" if it wasn't already one, a sentiment many of his colleagues shared. As a response to such criticism, Ronald Klatz, still president of the AAAM, admitted that consumers should be careful when choosing a particular antiaging product or therapy but maintained there was real science behind it. "Are we supposed to be pro-aging?" he asked, and not do everything we could to stop diseases like Alzheimer's? Questionable antiaging practices posed a real danger of making the whole field appear shady, however, as some other gerontologists pointed out. Robert Binstock, a professor at Case Western, for example, was certainly not "pro-aging," but he felt that the doubts about the legitimacy of antiaging medicine could hamper more rigorous research dedicated to helping people live healthier and possibly longer lives.[83]

The growing divide between the AAAM and mainstream gerontologists soon became a chasm. In his address at the organization's annual conference in Las Vegas in December 2003, L. Stephen Coles, a physician and researcher at UCLA, declared that while real breakthroughs could be achieved within two or three decades, there currently was "no such thing as anti-aging medicine." The statement understandably shocked many in the crowd, with some groans and even a few boos following the unexpected remark from a fellow member of the AAAM (who had long studied centenarians). Robert Goldman, cofounder and chairman of the organization, was especially upset, not surprisingly, and immediately addressed the audience to counter pretty much everything Coles had said. Goldman assured the eleven hundred physicians, nutritionists, physical therapists, plastic surgeons, chiropractors, and diet specialists who had gathered at the Venetian Hotel (and paid more than $1,000 to attend the conference) that there was much money to be made from antiaging medicines like HGH, nutritional supplements, and cosmeceutical creams. Indeed, the antiaging business now rang up billions of dollars a year in revenues, with apparently no limit to the number of patients and clients interested in treatments promising to make them look and feel more youthful.[84]

More spas and resorts, including Red Mountain Spa in Utah, the Mountain of Youth in Georgia, and the Maui Wellness Institute at the Wailea Marriott Resort in Hawaii, were offering "anti-aging vacations," promising travelers the unusual opportunity to go home younger than when they arrived.[85]

As the row escalated between the antiaging community and those who were convinced that humans did not have a choice when it came to getting older, Gary Null kept on doing what he had been doing for the previous three decades. Since the early 1970s, Null had promoted his own brand of antiaging program through nutrition and exercise, all the time arguing that aging-related diseases and conditions like Parkinson's, Alzheimer's, and arthritis were not "normal" and could be avoided. In his latest book, *Power Aging: The Revolutionary Program to Control the Symptoms of Aging Naturally*, Null offered ways in which readers could fight the visible and invisible signs of age by eating more healthfully and making lifestyle changes. Meat, dairy, sugar, wheat, caffeine, and alcohol were all no-nos for Null, a tough nutrition regimen for most to follow but still less draconian than the extreme or severe calorie-restriction plan that more fanatical antiagers were enduring.[86] Roy Walford, a UCLA pathologist and perhaps the country's most famous calorie restrictor, had subsisted on twelve hundred to sixteen hundred calories a day for many years and, at the age of seventy-seven in 2001, planned to live at least forty-three years more.[87] Walford was convinced his spare diet had slowed the progression of his Lou Gehrig's disease, something with which other scientists were coming around to agree.[88]

Indeed, over the preceding decade, more studies indicated that radically limiting calories was antiagers' best hope of living long lives. Eating just fruit, vegetables, nuts, berries, and grains could fundamentally alter the human body's basic metabolic functions, calorie restrictors and a growing number of scientists believed, ultimately slowing the aging process. Calorie counting was taken to an extreme, with the nutritional contents of every morsel closely monitored. Nibbling on the same thing everyday must have gotten old for these bony people, but the possibility of living past a hundred—perhaps well past—was worth the effort. An organization, the Calorie Restriction Society, had recently been formed; its sixteen hundred members shared the latest scientific information about their cause and exchanged advice, menus, and recipes for how to make what some would consider rabbit food tastier and more filling.[89] It was clear that some would do virtually anything to extend their lives, a pursuit that would only accelerate as America and Americans continued to age.

# 5

## The Silver Tsunami

The challenge is not, as many have argued, how to pay
for an aging society. It's how to harness the skills of a
vast, willing and able new crop of maturing Americans
who want to stay in the game longer, give something
back and help cure society's ills.
—Daniel J. Kadlec, coauthor of *The Power Years: A*
*User's Guide to the Rest of Your Life*

Like many areas across the country, Douglas County in Colorado had long been a desired spot for young families to put down roots. In 2007, however, local leaders and state legislators began to notice a pronounced demographic shift taking place in the county and surrounding areas. The over-sixty population in Douglas County was growing and would continue to grow at an alarmingly fast rate—nearly 60 percent between 2004 and 2009—with other counties in Colorado also experiencing a spike in the percentage of older residents. "We're looking at a silver tsunami," said Lafayette City (Boulder County) councilman Jay Ruggerri, foreseeing a greater need for services for the aging, such as meals for shut-ins, medical aid, and transportation.[1]

In the suburbs of Denver, however, schools and recreation facilities for children were being built at a cost of hundreds of millions of dollars, with no such "silver tsunami" taking place there. Two very different kinds of communities—one relatively old and one relatively young—were emerging in Colorado. State senators, especially those on the legislature's Joint Budget Committee, could see a tug of war over public funding coming as each kind of community lobbied for resources. "You never want to be in a place where you have to vote for taking care of old people or vote for educating young people," said Senator Abel Tapia, a Democratic senator from Pueblo, "but that's where we'll be."[2]

As the silver tsunami approached the nation's shores, significantly more attention was beginning to be paid to the aging of America. The oldest baby boomers were beginning to turn sixty, sparking an increasingly loud conversation about how they might choose to spend their remaining decades. Because of boomers' numbers and influence, their third act of life now under way presented major consequences to the social, economic, and political interests of the country. While many worried about an impending "aging crisis" due to a lack of financial and health care resources, others focused on how boomers could continue to grow as individuals and contribute to society. Discovering a cure for aging remained a hot pursuit, however, this despite more research showing that getting older was not the debilitating process many Americans believed it to be. As the battle between the antiaging community and its foes intensified, so did the effort by marketers to offer innovative products and services dedicated to older consumers. The age wave was now an incoming tide, and something that could no longer be ignored.

## A Reinvented Society

Concern about an aging population was hardly limited to a handful of counties in Colorado. The cultural geography of the nation as a whole was in transition as the demographic makeup of suburbs gradually became older. "Suburbs, which previously were considered youthful and family-friendly parts of America, will . . . become a fast-graying part of our national landscape," noted William Frey in a report released by the Brookings Institution in 2007. With the number of seniors expected to grow at a rate of nearly 36 percent over the following decade (four times faster than the nation as a whole), demographers like Frey were urging community leaders to start planning for the population shift. Given the history of the country over the past half-century, seniors outnumbering children in the suburbs was, for many local politicians, an understandably difficult concept to accept, making the planning process a slow one. The suburbs of Atlanta, Washington, and Dallas were aging particularly fast, however, with Chicago and Los Angeles soon to follow the trend.[3]

It was a surprise to many that it was the suburbs of major cities rather than traditional areas of retirement in states such as Florida and Arizona that were rapidly aging. The common perception that massive hordes of older people continually moved to warm places after retiring was clearly wrong. Fewer than 2 percent of those between the ages of fifty-five and sixty-four moved across state lines each year, another study by the Brookings Institution found, with the number even lower for people older than sixty-five. Contrary to popular belief, older people simply didn't move that much, making it highly probable that baby boomers would "age in place"—that is, stay in their current homes. The idea of leaving an expensive-to-heat house in the snowy north for a condo where it was endless summer was perhaps an appealing one, but the reality of retirees staying put made more sense. Many boomers grew up in the suburbs, became urbanites as young singles, and then moved back to the burbs after marrying and raising kids, making the prospect of relocating to an unfamiliar community hundreds or thousands of miles away not particularly attractive. In short, boomers were much more likely to remain in their house or possibly move across town to a more affordable, senior-friendly home than head south after working full time.[4]

Although there was considerable variance based on local demographics, a good number of communities in the United States had begun to address to some degree the growing wave of aging residents. Baltimore was being looked to as a model of proactive planning in this regard. Community leaders, led by John P. Stewart, executive director of the city's Commission on Aging and Retirement Education (CARE), were determined to create what they considered nothing less than "a reinvented society." (Part of this approach likely had to do with the hometown Baltimore Longitudinal Study, which was still going strong as it neared its own half-century mark.)[5] "We're trying to create a blueprint for the design of an elder-friendly city which, when you come right down to it, will be a citizen-friendly city," Stewart told the editor in chief of *Nursing Homes/Long Term Care Management* in a 2006 interview. Developing sufficient resources for health care, transportation, public safety, job opportunities, and continuing education were all ways in which neighborhoods in Baltimore would be improved, he held, not just for seniors but for everyone. Already 38 percent of the city's homeowners were more than sixty years old, making CARE's biggest priority to make it possible for those residents to age in place should they wish to as they got older.[6]

Although reinventing their respective communities was a major challenge, local leaders felt there was an urgency attached to their mission. On January 1, 2006, another landmark in the history of aging in America was reached when the oldest baby boomers turned sixty. Sixty may have been the new fifty, to paraphrase the popular saying going around, but there was no denying the fact that boomers were beginning to enter their senior years. It was equally obvious that this generation of budding seniors looked and acted a lot different from any previous one. The concept of retirement was in flux, for one thing, and more boomers were single, a result of the much higher divorce rate over the preceding few decades.[7]

It was also unlikely that members of any other previous generation were so interested in redefining themselves. Charting a new course at about the age of fifty was no longer such an odd thing to do; so many people were doing it, in fact, that it had earned a term: "creative aging." Creative aging represented an approach to getting older that was much more upbeat than what Steven Mintz called in his 2015 book *The Prime of Life* "the angst of midlife." That period of adulthood was characterized by "fretfulness, brooding, and wide-ranging sense of distress associated with parental death, marital conflicts, job setbacks, financial strains, children leaving home, severe illness, or the symptoms of physical aging and declining cognitive functioning," Mintz wrote, hardly a sanguine scenario of middle age.[8]

Unlike the decidedly negative "midlife crisis," then, creative aging was not typically sparked by a confrontation with mortality, bad marriage, or career roadblock. Rather, it was the admirable desire to do something different and challenging in the years that one had left that triggered a sweeping change in lifestyle. Going to graduate school, adopting a child, exploring a form of spirituality, or writing the Great American Novel were just a few of the many possibilities of creative aging. Importantly, creative aging was about enhancing one's old life, while a midlife crisis was about rejecting it; the former was considered a much healthier transition. Adventure travel was a common theme. Some fiftyish boomers were deciding to hike in the Himalayas, while others were opting for snorkeling in the Galapagos. Still others were signing up for a wide variety of "fantasy camps" in order to cross off one line (such as "play guitar with a real rock 'n roll star" or "drive a racecar at two hundred miles per hour") from their "bucket list."[9]

The concept of creative aging could certainly be found in the latest book by America's loudest cheerleader for aging boomers, Ken Dychtwald. Dychtwald and Daniel J. Kadlec's *Power Years: A User's Guide to the Rest of Your Life* advised that boomers seize the vast possibilities that could be found in their later years. For those who had the resources, retirement offered a host of opportunities, the authors cheerily proclaimed, whether those involved deepening friendships, pursuing romantic relationships, or starting new careers.[10]

Quite a different picture of retirement, however, was painted in a 2005 PBS documentary, *The Open Road: America Looks at Aging*. Through the lens of thirteen recent or soon-to-be retirees, filmmaker Nina Gilden Seavey showed that retirement was not necessarily years of "power." Some folks had to continue working even after leaving a full-time career, demonstrating that the kind of personal growth that Dychtwald and Kadlec described in their book was a luxury that only a segment of the population could afford. Interestingly, the film was used as part of a grassroots outreach program dedicated to the future of retirement. *The Open Road* was shown in town meetings in nine cities across the country, sparking a dialogue about what retirement might or should look like as the floodgates opened.[11]

## Merchants of Doom

Not surprisingly, the morphing concept of retirement was a main topic at the 2005 White House Conference on Aging. Keeping with tradition, the conference, sponsored by the Bush administration, was held a decade after the previous one. (For the first time in the forty-plus-year history of the conference, the standing president did not attend.)[12] At the event, twenty-five hundred delegates discussed fifty resolutions related to aging over the course of four days in December, with the goal being to direct national policy regarding older Americans for the next decade. Baby boomers were, naturally, a focus of the conference (its theme was "The Booming Dynamics of Aging: From Awareness to Action"), a clear acknowledgment that the first wave of the group was about to turn sixty.[13]

In addition to issues surrounding retirement, the usual topics—Social Security, job opportunities, social services, health care, and housing—were discussed at the 2005 conference, with delegates interested in strengthening both the Medicare and the Medicaid program and having Congress reauthorize the Older Americans Act.[14] Pundits' warnings about a coming economic apocalypse as tens of millions of baby boomers retired had clearly seeped into the agenda of this conference. Also, many boomers had had a distrust of authority since their counterculture days and thus were skeptical that the government would be putting their monthly checks in the mail when they became eligible for them. Some boomers were planning to file early for Social Security benefits when they turned sixty-two, nervous that the money might not be there in a few years when their full benefits were promised.[15]

If James H. Schulz and Robert H. Binstock were right, baby boomers' concerns that the federal government would be short of cash when they qualified for Social Security and Medicare were unwarranted. In their *Aging Nation: The Economics and Politics of Growing Older in America*, the coauthors made the interesting case that the looming aging crisis was much ado about nothing. The widely held notion that aging boomers would crash the nation's economic system was created by "merchants of doom" (academics, journalists, pundits, and politicians) who used "voodoo demographics" to forge their apocalyptic scenario, they argued. If the so-called experts used more probable projections of the number of children to be born over the next few decades, Schulz and Binstock pointed out, the percentage of beneficiaries through the year 2040 would be about the same as that in 1960. Social or economic panics about the aging had taken place in the United States in the eighteenth and nineteenth centuries, the coauthors correctly informed readers, with the one that took place during the Great Depression a good example of the degree to which policy could be affected when politicians believed a crisis was at hand.[16]

In addition to the economic calamity that perhaps lay ahead, wonks in both the public and the private sector fretted about an impending crisis in health care. A report issued by the Institute of Medicine (IOM) in 2008, "Retooling for an Aging America," warned that the country's medical system was not at all prepared for the coming wave of aging baby boomers. There would be vast shortages of health care workers, the report cautioned, a situation made worse by the likelihood that those in the field of geriatrics would be undertrained. Even at the current time there were simply not enough professionals in the field; just one physician was certified in geriatrics for every twenty-five hundred older Americans, according to the report, and turnover among nurse's aides was a startling 70 percent a year. While boomers would likely have fewer chronic disabilities and live longer than previous generations of the elderly, the IOM report continued, the sheer numbers of them would overwhelm the system. About five times more geriatricians would be needed in a couple of decades—many more than the number expected to go into the field. Furthermore, "the geriatric competence of virtually all members of the healthcare workforce needs to be improved," the report added, recommending additional education for physicians, social workers, nurses, nurse's aides, physical therapists, home health aides, and anyone else dealing with older patients.[17]

While health care, entitlements, and retirement were no doubt important issues, it was the subject of volunteerism that perhaps stood out most at the 2005 White House Conference on Aging. Specifically, the delegates were charged with developing policies that would encourage older Americans, especially the fast-approaching wave of boomers, to devote their energy and expertise to volunteerism, nonprofit work, or other forms of "civic engagement." Nonprofit groups were a visible presence at the event, knowing that boomers represented the key to their future.[18]

Volunteerism and the dozens of other resolutions debated at the 2005 White House Conference on Aging were certainly central to the lives of aging Americans, but following the conference more than one critic wondered if there should be another. Previous conferences hosted by presidents held over the years (notably the ones in 1961 and 1971) had had a major impact on shaping governmental polices related to the elderly, Michael J. Stoil observed in *Nursing Homes/Long Term Care Management*, but times had changed a great deal. There were now many more seniors, and as a group they were significantly more affluent than three or four decades before. Also, the senior constituency wielded much more power than it used to, greatly in part due to the successes achieved at previous such conferences. Ironically, Stoil felt, the social and economic advancements made by older Americans over the preceding half-century had made the White House Conference on Aging less relevant and less capable of producing a road map for future policies. Should the event itself be retired, he legitimately asked.[19]

### Ripe

One other thing that made the most recent White House Conference on Aging appear anachronistic was the rise of the Internet. Meeting face to face in a large setting once every decade was certainly valuable, but websites, e-mail, and social media had radically transformed the communications landscape. Seniors, like everyone else, were connected in a way that people in 1961 and 1971 couldn't imagine, making it relatively easy to discuss and debate relevant issues on day-by-day basis. Expectedly, Internet usage among older people was less than among the general population; by 2005, only 31 percent of people over sixty-five had ever gone online, according to the Kaiser Family Foundation. Even so, there were a surprising number of blogs that appeared to be written by and for older folks. Many of these blogs were anonymous, making it impossible to know who was really hosting them.[20]

Like any blog, "elderblogs," as they were sometimes called, could be personal musings, summaries of scientific and medical advances, or meeting places where visitors could swap stories. Members of the antiaging community hosted a fair share of blogs, most of them endorsing particular avenues of extending the human life span. To their credit, elderbloggers were providing content in an area mostly ignored by the mainstream media—that is, the experience of getting older that was not focused on physical or mental decline. For the hosts themselves, especially those feeling socially isolated, blogging could be a means of creating relationships with others around the world, a wonderful use of the relatively new technology.[21]

While some elderbloggers used their platform to detail how and why it was no fun getting old, most offered a decidedly upbeat take on aging. Younger people could have learned a lot by reading an elderblog once in a while. Because they simply did not understand what it was like to be old, most Americans tended to fear being old, something borne out in survey after survey. A 2005 USA Today/ABC News poll on aging, for example, found that many viewed the *idea* of growing old as scarier than the actual experience. The older people got, the less they worried about aging, according to the poll, a reflection of younger people's assumption that a rapid decline in health was the norm in one's later years.[22] The media tended to support the idea that growing older was mostly about physical decline, and so it was hardly surprising that Americans held a generally negative view of aging. "Eyesight dims, joints get stiff and achy, teeth go bad and, in general, things just keep getting worse until death arrives," a journalist rather depressingly wrote for *Popular Mechanics* in 2008. "Aging is breakdown," he continued, reinforcing the all-too-common dread of getting older.[23]

Someone many considered to be America's best-known doctor had no doubt that the country as a whole had a very distorted view about the natural process of getting older. "Never before in history has human society been so sunk in such a wrong and unhealthy concept of aging as ours is," Andrew Weil told a standing-room-only crowd at a Denver-area bookstore in 2005. The sixty-three-year-old Weil was there to promote his new book, *Healthy Aging*, which had become a number 1 *New York Times* best seller (and landed the doctor on the cover of *Time* magazine). Weil was not at all a fan of antiaging medicine or the antiaging philosophy that framed it, seeing the better approach as accepting the inevitable while doing everything possible to postpone the development of age-related diseases. The basics—healthy diet, regular exercise, stress management, and taking on new challenges—were the key to living long and well, he argued in the book, urging that we should begin celebrating age rather than abhoring it. (Weil often used the people of Okinawa, Japan, as a prime example of positive aging; older people were highly respected in that part of the world, making it not coincidental that they enjoyed the highest longevity rate in the world.) "We're a totally youth-obsessed culture where aging is viewed as a catastrophe," he protested, doing all he could to try to change the abysmal image of getting older in America.[24]

While progress was being made with regard to aging in America, the social bias against older women remained very much in play. Nowhere, per-haps, was the double standard more evident than in politics. Conservatives focused a lot on Hillary Clinton's looks during her 2008 run for president, making her a model for different cultural standards of aging based on gen-der. "Men aging makes them look more authoritative, accomplished, distin-guished," noted uberconservative Rush Limbaugh at the time, but, "sadly, it's not that way for women." Americans would not want to watch Clinton "get older before their eyes on a daily basis," the radio personality added, which would ostensibly disqualify her as a viable candidate. Voters would have no problem observing Mitt Romney get more wrinkles and gray hair while in office, on the other hand, as there was a very long history of aging white male presidents. As the first serious female contender for president, Clinton was helping to highlight not just gender discrimination in Ameri-can society but age discrimination as well, proving that our playing field was a long way from being even.[25]

Nora Ephron was doing much the same but a lot more humorously. Eph-ron's *I Feel Bad About My Neck,* published in 2006, was filled with funny an-ecdotes regarding aging; the title itself was an amusing commentary on the changes that had taken place in a certain part of her body over the years. The sixty-five-year-old author and screenwriter made it clear, however, that getting older was not easy for her and other women her age. The time and money that went into maintaining one's looks were ludicrous, Ephron re-marked, and, even worse, ultimately a losing battle. "The honest truth is that it's sad to be over 60," she confessed, illustrating that even brilliant women like her often considered aging to be a period of decline, at least in a physical sense.[26] (She would die just six years later.) On the other hand, Janet Champ and Charlotte Moore's *Ripe: The Truth About Growing Older and the Beauty of Getting On with Your Life* offered a useful alternative for postmenopausal women getting caught in the beauty trap. It was not just possible but impor-tant for women to rise above the portrayal of attractiveness as presented in popular culture, the coauthors maintained, nicely using "ripeness" as a meta-phor for women's later years.[27]

Lillian B. Rubin's *60 On Up: The Truth About Aging in America* echoed Ephron's musings while pinpointing the reasons why people over sixty felt so inadequate. Baby boomers' considerable efforts to preserve their beauty could do nothing to stop the relentless ageism that was directed at them on a daily basis, Rubin (an octogenarian) indignantly contended, seeing antiaging as a silly and wasteful exercise in vanity. Aging simply could not be controlled or cured, she argued, reasoning that the better solution was to accept and plan for it.[28] Despite the fact that many boomers did try to slow their own aging process through diet, exercise, and more extreme methods, most of them actually sided with Rubin on a purely intellectual basis. Just 22 percent of boomers believed they held a significant amount of influence over the physical aspects of getting older, a 2007 survey by C&R Research found, more evidence that what they thought about aging was not entirely consistent with what they did about it.[29]

## The Art of Aging

While Americans continued to view aging as the next-to-worse-case scenario (dying was a significantly less attractive alternative), the link between older people and creativity continued to rise. Anecdotal evidence suggested that seniors were making more art or were more often the subject of others' creative expression. Perhaps because it was such a mysterious human trait, creativity was frequently portrayed as something that somehow endured the physical toll of aging. In her 2006 book *Aging Artfully*, for example, Amy Gorman profiled twelve visual and performing women artists who lived in the San Francisco Bay Area and happened to be at least eighty-five years old. (The oldest was 105.) Old age could be as rewarding a time in one's life as any, the book made clear through the lives of the dozen women, and filled with creativity.[30]

That was certainly the message being sent by the National Center for Creative Aging, which had been founded a few years earlier. The mission of the organization was to increase arts activities among seniors not just for fulfillment but also for health reasons. Research showed that older people who were involved in some kind of arts-related program were in better health (and used fewer drugs) than those who were not. Programs had been started in local communities all across the country, offering seniors a vehicle to tap into their still very active imaginations. Whether through theater, storytelling, poetry, painting, sculpting, or even living history (where performers acted out their own personal past, recalling Robert Butler's "Life Review" therapeutic process), creative expression was perceived as something that was literally good for you.[31]

A prime example of aging artfully could be found in the presence of poet and best-selling author Maya Angelou. Angelou, who was seventy-eight in 2007, was still producing work at a steady rate and was showing no signs of slowing down. More than that, however, she had developed her own simple but spot-on philosophy on aging and was happy to share it with people interested in how they could embrace getting older as an affirmative experience. "I would encourage you to see each day as a gift," she told attendees of the "Being Ageless" conference organized by the Omega Institute for Holistic Studies in 2007, taking special issue with those who whined about how better life was for them when they were younger. "I'm the same person I was back then," Angelou made clear, fully expecting others to see her similarly.[32]

While the media was for the most part no friend to older people, positive representations of aging could occasionally be found on television. A series called *Life (Part 2)* that aired on various PBS stations in 2007, for example, featured news, interviews, and discussions about the ways in which older people were finding meaning and purpose in their lives. The thrity-minute weekly program helped to counteract negative stereotypes about aging by illustrating that people in their later years could indeed be contributing members of society. Actor Ed Asner and author Frank McCourt, each in his late seventies at the time, appeared on the show; the two men, still active in their respective careers, could be said to have been excellent examples of "successful aging." The Academy Awards ceremony in 2007 also sent an affirmative message about the possibilities in later life. A video about Sherry Lansing, former chairman of Paramount Pictures, was shown on the broadcast, which included a section about PrimeTime, an organization that put retired people to work as volunteers in the public schools. Millions of television viewers around the world learned about the program that Lansing's foundation had recently started, triggering interest from hundreds of people to sign up.[33]

Living proof that notable older people were not only alive and well but continuing to pursue their artistic careers served as an important and affirmative message about aging. Angelou's declaration that she was the "same person" despite having acquired the physical signs of age was as good a point as any to make on the subject and something to which anyone who had become older could relate. Some older people were sick or had dementia, certainly, but many did not; still, Americans tended to view anyone in his or her later years as somehow less than the person they used to be. Even many of those who provided services to the elderly saw them collectively as frail and dependent, research showed, with a kind of wall dividing between what was perceived as "us" and "them." Studies of aging had until relatively recently been based primarily on interviews with residents of nursing homes, which further contributed to a picture of older people as depressed and reliant on others.[34]

While gerontologists were of course dedicating their professional lives to the well-being of older people, those in the field naturally spent much of their time focusing on issues related to decline and the problems the elderly faced. This could be seen as another reason why aging was heavily imbued with what could be considered negative stereotyping. That the third act of life was often a period of better emotional health than the second was an idea that many people, even some professionals in the field, could simply not accept as true. In short, the narrative of aging in the United States remained narrow and medicalized, begging the question of whether this story would persist as our population grew demonstrably older. "We need an image of society enriched by growing numbers of old people," suggested Bill Thomas, author of *What Are Old People For? How Elders Will Save the World*, hoping that baby boomers would create a "new myth" for aging.[35]

Baby boomers themselves were often shocked when encountering any kind of age-related health issue, thinking they were invulnerable to such things, which only older people experienced. The first hot flash for women, initial occurrence of erectile dysfunction for men, or a diagnosis of arthritis could each be a disturbing milestone for boomers assuming they would always be young, or at least not old. Dental, hearing, and vision problems typically rose after the age of fifty, all serving as wake-up calls for those in denial about aging. Having to start wearing reading glasses was not uncommon at midlife, but a fair share of those in that age group were putting off purchasing a pair for months because of what it represented. Once getting over their renunciation about aging, however, boomers were inclined to attack the process with a vengeance. Remembering how their parents had aged (not well, more often than not), many boomers did whatever they could to preserve their remaining youth, including undergoing various medical interventions, adopting healthier diets and lifestyles, or trying different forms of exercise. Yoga and Pilates were now especially popular activities for those fighting off the physical signs of age, each something mom or dad was unlikely to have done when she or he reached the midcentury mark.[36]

In his 2007 book *The Art of Aging*, Sherwin B. Nuland took a refreshingly

optimistic look at what he accurately described as the rude surprise of becoming an older person. Aging crept up on each of us while we watched other
people get old, he observed, with many people imagining they possessed a
kind of immunity against the physical and mental signs of fading youthfulness. While that wasn't true, age "concentrate[d] the mind," wrote Nuland, a
professor of surgery at Yale, and it acted as a catalyst for "new bursts of creativity, perceptiveness and spiritual intensity." Rather than the debilitating force
it was typically made out to be, he argued, aging was an ideal path toward
achieving the much-desired goal of wisdom in life. Nuland's take on aging,
which drew from interviews with many older people, was a virtually complete turning of the tables on the subject. Like Weil's *Healthy Aging*, it did as
much as any single book could to correct common misperceptions regarding
what was generally considered to be a bad ending to an otherwise good life.[37]

A study done by Elizabeth Head, a neuropsychologist at the University
of California at Irvine, revealed other positive insights about the aging mind.
Vocabulary and arithmetic abilities did not diminish with age, she found, nor
did learned and specialized skills, such as playing chess or the piano. But it
was, as Nuland suggested, wisdom where older people really shone. Seniors
consistently scored higher than younger adults on tests of life choices, handling conflict and ambiguity, and setting priorities, Head's research showed,
strong evidence that experience was a valuable asset.[38] A team of researchers
from Duke University and the University of Alberta found another brain-
related benefit of aging: forgetting the negative memories but retaining the
positive ones as we get older. Authors of the study, which was published in
*Psychological Science* in 2009, suggested it was this ability of the brain that
helped increase older people's emotional well-being, just as Nuland's interviews had indicated.[39]

Additional research showed that while the human brain often went
through some not very pretty changes as it got older—including shrinking
and taking on a form not unlike Swiss cheese, resulting in short-term memory and attention problems—some mental functions actually improved. In
addition to possessing greater "expert knowledge," as Head's study had found
(very useful for playing bridge, it turns out), older brains had a kind of automatic recognition system allowing for more efficient problem solving. "I think
I do science better than I did when I was younger," observed Eric Kandel, the
seventy-seven-year-old Columbia University professor who shared the 2000
Nobel Prize in medicine, believing he now had "a better understanding of
which problems are important and which aren't." Lawyers too were claiming

they had gained superior information-sifting abilities as they got older, an ideal skill to have when involved in particularly complex cases.[40]

Verbatim comments from older people in the Washington, D.C., area lent additional credence to the good news regarding aging that scientists were reporting. Seniors clearly did better when they had the chance to keep doing what they were doing, something not always the case in our society, which favored youth over experience. In 2009, the *Washington Post* asked readers: "What does 'aging well' mean to you?" Almost all of the responses (at least those published) were reassuring. "Activity," was the short and sweet answer from a sixty-seven-year-old retired postal supervisor, while a sixty-two-year-old school counselor replied, "Not trying to be younger than you are." One reader happened to be Herb Kohl, the seventy-four-year-old Democratic senator from Wisconsin who chaired the Special Senate Committee on Aging. "Aging well means being able to stay engaged in the things that excite and motivate you," Kohl wrote, and then did exactly that by putting in a plug for his committee's major initiatives—a secure retirement, access to health care, and support for long-term care.[41]

## Age Well!

Encouraging news about the aging mind did not preclude efforts to slow, stop, or even reverse the body's insistence to get older. Scientists were still investigating the causes of aging, hoping that a cure could be found for it once the precise biological "defect" was identified. Genetics—specifically a "faulty" chromosome—remained the most likely suspect for aging, making this line of inquiry the choice for most scientists in the field. A decrease in cellular efficiency was likely the cause of both physical and mental deterioration, it was generally agreed, a perfectly natural occurrence despite all the negative associations assigned to it.[42]

Locating the wear-and-tear theory of aging within a cellular framework seemed to satisfy many scientists trying to put the complicated biological puzzle together. Aging was "a life arc of the inter-related and overlapping processes and changes in the body's 100-trillion or so cells that take you from birth to death," stated Robert Palmer, a geriatrician and author of *Age Well!* "You can slow it but you can't stop it." Like the filament of a light bulb, the cells in our body burned out over time, said Palmer of the aging process, this slow but sure series of failures accounting for the common ailments of older people. Genetics may have been the wiring system of aging, but lifestyle and diet were contributing factors, researchers also concurred; the degree to which the workings of our bodies were stressed had a significant effect on the rate at which people aged.[43]

Viewing the human body in mechanical terms was a useful model by which to design a body that would have better functionality and not wear out so fast. Indeed, biogerontologists such as Aubrey de Grey were firm in their conviction that longevity was fundamentally an engineering problem that could be solved. Much like any machine, the human body could last significantly longer with a good maintenance program, insisted de Grey, coauthor of *Ending Aging: The Rejuvenation Biotechnologies That Could Reverse Human Aging in Our Lifetime*. De Grey had even come up with a plan to fix the aging problem. His "Strategies for Engineered Negligible Senescence" (SENS) outlined seven biological malfunctions and ways to repair each of them based on his success in extending the lives of mice.[44] He and his partners were in active pursuit of designing the "Methuselah mouse," as he referred to it, the ultimate objective being to extend the healthy human life span by advancing tissue engineering and regenerative medicine therapies.[45] With such fix-its, the human being was capable of living to be a thousand years old, the British researcher believed, labeling his many doubters as being in a "pro-aging trance."[46]

Some in the nascent field of systems biology, however, thought that aging resulted not from some kind of mechanical failure or from something lurking menacingly in humans' complex DNA code. A new, provocative theory posited that it was instead our inflammatory or immune system that was responsible for aging. While protecting us against infectious diseases and harmful substances by destroying antigens—substances (usually proteins) on the surface of cells, viruses, fungi, and bacteria—the system sometimes overreacted and inflicted major collateral damage on our organs and tissues. The good news was that an overactive immune system was treatable, giving some scientists hope that an anti-inflammatory drug could be the magic pill allowing us to live both healthier and longer lives.[47]

Until aging could be vastly slowed down through such pharmaceutical alchemy or by building a much more efficient human machine, however, the best option for living longer remained caloric restriction. A new book, *The Longevity Diet*, was helping to spread the word about what its coauthors legitimately described as "the only proven way to slow the aging process." The book, by Brian M. Delaney (the president of what was now called the Calorie Restriction Society International) and Lisa Walford (co-author of

*The Anti-Aging Plan* along with her father Roy Walford, the dean of caloric restriction), outlined a plan for "CR," no doubt attracting more subscribers to the rather extreme way of eating (or, more accurately, not eating). Consuming fewer calories and carefully selecting what one ate lowered cholesterol and blood pressure and reduced body fat, Delaney and Walford correctly advised, and was the most documented means of extending one's life span. Critics warned about the health risks of extreme caloric restriction (including starvation), but the method was clearly gaining followers, as it did appear to work if one was willing to adhere to what most people would consider a highly limited diet.[48]

For many scientists, however, CR was too simple and too radical a method of adding years to one's life. They maintained that extending longevity on a grander scale relied on altering the biochemical pathways of the body in order to suppress those diseases that often led to death.[49] Rather than attempting to design a life-extension pill, however (a long shot at best at this point), researchers were focusing on their efforts on creating a drug that mimicked the effects of caloric restriction.[50] In fact, a drug intended to do just that was in development: Sirtris Pharmaceuticals of Cambridge, Massachusetts, was conducting clinical trials of a synthetic version of resveratrol, a sirtuin activator found in grapes and red wine. The team of researchers was led by Leonard P. Guarante of MIT and David A. Sinclair of the Harvard Medical School, each of whom had spent a considerable number of years searching for genes that could extend life in lower forms of life (yeast and mice, respectively).[51]

Unlike the case with many researchers working in basement university labs, Sinclair's linking of resveratrol to longevity had led to fame and fortune. In addition to appearing on *60 Minutes*, the young-looking Australian was featured on a 2008 ABC News TV special hosted by Barbara Walters called *Live to Be 150: Can You Do It?* In 2008, GlaxoSmithKline purchased Sirtris Pharmaceuticals, the company Sinclair had cofounded, for $720 million. Soon, however, companies hoping to cash in on the red grape extract phenomenon were using Sinclair's name to sell resveratrol on the Internet. Resveratrol had not yet been proven effective in large-scale clinical trials with humans, Sinclair pointed out, and, even if it did work, massive quantities (about eighty pills a day) would have to be taken to get some benefit. (Besides all that, Sirtris was testing the ability of its drug, which was many times more powerful than natural resveratrol, to treat diseases associated with aging rather than aging itself.) With both Oprah Winfrey and frequent guest Columbia University medical professor Mehmet Oz each talking up the potential of resveratrol on her show, however, red grape extract was selling briskly online and in health food stores.[52]

Those in the chocolate business were no doubt happy to hear the hype about resveratrol, as it also happened to be a naturally occurring compound found in cocoa beans. Should Sirtris's findings be positive, dark chocolate and cocoa could be presented not just as tasty treats but also as products that could potentially help consumers live longer—quite a selling point. The Hershey Company had in fact already determined how much resveratrol was in cocoa powder, baking chocolate, and dark chocolate (14.1 to 18.5 micrograms per serving). While the excitement over resveratrol in chocolate was new, a direct result of all the media attention, many ancient cultures believed that cocoa beans possessed antiaging properties, lending further credence to the pleasing idea that a Hershey Bar could perhaps be very good for you.[53]

Even if it didn't work, resveratrol was one of the more innocuous antiaging treatments being pursued. Radically changing one's eating and exercise routines was a more aggressive route, followed by daily injections of human growth hormone (a substance secreted by the pituitary gland that promotes growth during childhood and adolescence) and weekly shots of testosterone. It was estimated that twenty-five thousand to thirty thousand Americans were injecting HGH for antiaging purposes, despite it being illegal to dispense HGH and other hormones for such purposes.[54] Spending more than $1,000 a month on such a course of action was not unusual, but antiagers who reported feeling healthier, more energetic, and more mentally sharp believed it was well worth the money. The classic examples of avid antiagers were wealthy males with A-type personalities who were happy to part with a little of their money to buy more health and time. The truly devoted were trying very odd techniques said to slow the aging process, such as fetal cell injections, inhaling radon gas, and even removing testicles (the latter to lessen overexposure to reproductive hormones).[55]

Hyperbaric chambers were another option for more committed antiagers. Ever since a tabloid photo dating from about the mid-1980s depicting the youth-obsessed Michael Jackson lying in a hyperbaric chamber was published, more people had chosen the treatment for any number of health-related purposes. Climbing into the coffin-like compartment filled with slightly elevated air pressure and raised oxygen levels for some time on a regular basis could not just cure cancer and other chronic diseases, proponents believed, but possibly slow or reverse the aging process. Some spas and alternative health clinics had installed hyperbaric chambers, and home units were available to rent or purchase. At American Medical Aesthetics, which had clinics in Santa Monica and Irvine, California, for example, clients received hyperbaric treatment as a "potent anti-aging therapy" that energized the body and eliminated toxins. Like virtually all other antiaging treatments, however, hyperbaric chambers were no fountains of youth. Physicians specializing in hyperbaric medicine pointed out that, if anything, oxygen in fact accelerated aging rather than slowed it by fostering the development of free-radical compounds that gradually damaged cells.[56]

## Un-Wrinkle Pressed Powder

While hyperbaric chambers were certainly one of the more exotic methods of antiaging, human growth hormone could be purchased at any number of spas, clinics, and physician's office across the country. Although scientific evidence supporting the use of HGH as an antiaging treatment was scant at best, use of the hormone continued to rise. Hard research was, however, finally catching up with some of the more popular antiaging methods. DHEA supplements and testosterone patches just didn't work, according to one of the first serious studies to put them to the test, something that members of the anti-antiaging movement had been saying all along. Those who had been using one or both of these popular treatments realized no gains in strength, physical performance, or other measures of health, a study published in the *New England Journal of Medicine* reported in 2006. The good news was that no harmful side effects were reported either, but the authors of the study, led by K. Sreekumaran Nair of the Mayo Clinic, remained reluctant to deem them completely safe.[57]

No one, perhaps, was happier to hear the findings of this particular study than S. Jay Olshansky. A few months after he gave his Silver Fleece award to the American Academy of Anti-Aging Medicine in 2004, Robert Goldman and Ronald Klatz sued Olshansky to stop what the leaders of the organization called a "ruthless campaign" to ruin their careers. The osteopathic physicians had filed a $120 million defamation lawsuit in Cook County (Illinois) Circuit Court, claiming that the University of Illinois at Chicago professor had purposely killed their budding antiaging dietary supplements business. Olshansky had then filed a countersuit against Goldman, Klatz, and their organization, and the lawyers took over. Two years later, the battle ended in a draw, with neither side paying damages. Olshansky, however, claimed victory. "We consider this a win," Olshansky said after the settlement was reached, seeing the result as a triumph for academic freedom and for "the ability of scientists to speak freely about what we know and what we don't know."[58]

True to form, the antiaging community ignored the outcome of the law-suit as well as the important findings from the Mayo Clinic study, seeing them as just distractions propagated by those who were "pro-dying." That year's an-tiaging conference in Las Vegas went off without a hitch, with attendees firm in their belief that getting old was a treatable medical condition. The exhibit hall of the Venetian Resort Hotel Casino was packed with marketers promot-ing the usual array of vitamins, hormones, drugs, and paraphernalia intended to stop the march of time. ("Detoxifiers" and "oxygenators" were particularly popular.) Dozens of lectures and workshops were offered to the several thou-sand attendees, most of them physicians, who were eager to know more about the treatment options for patients interested in looking and feeling younger. The lack of proof that they actually worked did little to take away from the fact that antiaging was a highly profitable business.[59]

The growing sense that antiaging medicine was an oxymoron was also having no effect on marketers generating sizable revenue from cosmeceuti-cals. Antiaging skin care was hotter than ever, not too surprising given that the nation was getting older everyday. More men had recently started to use antiaging skin care products, with all kinds of gels, serums, and creams promising to smooth out wrinkles on their faces as well.[60] With the industry now no longer new and more competitive than ever, marketers had to offer more innovative products to get consumers' attention. One new product for women, for example, was Peter Thomas Roth's Un-Wrinkle Pressed Powder, which contained myriad active ingredients, including antioxidants and a syn-thetic version of snake venom (that was said to have a Botox-like effect by re-ducing wrinkles through inhibiting muscle movement). Some other new skin care products not only had "rejuvenating" properties but gave their users a tan, presumably a way to lessen potential damage from the sun. The FDA still had not approved cosmeceuticals, however, so it was impossible to know the actual efficacy of any product in the category. Ingredient lists were another fuzzy area. Ingredients that were 1 percent or less of the formulation (usually quite a few) could be placed in any order, leaving consumers in the dark about how much of the supposedly "active" agents were in the product.[61]

Spurred on by the success of cosmeceuticals, cosmetics marketers were rapidly expanding their product lines. Brands of antiaging makeup were being introduced at an especially fast rate. Fifty such products, distributed in drugstores, department stores, and online, had made their debuts in 2004 alone. If antiaging skin care products helped one look younger, consumers figured, why not use antiaging lipstick, blush, and foundation as well? Revlon's Age-Defying Light Makeup and Clinique's Repairwear Anti-Aging Makeup were just two products in the increasingly crowded category. Many dermatologists were highly skeptical that any brand of antiaging makeup, like cosmeceuticals, really did much if anything, but that did not stop consumers from adding them to their skin care arsenal.[62]

Other dermatologists, however, seeing little harm in such products, were following Nicholas Perricone's lead by entering the cosmeceuticals business with their own brands. Jeffrey Dover, a well-known Boston dermatologist, for example, had launched his own line of antiaging creams called Skin Effects that could be purchased at CVS stores in the area. Dermatologist-branded cosmeceuticals could first be found at spas and then the doctors' own offices; now, however, they were appearing in the retail arena, vastly increasing their availability. Many wondered about the ethics involved in this kind of enterprise, as such products did not approach the efficacy of prescription medications. Not only were they not FDA approved, over-the-counter creams typically relied on an inflammatory agent to stimulate collagen production and thus temporarily reduce wrinkles by puffing up the skin; no long-term effects were achieved as with clinical-strength products.[63]

Even a temporary smoothing out of the skin appeared to be good enough for many consumers, however, especially when doctors wearing white lab coats on TV infomercials and websites promoted the products. Scientific-sounding names like StriVectin-SD added to the effect, accounting for what was a fast-growing segment of the cosmetics industry. Some major cosmetics companies were reaching out to physicians with academic affiliations in order to bolster their scientific image and to convince consumers that their products were not just beauty aids but medications. Estée Lauder, for example, was working with a doctor who taught at Stanford University School of Medicine, while Bath & Body Works was partnering with a physician associated with the Albert Einstein College of Medicine of Yeshiva University. With such credentials, was it any surprise that the antiaging movement continued to gain momentum?[64]

## The Lifestyle of the Future

Cosmeceuticals were of course just a portion of the vast marketing effort being directed at aging baby boomers. Throughout the second half of the twentieth century, youth-obsessed marketers had largely ignored consumers over forty years old, but this was fast changing in the early 2000s as the demographic pig worked its way through the proverbial python. "All of a sudden corporate America is waking up to what's going on," said marketing consultant David Wolfe in 2006, as food companies, fitness clubs, clothing retailers, and car manufacturers turned their attention to middle-aged boomers. Advertising revenue in AARP's magazine was up, another sign of marketers' rather sudden interest in older consumers. Marketers had aggressively targeted baby boomers since they were tots, of course, but were now heading into unfamiliar waters because of their historic slighting of anyone who was not considered young. By middle age, they (incorrectly) believed, consumers had formed their purchasing habits and brand loyalties and thus were resistant to trying anything new or different. Marketers were quickly changing their tune, however, as it became clear that boomers were different from previous generations of older consumers. Boomers were "professional" consumers, it could safely be said based on their lifelong experience of being marketed to, and appeared to be as interested as ever in trying new things and experiences. They also had, as a group, boatloads of money, making them now an essential target audience to consider when marketing any product or service.[65]

One did not have to be a financial genius to know that the aging boomer market also represented, on paper at least, a good investment opportunity. Wall Street was thus understandably keen on industries and companies catering to the group or with plans to do so. Companies in the pet care, cruising, financial advice, home building, cosmetic surgery, and orthopedic businesses were all benefiting from the age wave as investors bet on the future.[66] Savvier makers of appliances and bath fixtures were in fact already, as the *Wall Street Journal* put it, "designing for the senior surge." Thermador had come up with a range that made sure pots wouldn't boil over, while Dacor was selling an oven with control panels whose typefaces could be made larger. Kohler had invented a toilet that not only had a nightlight but was motorized to rise for easier use. Home builders, meanwhile, were beginning to make halls and doorways wide enough for walkers and wheelchairs and putting bedrooms on the ground floor so that residents would not have to use stairs.[67]

Marketers trying to figure out how to effectively reach aging baby boomers might have looked at what was taking place in the tech sector. Engineers at MIT's AgeLab, for example, had for the past decade been working with businesses to design products and services for older people, or what the founder of the lab called "the lifestyle of the future." More readable labels and more easily opened packages were just the beginning; food producers, carmakers, and insurance companies were paying AgeLab big consulting fees to come up with practical ideas that older people would like without making younger people run away.[68]

Technology companies also saw opportunity in providing much needed help to caregivers by coming up with innovative products and services for boomers' parents. Of boomers who had a living parent, 41 percent were helping to care for him or her, according to a USA Today/ABC News/Gallup Poll, suggesting there was a huge potential market for anything that could make the job easier. Also, outside-the-home care was expensive: an assisted-living residence cost roughly $36,000 a year, and a private room in a nursing home was going for more than $77,000 annually.[69] Via a new scheme called GrandCare System, those who were apprehensive about living alone without some in-home care or were uncomfortable with outside-the-home care or were unable to afford it had a new choice: a "wired" home. The system used sensors to record motion around a living space, allowing someone else in a different location to monitor any movement, including footstep patterns, on a computer. (Webcams were another option.) Adult children far away from an elderly parent were using the new technology to keep track of their loved one, a godsend for those worrying if he or she had fallen or had wandered off. The technology was a perfect example of the advances being made in the aging-in-place movement that was fast becoming the gold standard for senior living, and offering adult children peace of mind. Other technologies leading to the much anticipated "smart house" were in development, including a system telling those concerned whether their loved one was taking his or her medications.[70]

The new industry of care managers or coordinators was also helping distant adult children monitor the status of their older parents. An estimated two hundred thousand nurses, social workers, and counselors filled the gap between generations, especially when they were geographically separated. The care managers served as the "eyes and ears" for faraway family members, an invaluable service for those concerned about the well-being of their loved one and fortunate enough to afford the care.[71] Care management would undoubtedly play a larger role in the future, when baby boomers themselves would require such services in their elderly years. As the Institute of Medicine would soon report, a shortage in the caregiving labor pool was almost a certainty because of the number of boomers who were going to have physical or mental challenges. The problem was compounded by the industry's notoriously low wages (less than $10 an hour, on average) and very high turnover—each something that would have to change if there was any hope of making geriatrics a more attractive field.[72]

## Happy Neuron

While helpful for caregivers, technology could only do so much to alleviate what was typically a complicated, life-altering experience for everyone involved. Compounding the caregiving problem was that both boomers and their parents treated aging as a taboo subject; almost 70 percent of adult children had not talked to their mother or father about issues related to getting older, a recent AARP survey found.[73] Such talks between adult children and their parents were a good idea given the strange situations that could arise when an elderly person developed cognition problems. Friends from the distant past might appear in conversations, or the police be repeatedly called when the parent was convinced someone was in his or her house. Fantasies and forgetfulness were routine occurrences for those with the onset of senility or dementia, accounting for the odd behaviors that were likely rooted in loss of control. A parent going missing was a not infrequent problem, with he or she sometimes turning up in a neighbor's house. The fear of being placed in a nursing home had much to do with the disappearances, as was the gradual recognition that the parent was losing his or ability to think and reason. Trying to stop elderly parents from driving due to the concern they would injure themselves or others was a common but difficult issue, though relatively minor compared to having to tell the loved one that he or she could no longer live alone. Declaring a parent incompetent was an even more painful experience; the knowledge that one was likely doing the right thing offered little comfort.[74]

The issues surrounding caring for older parents were made clear in a television documentary produced by Boston-based WGBH and aired by a number of PBS stations in 2008. The aptly titled *Caring for Your Parents* viewed the subject through the prism of five Rhode Island families from a cross-section of economic classes, illustrating the variety of challenges that people in such situations often faced. While the stories naturally differed—some of the parents lived with their families and others in nursing homes—all of the caregivers featured in the film struggled in some way to manage the task. The strain of having to care for a parent could very well be exhausting or even overwhelming, the film showed, and was capable of breaking up a child's marriage or causing his or her health to suffer. Should a parent get sick, the caregiver often assumed the role of health care provider, so much so that his or her own life had to be put on hold.[75] If there was any unifying theme among the diverse families, it was that a daughter (versus a son) typically served as the primary caregiver to her parents. (The typical unpaid caregiver was a woman in her mid-forties who worked outside the home, according to AARP.)[76] Although difficult to watch ("It's a major downer," noted a reviewer for the *Pittsburgh Post-Gazette*), the documentary did include special moments of joy known to take place between caregiving children and their elderly parents.[77]

Such moments could also be found when one aging spouse became a caregiver to his wife or her husband with cognition problems, an increasingly common experience as the population became older. Because of its intensity, more people were documenting this aspect of life. In *The Caregiver— A Life with Alzheimer's*, for example, Aaron Alterra traced his relationship with his wife of more than sixty years, in the process exposing many of the shared experiences that came with living with a loved one with Alzheimer's (the gradual realization that something was wrong, finding the right doctor, determining a diagnosis, considering treatment options, experimenting with different medicines, and figuring out how to pay for it all). While the journey with his wife was no doubt difficult, Alterra demonstrated how his life had in some ways been enriched by becoming a caregiver.[78]

With such stories, the controversy surrounding Peter L. Whitehouse's *Myth of Alzheimer's Disease*, published in 2008, could easily be understood. As the title of the book boldly proclaimed, Alzheimer's was not a disease at all, according to the author, a professor of neurology at the Case Western Reserve University School of Medicine. Rather, he proposed, the symptoms assigned to Alzheimer's were just normal aging of the brain, something that occurred at a faster rate in some people. (Graying hair was a fair analogy.) Everyone would get Alzheimer's or some other form of dementia if they lived long enough, Whitehouse stated, challenging scientific evidence that degeneration of a part of the hippocampus was responsible for the condition. Going even further, Alzheimer's was essentially a "constructed" disease, he suggested, a product of a culture that could not make sense of or control such a frightening mental state. Because of his credentials (he had not only treated thousands of patients with deteriorating brains but cofounded the university's Alzheimer Center, making him nothing less than a guru in the field), Whitehouse's contentious theory could be challenged but not summarily dismissed.[79]

Whether or not Alzheimer's was a real disease or a cultural myth, it could not be argued that many in the general public were terrified of acquiring the symptoms themselves as they aged. To this end, a growing number of companies were offering "mental fitness programs" to help users maintain or improve their memory and cognitive functioning. Over the preceding few years, a handful of so-called brainpower-boosting programs had been introduced, with Americans spending about $225 million in 2007 on products with names like MindFit, Happy Neuron, Brain Fitness, and Lumosity. Nintendo had even got into the business, offering a video game called *Brain Age;* the product had already sold ten million copies worldwide. The marketers claimed that their products, which could be used online or on a hand-held device, could "tune up" the brain, strengthen memory, and delay age-related "cognitive slippage," but it was unclear if and how they worked. Still, the industry had tripled in sales over the previous four years, a strong indication that aging consumers would continue to invest in their brains in order to stay in shape, cognitively speaking.[80]

A trip to the cavernous Nintendo store in Manhattan would certainly suggest that mental fitness in the early twenty-first century was analogous in some ways to the physical fitness craze of the 1970s and 1980s. Hordes of silver-haired people could often be found there on weekends playing *Brain Age* while their grandchildren played *Super Mario* in another part of the store. The business community saw a bright future for the mental fitness industry as the number of "gray gamers" grew. "As baby boomers march toward senior citizenship," *BusinessWeek* observed, "hiding their mental age may prove as important to them as concealing their gray hair." Much as how cosmeceuticals had come to be a hugely profitable business despite the glaring lack of evidence that the products actually worked, no empirical proof that brain exercises slowed cognitive decline did not appear to diminish marketers' expectations.[81] As more Americans marched toward senior citizenship, attempts to thwart aging continued, and efforts to maximize one's time on Earth intensified.

# 6

Raging Against Aging

I believe the word retirement in a decade will be a
quaint, charming term that people used to use.
—Larry Minnix, president of the American Association
of Homes and Services for the Aging, 2010

Do you know your "RealAge"? Tens of millions of Americans do after
taking a test on sharecare.com, a health care website codeveloped in
2010 by Mehmet Oz, the well-known surgeon, author, and television
personality. The test poses a wide range of questions about visitors' medical information, genetic history, marital and job status, eating and exercise
habits, and even frequency of socializing. After completing the test, visitors
learn their RealAge, and the difference, if any, between it and their calendar
or chronological age. A few composite characters are featured on the popular website to give visitors an idea of how they might score on the test. One
woman featured has never been married, walks her dog every day, goes to
dinner with friends every weekend, eats fruits and vegetables every day, fol-
lows her doctor's instructions, and does not stress about life's little problems,
making her RealAge 28.4 years (4.2 years less than her calendar age of 32.6
years). Another featured woman, however, often eats red meat, stresses over
minor things, does light exercise, spends most of her time alone, and fails to
take her prescribed medications and vitamin D, giving her a RealAge of 67.5
years (7.3 years more than her calendar age of 60.2 years).[1]

The interest in determining one's RealAge was a solid indicator of the
unrelenting allure of youngness and equally persistent aversion toward "oldness." As the oldest baby boomers reached the traditional retirement age of

sixty-five in January 2011, aging took on a new significance, and battling it a new urgency. Rather than accept their advancing age, many boomers were rebelling against it and actively seeking ways to postpone their entry into senior citizenship. Ageism wasn't helping matters, further pushing boomers to make themselves seem younger than their years. With youth still one of the most valuable and highly sought social currencies, Americans as a whole were "raging against aging," as the *Wall Street Journal* put it in 2011, with few affirmative interpretations of getting older to be found. The entry of wealthy individuals and corporations into the antiaging movement has only intensified our antipathy toward the natural course of our bodies, leaving us with no clear way of how we should age except through resistance.

## The Nasty Little Secret

Americans' long war on getting older was in some respects a microcosm of what was a global fear of aging. Not just the United States but also many other countries were rapidly aging, making many demographers believe a major social and economic crisis was a few decades away. The United Nations was forecasting that the world's population would increase by about one-third by 2050, a huge demographic shift in historic terms. Put another way, the global population of children under five was expected to fall by forty-nine million as of the mid-twenty-first century, while the number of people over sixty was predicted to grow by 1.2 billion.[2]

With such a big jump in a relatively short time, it can be understood how and why many economists and health care professionals were so concerned about the future older population of the world. Those with some sense of history knew, however, that the previous crisis about global population turned out to be a false alarm. In his 1968 best seller *The Population Bomb*, Paul Ehrlich predicted that hundreds of millions of people would starve to death over the following two decades because of a rising global population. But the baby boom had already become a baby bust by the time of the book's publication, making Ehrlich's dire warnings great copy but, from a demographic perspective, methodically challenged. In fact, demographers are today worried about there being too few people on the planet rather than too many, making one wonder if the prospect of an older global population is as worrisome as some claim.[3]

With the oldest baby boomers turning sixty-five on January 1, 2011, yet another milestone in the history of aging in the United States was reached.

Each day since then and until 2030, about ten thousand more Americans will have reached that age, the Pew Research Center forecast; 8 percent of the nation's population would be at least sixty-five in 2030.[4] As would be expected in an aging population, the number of American grandparents was high and still growing. There were about sixty-five million grandparents in the country in 2010, reported a study by the MetLife Mature Market Institute, a number that represented an all-time high. Because the number of grandparents was growing at twice the overall population rate, however, there would be even more of them. The number of grandparents was projected to be eighty million in 2020, nearly one in three American adults, according to the MetLife report. And rather than little old ladies and men puttering around the house and knitting sweaters, most grandparents were baby boomers who were still working full-time, casting a much different light on what older people looked and acted like.[5] As with the attempt to come up with a better alternative to the words "seniors" and "elderly," in fact, some were trying to replace the term "grandparent" with a new one that did not automatically conjure the image of *Whistler's Mother*.

With that many people to be that old in less than two decades, more attention was being paid to whether and how boomers would define and redefine old age in America. A 2012 report released by AARP and the research group Focalyst shed some light on what might happen by doing some myth busting. Contrary to what some believed, most boomers were not retiring early or downsizing their homes, a clear indication that they were not ready to embark on a life significantly different from the one they were living. In addition, most boomers were neither wealthy nor married empty nesters, suggesting they currently had neither the time and nor the money to do whatever they liked in their third act of life. It was still too early to be sure, but it appeared that boomers' version of seniority would indeed be different from that of previous generations who had "cashed in" to make possible a leisure-based model of retirement. Rather than a clearly defined post-work life, in order words, it appeared that boomers version of "retirement" would look a lot like the life they had led for most of their adult years.[6] Was this recasting of older age a good thing, one had to ask, or simply evidence that people were in denial about entering their senior years? Is it possible that because of their deep connection to youth, many boomers were and remain just not capable of contemplating Laslett's Fourth Age, in which decline and disease will become unavoidable?

Regardless of the answers to those questions, where baby boomers planned to live as they aged had a lot to do with how they would live. Much was being made about boomers' need for senior-friendly homes as they aged, with some builders already offering residences on a single floor, having little or no lawn to mow, designed with extrawide hallways to accommodate wheelchairs, and featuring easy-to-reach light switches and door knobs. But contrary to such recommendations put forth by prestigious organizations, including Harvard University's Joint Center for Housing Studies and AARP, a new survey from the Demand Institute showed that boomers had very little interest in a senior-friendly home now or in the future. Not only were most boomers planning to stay put in their current homes (that is, aging in place) and were not considering modifying them to any significant degree, the survey by the non-profit institute (managed by the Conference Board and Nielsen) revealed, but if they did move they might very well upsize versus downsize. Even taking out a new mortgage on a bigger home—something traditionally considered anathema for budget-conscious retirees—was a possibility, the poll among four thousand boomer households reported, more evidence that retirement would indeed likely be quite a different proposition for this generation.[7]

Health too was a major consideration when considering the future of aging boomers. Although both obesity and diabetes had jumped over the past few decades as fast food and sugary drinks invaded the nation's culinary landscape, many boomers were in better health than their parents and grandparents had been when they were in their sixties. Boomers had, after all, been active participants in the running/jogging craze of the 1970s, had joined health clubs in droves in the 1980s, and had signed up for yoga and Pilates classes since the 1990s. Many boomers still belonged to gyms but were finding that the kinds of workouts to be had there were not an especially good fit because of their age. While yesterday's senior might have been content with a simple stroll around the park or some low-impact aerobics, more-active boomers were heading to new kinds of gyms or health clubs conceived just for them. À la Curves fitness centers for plus-size women, gyms for the fifty-plus crowd were opening up across the nation. At Nifty After Fifty, a Los Angeles area chain of gyms, for example, members fifty or older could take classes that were not designed for bodies half their age. (One such class was something called "Cane Fu," in which a walking stick was made part of a martial arts course.) Other health and fitness brands were aiming for the huge boomer market as they aged. The YMCA introduced a "50 Moving Forward" program at some of its locations, which taught fifty-plussers how to eat more healthfully, for instance, while Jane Fonda, who had told boomers some thirty

years before to "feel the burn," had created a line of more body-friendly fitness videos for those very same people.[8]

Major advances in nutrition and much improved medical care were other
reasons why many baby boomers were in better health than previous generations of fifty- and sixtysomethings. Boomers also smoked and drank less than
their parents had, as any episode of *Mad Men* would suggest. Still, boomers'
history of excess in their younger days was now making itself known via various physical ailments. Many had hearing loss after years of listening to rock
'n roll at jet engine volume levels, and others had hepatitis C from injecting drugs. (The Centers for Disease Control and Prevention urged that all
boomers get tested for hepatitis C.) Gerontologists believed, however, that
the larger potential health hazard for boomers was psychological rather than
physical. Boomers' denial of aging would one day catch up with them, they
worried, with a collective rude awakening lying in wait. "What really scares
the hell out of me is that they're totally unprepared for old age," said Robert
Kane, director of the University of Minnesota's Center for Aging, thinking
that aging was "the nasty little secret no one talks about."[9]

Other experts, however, believed that the scariest thing about the aging
of baby boomers was the impact they would have on the nation's health care
system. Boomers would overload the government's senior citizen health care
program, people like Merrill Goozner warned, stirring up a big ruckus over
the funding of both Medicare and Medicaid. Each of those programs had
long been considered immune to political wrangling, but that had gradually
changed over the years, leaving Medicare in particular vulnerable to financial
scrutiny. Would Gen Xers and millennials as working-age taxpayers be willing to pay whatever it was going to take to keep boomers healthy as they got
older? Goozner, writing in *Modern Healthcare*, in 2015, wasn't so sure, seeing Medicare as a major battleground in the prophesized generational war to
come. Already Republicans were beginning to propose cost-cutting measures
like "means-testing" and "defined-contribution," ideas that may very well appeal to younger generations who will likely have to foot much of the bill for
their parents' and grandparents' considerable healthcare needs.[10]

## Live Long and Prosper

As pundits speculated about the later years of life for baby boomers and the
implications for the country, Americans continued to struggle with the very
concept of aging. As always, much was made of older people who were defy-

ing stereotypes by leading especially active lives. Robert Butler, the legendary gerontologist who had coined the term "ageism," was presented as a natural choice for others to look to and be inspired by. At eighty-two years old in 2010 and still head of the International Longevity Center, Butler was as busy as ever, flying around the world to make celebrated appearances at aging conferences. Butler was, according to *U.S. News & World Report* in February 2010, "living proof that humans, like fine wine, can deepen in complexity with time," quite an accolade.[11] (Butler died just five months later.)

If they looked hard enough, journalists interested in putting a positive spin on aging were able to locate seniors like Butler who were doing extraordinary things. Readers of *U.S. News & World Report* learned about an eighty-five-year-old woman who was a Peace Corps volunteer in Morocco, a ninety-one-year-old woman who was still teaching aerobics, and a hundred-year-old woman who was continuing to put in forty-hour work weeks. Stories of individuals like these who were obviously not representative of the general population gave readers an overtly optimistic and thoroughly unrealistic view of aging (that could perhaps be interpreted as an inverted form of ageism). In short, media coverage of aging was (and remains) highly polarized, with either the economic and health care apocalypse waiting in the nation's wings or, conversely, an approaching golden era of seniordom composed of the healthiest, most affluent, and most active generation in history.[12]

George Takei, who had played Sulu on the original *Star Trek* television series, was another older person who exemplified how one should age, according to the media. Seventy-seven years old in 2014, Takei had seemingly embraced the human-Vulcan Mr. Spock's famous line "Live long and prosper," something enhanced by his exuberant personality. Takei did one hundred push-ups and fifty sit-ups every morning, part of his formula of longevity. Besides regular exercise, he believed, sufficient sleep and an engaged mind were the keys to a long, healthy life, with a good sense of humor another thing that kept a person young. The actor and spokesperson for LGBT equality had a YouTube series called *Takei's Take* that was sponsored by AARP but attracted an audience of all ages. The man had a cultlike following because of his outspokenness, in fact, making him a kind of folk hero among millennials who admired people who were not afraid to express their opinions and individuality.[13]

The neurologist and best-selling author Oliver Sacks appointed himself as a role model for dynamic aging. On the cusp of his eightieth birthday, Sacks used the *New York Times* op-ed page to describe what he called without any irony "the joy of old age." Best known for his book *Awakenings,* which was turned into an Academy Award–nominated film, he was clearly pleased with his current life and considered his advanced age to be more of a surprise than anything else. "I often feel that life is about to begin, only to realize it is almost over," he remarked, happy to report that none of his medical problems was disabling. Sacks was very much looking forward to his eighties, feeling that he was continuing to grow intellectually. "I do not think of old age as an ever grimmer time that one must somehow endure and make the best of," he wrote, "but as a time of leisure and freedom, freed from the factitious urgencies of earlier days, free to explore whatever I wish, and to bind the thoughts and feelings of a lifetime together." Still, he thought he should be trying to complete his life, whatever that meant, as it was not unusual for some kind of catastrophic illness to develop among people his age. "Perhaps, with luck, I will make it, more or less intact, for another few years and be granted the liberty to continue to love and work, the two most important things, Freud insisted, in life," he ended his essay.[14]

Sacks's story was an encouraging one but not reflective of reality. Some kind of health issue often made itself apparent by age eighty, if one was lucky to live that long. (The average life expectancy for an American was 78.74 years in 2012.) More than half of Americans older than eighty-five had a number of chronic illnesses or disabilities, making the appealing idea of a quick death after a long, mostly healthy life unlikely to happen.[15] Sacks himself learned he had terminal cancer in early 2015, something that was sure to cut short his life as an octogenarian. "My luck has run out," he wrote in a follow-up *New York Times* op-ed, his recent diagnosis (multiple metastases in the liver) making him more determined than ever to "live in the richest, deepest, most productive way I can" in what in all likelihood would be less than a year. Sacks died in August of that year.[16]

As Susan Jacoby observed in *Newsweek,* the media's focus on those who were aging "gracefully" was a distortion that did more harm than good. For every eighty-nine-year-old Betty White or eighty-year-old Warren Buffett, there were hundreds of thousands of octogenarians with significant mental or physical disabilities, she pointed out, with financial hardship also common in older people. "Americans must prepare for the possibility that not the best, but some of the worst years of our lives may lie ahead if we live into our ninth and 10th decades," Jacoby wrote, a thought echoed in Muriel R. Gillick's *Denial of Aging.* Pretending that age no longer mattered (or that "90 is the New 50," as a panel at the 2008 World Science Festival was absurdly titled) was not a good way to have much needed conversations about how to provide long-term care and community-based services for the growing number of older people.[17] One indicator alone—the number people who were replacing their knees or hips with artificial ones—proved that age was something that could not be completely denied. In 2014, the number of Americans with new joints topped seven million, with orthopedic surgeons predicting that number would grow as tens of millions of baby boomers reached their seventies.[18]

Because chronic conditions that were virtually impossible to cure completely tended to come with the territory of aging, any geriatrician would agree that providing medical care to older adults was a difficult-at-best job. The stress of the job was reflected in the numbers: there were only six thousand geriatricians in the United States in 2015 (out of about one million physicians), with the number shrinking.[19] It was not unusual for a geriatrician's patient to have at least three chronic conditions, in fact, such as Alzheimer's, heart disease, and diabetes. Patients might very well be taking a dozen medications prescribed by various doctors, some of them interacting dangerously with each other. Doctors were often at a loss as to how they could help, knowing there was no magic pill or treatment that could reverse their patients' dire conditions.[20]

Like its sister field of geriatrics, gerontology has in recent years become a difficult field to which to attract talented professionals. Aging was "a hard sell," a reporter for the *Boston Globe* noted in 2013 after officials at the University of Massachusetts in Boston decided to suspend its undergraduate degree program in gerontology. Enrollment in the program had fallen by two-thirds over the preceding decade, and a relaunch in 2010 had failed to attract more students. Gerontology was obviously a field that would offer innumerable career opportunities, even more so in the future than in the past few decades, but its inherent challenges were now simply too great to make enough young people want to train for it. The situation was "unfortunate," the *Globe* correctly observed, "because the issues at stake will only grow in importance as the baby boom generation moves into retirement." One gerontologist suggested that the field should be rebranded, as its very name, which brought to mind frail patients edging ever closer to death, scared off potential prospects. "For gerontology to thrive as a separate area of study," the reporter concluded, "researchers need to make it clearer to students how the field connects to the future of the country and the economy."[21]

It would perhaps have been a good idea for gerontologists to take a look at the success the Mailman School of Public Health at Columbia University was enjoying. Enrollment in the school's graduate programs rose by more than 25 percent between 2008 and 2012 after the curriculum was revamped to address health issues pertaining to people of all ages. Applications and grants were also up, a reflection of Mailman's interdisciplinary approach that made it different from all other schools of public health. Aging was at the heart of the program, proving that gerontology did not have to be a field that talented young people found uninteresting or depressing. Mailman had the potential to help "reframe our understanding of the benefits and costs of aging," said epidemiologist and geriatrician Linda P. Fried, who served as dean of the school. Research into aging was key to finding solutions to public health problems in the twenty-first century, Fried told the *New York Times* in 2012, those problems being not just medical but financial and social as well. Presenting aging as a vital global issue that had direct relevance to everyday life now and in the future would clearly be in the best interests of the field and to the growing number of people getting older by the second.[22]

## Chasing Methuselah

The stigma associated with aging was made even more apparent by the millions of Americans who were doing everything possible (or, more accurately, impossible) to prevent themselves from getting older. Following the longevity plan of Jeanne Calment, a Frenchwoman who died in 1997 at the age of 122 (the oldest age of an individual on record), would certainly have been a lot simpler than the steps many were taking to add years to their lives. Calment, who had taken up fencing at eighty-five, claimed that copious amounts of port wine and olive oil were the secret to her long and active life, making one wonder why antiagers were not consuming massive quantities of each to achieve similar results. Almost one hundred million Americans were currently using some kind of antiaging product or practice, an astounding number by any measure. There was no doubt that antiaging, once a pursuit limited to what could be described as a fanatical fringe, was now a mainstream activity, cause for *Christianity Today* to assert in 2011 that Americans were "chasing Methuselah." The decidedly mainstream magazine *Good Housekeeping* had recently come up with something called the "Anti-Aging Awards" (which informed readers which of ninety antiaging skin care products offered the best results), an indicator that the movement had spread to a mass audience. One could also learn from the magazine how to "age-proof" one's hair, another solid sign that antiaging had reached (or perhaps had crossed over) the tipping point.[23]

Scientists in the antiaging arena, meanwhile, were interested in finding a way that one would not have to age-proof one's hair through some beauty product. Going back to Aristotle, who wrote a book on aging more than twenty-three hundred years ago, biologists had for the most part seen the process of getting older as one of gradual physical breakdown. Evolutionary biologists like Michael R. Rose were challenging that theory, however, thinking that there was more to it than biochemistry. "We now understand that ageing is not a cumulative process of progressive chemical damage, like rust," he wrote in *New Scientist*, but "a pattern of declining function produced by evolution." Rose and his coauthors Laurence D. Mueller and Casandra L. Rauser described in *Does Aging Stop?* how aging appeared to slow down at some point, evidence that the process was not one of constant bodily deterioration.[24] He believed that evolution or, more specially, natural selection played a key role in aging, the reason he and others in his field were confident that radically extending the human life span was a real possibility. Living longer could be achieved through better adaptation to one's environment, they deduced, while the wear-and-tear theory of aging based in continual physical decline until death occurred was an unbeatable hand.[25]

Others who rejected the wear-and-tear or "stochastic" theory of getting older—that damage to the body accumulated over time until it was no longer able to repair itself—held that oxygen was the key to aging. Biochemistry was basically a complex series of chemical reactions in which the body took electrons from food, proponents of the free-radical school of aging pointed out, with oxygen essential to the process. But as oxygen released free radicals—molecules or atoms with an unpaired electron—the body was damaged, a process that triggered the physical signs of aging.[26]

For some scientists, however, the fact that humans relied on oxygen to live made any chance of immortality or radical life extension impossible. Without oxygen, they reminded colleagues in search of a fountain of youth, cells will die, as will the host organism, making aging an unavoidable part of life. Thomas Kirkwood, professor of medicine and director of the Institute for Ageing and Health at Newcastle University in England and author of *Time of Our Lives: The Science of Human Aging*, was one such scientist who could not foresee the discovery of a remedy for reversing accumulated damage to cells. "It may be possible to combat aging by altering important mechanisms that cells use to counteract the buildup of damage," he noted in *Scientific American* in an article entitled "Why Can't We Live Forever?" But organ failure and ultimately death were inevitable. "Solutions will not come easily, despite the claims made by the merchants of immortality who assert that caloric restriction or dietary supplements, such as resveratrol, may allow us to live longer," he insisted.[27]

Given that aging was fundamental, it was interesting, to say the very least, that there remained no consensus of how and why humans aged. Five years later, in fact, scientists were still debating the question, and coming up with new possibilities. In 2015, an international team of scientists claimed that it was "DNA disorganization" that caused aging, a spinoff of the cellular-based theory that had become the most accepted view. A kind of chaos took place within cells as they got older, reported the team's study published in *Science,* a function of the way in which DNA was tightly packed inside them. Everything from gray hair to brittle bones was the result of cells "gone wild," wrote the team, who had used a human stem cell line with a faulty Werner gene as the basis for its research. This was the latest of many studies to use Werner syndrome (or adult progeria) as a means of exploring the progression of aging, as it was this genetic disorder that some scientists believed most closely mimicked the process by which otherwise healthy people became physically older.[28]

Although there were many attempts being made to delay the aging process without exactly knowing why and how it occurred, it was generally agreed that understanding the biological foundation for it would lead to much more effective solutions. One of many pesky problems thwarting the merchants of immortality was that it was almost impossible to predict how fast or slowly an individual would age. Researchers visiting nursing homes to interview subjects were constantly amazed at the longevity of some older people who had eschewed healthy lifestyles and the lack of longevity among others who had lived like ascetics. It was not unusual to find a centenarian who had the diet of a caveman and had never been near a gym or, conversely, an ancient-looking seventy-year-old who had long had a Spartan diet and had regularly exercised. It was obvious that genetics played a huge role in determining how long one would live, diminishing the effect any antiaging treatment could potentially have. "It's hard to live past 90 without getting lucky in the genes game," explained David Stipp, author of *The Youth Pill,* a book that explored how gene mutations could double the life spans of certain animals. The only real common denominator among centenarians was the absence of alcoholism, Stipp had found, as it was almost certain that excessive drinking would shorten one's life.[29]

The power of genetics in determining the pace of aging was just one major obstacle facing scientists attempting to stop it in its tracks. Despite the still rising membership of the AAAM, the term "anti-aging medicine" remained an oxymoron, with no drug yet proven to slow the body's insistence to get older. Still, it can be understood why scientists working in the antiaging arena believed they had a fair chance of finding the proverbial fountain of youth. Biotechnology had been around only thirty years, but even the most vocal of antiaging critics would have to admit that major and useful discoveries had been made. Treatment for AIDS was perhaps the most notable example; what had been an almost sure death sentence had been turned into a chronic illness that typically could be managed through a cocktail of drugs. Likewise, certain cancers that had previously meant almost certain fatality in a short period of time were being treated with monoclonal antibodies that allowed patients to live for years or even decades.[30]

In general, in fact, biotechnology had transformed many acute and lethal illnesses into long-term, controllable diseases, in the process considerably lengthening patients' life spans. Biotechnology focused on antiaging was similarly dedicated to extending lives, making such efforts not the stuff of mad scientists working in the shadow of Dr. Frankenstein. Many biotechnologists were coming to believe that the study of basic aging itself was a smarter use of their resources than finding medications to treat particular diseases. Even more to the point, curing a disease like cancer would itself be a miraculous discovery, but why devote the tremendous amount of time and money that would be required if people who might have contracted it died of another age-related illness just a few months later?[31] It was only a matter of time before researchers figured out how to slow aging at a molecular level, biologists held, something that had already been achieved with mice.[32] Given all that had been achieved in biotechnology in just three decades, was it completely unreasonable to think that equivalent strides would be made in the next three?

## Liquid Gold

Not at all, at least according to a growing number of scientists receiving grants from institutions and individuals committed to solving the aging enigma. Boosting the cause of the antiaging scientific community was the taking hold of the once radical idea that delaying aging versus curing disease was the smarter way to enable people to live longer and healthier lives. A study conducted by scientists from the University of Southern California, Harvard University, Columbia University, the University of Illinois at Chicago, and

other institutions and published in *Health Affairs* in 2013 essentially canon-
ized this new way of thinking. Slowing the aging process and its associated
maladies would not only lead to a healthier human being, the authors of the
study pointed out, but potentially save trillions of dollars in health care costs
over the next half-century. While it was a noble effort, curing diseases like
cancer and heart disease would have less impact on longevity and quality of
life than delaying aging itself, they added, as it was typical for older people
to suffer from a variety of illnesses. "When we treat someone with cancer, or
heart disease, or stroke, we are treating a manifestation or byproduct of biological aging," said Jay Olshansky, a coauthor of the study, but "the underlying
process marches on unaltered by this approach to disease."[33]

With scientists now focusing on the biology of aging, extending one's
"healthspan" (much like one's "RealAge") was becoming a more important
aim than adding a few more months or years to the end of an individual's
life. Some scientists were predicting that as many as half of the children born
since 2000 would become centenarians, but, for the moment, that was simply
the stuff of futurism. The fact was that the dramatic rise in longevity made
through medical breakthroughs over the course of the twentieth century had
slowed down considerably, making biologists realize that an exponential leap
of a different kind had to be made if humans were going to live to an age of
which they were believed to be capable (120 years was most commonly cited).
Americans exploring the biology of aging (some had begun to refer to the
new field as "geroscience") in particular felt some pressure to figure out how
to push the human body into three digits. In the World Health Organization's ranking of longevity, the United States was currently thirty-fourth in
the world with a life expectancy of seventy-nine years—lower than countries
like Cuba, Lebanon, and Costa Rica, and more than four years behind the
leader, Japan. Also, 80 percent of Americans sixty-five and older had at least
one chronic condition, such as cancer, heart disease, arthritis, diabetes, or
dementia (50 percent had two), meaning most older people in America were
facing major health problems throughout their golden years.[34]

The biology of aging or geroscience was an ideal fit for a large health-
care-based institution like the Mayo Clinic. Beginning in 2009, the famed
medical clinic in Rochester, Minnesota, had become one of the largest aging
centers in the country, with no fewer than forty-eight geriatricians and ten
geriatric psychiatrists on staff. The clinic's orientation was clearly more health
span than life span, meaning that helping patients be free of chronic disease
was considered more important than extending longevity. The two were in-

extricably linked, however, as delaying the onset of illnesses like Alzheimer's disease, cancer, heart attacks, strokes, and diabetes was the best way to add years to a person's life. Growth hormone was another area of study at Mayo, with researchers there trying to determine whether a decline in the substance was either a cause or an effect of aging, and if drugs targeting its decline could affect the aging process.[35]

Hyped by Mehmet Oz on his television show and in women's magazines, such as *Allure*, growth hormone therapy was reaching a new level of popularity despite growing concerns that it was unsafe. Some famous fifty-year-old actresses looked more like thirty-five, sparking rumors that they were using HGH as a youth serum. Others in the public eye—models, athletes, politicians, and CEOS—were likewise suspected of being "on the juice," as it was said, making ordinary folks want to get in on the action. With its apparent benefits—reduced body fat, increased muscle mass, heightened mood and sex drive, more energy, and tighter skin—who would not want to use HGH? it could fairly be asked.[36] When combined with a change in diet, HGH could not just help make users' skin smoother and firmer but also take off pounds, an irresistible thing for those who had never before been able to lose weight.[37]

One can only imagine how many Americans would be committed antiagers if HGH or any other treatment worked over the long term and were determined to be completely safe. While HGH typically had a direct effect on the body, there was no clinical evidence that it or any of the other popular methods being used actually slowed the aging process or added years to one's life. The demand for them, however, remained greater than ever. On a global basis, consumers were spending almost $300 billion on all antiaging products and treatments by 2015, which included human growth hormone therapy, prescription or over-the-counter "smart drugs" (or nootropics), supplements such as DHEA, testosterone replacement, and vitamin and mineral infusions.[38] Researchers had been able to slow aging in multicellular organisms and animals through a variety of other methods, but applying those methods to humans remained just a dream, especially among those hoping to get rich from the realization of a fountain of youth.[39]

With the clock ticking, some antiagers were not about to wait for a scientist in a lab to figure out how to translate the ability to double the life span of a worm, fruit fly, or mouse to a human. More exotic therapies were appearing on the scene, offering takers the hope of checking their aging process before it was too late to do anything about it. Some of the more adventurous (and wealthy), for example, were heading to the Thermes Marins Monte-Carlo

Spa for a cryotherapy session that was said to both relieve stress and slow the aging process. Participants stripped down to the bare essentials and then entered a chamber that was cooled to minus 166 degrees Fahrenheit, where they spent a few (painful) minutes. After exiting the ice-cold room, however, clients (including actress Lindsay Lohan) reported feeling extremely rejuvenated, a result of super oxygenation of the blood and increased serotonin level. "The shocklike extreme cold stimulus, and the severe reduction in skin surface temperature over minutes, brings about a cryogenic influencing of the functions of neural structures as well as induction of neuroreflexive process that exert effects on various regulatory pathways," explained the spa's manual and high-tech therapy manager.[40]

Those not interested in traveling to Monte Carlo to be flash-frozen like a package of peas but still interested in looking and feeling younger could opt for a stem cell treatment. At any of the growing number of stem cell clinics across the country, a mix of blood and fat (termed "liquid gold" because of its financial value in the trade) were harvested from a patient's backside, treated with a chemical and run through a processor to isolate the stem cells, and then reinjected into the patient's body. Dozens of ailments could be healed through stem cell treatment, its proponents claimed, making its high cost (thousands of dollars per procedure) well worth it. The Beverly Hills–based Cell Surgical Network was the largest stem cell chain in the nation, with one hundred doctors offering treatment in sixty-seven locations in twenty-two states. As with all antiaging methods, there were no evidence-based studies to indicate that stem cell therapy was effective, but clinics offering it were popping up at a faster rate than McDonald's franchises.[41]

Not surprisingly, anyone choosing to undergo a medically based antiaging treatment like stem cell or cryogenic therapy were typically first given a laundry list of warnings about the process and asked to sign a consent form. (Patients in all kinds of allopathic settings were similarly informed and required to release the clinic from any liability.) All forms of antiaging therapies were receiving greater scrutiny regarding potential health risks, in fact, the result of some fatalities that were widely reported in the media. One fifty-six-year-old woman died of cancer after six months of injecting HGH that was prescribed by doctors at Cenegenics, for example, lending support to the FDA's warnings that the substance carried significant health risks. While antiaging was still not a specialty recognized by the American Board of Medical Specialties, meaning doctors could not be officially board certified in the field, thousands of American physicians were practicing it. Membership in the AAAM was up to twenty-four thousand worldwide, a clear sign that some physicians believed the potential financial benefits outweighed the potential risks.[42]

Beyond the providers' ability to charge patients thousands of dollars for a single procedure, the fact that most antiaging treatments were not covered by health insurance was a major draw, as physicians could be paid out of pocket. (Managed care was dipping heavily into physician reimbursements from insurance companies.) Because of the money to be made, even radiologists and emergency room physicians were beginning to call themselves antiaging doctors and offering treatment, usually by prescribing HGH or some other hormone. As in any field, jargon was considered important to draw in potential customers. "Adrenal fatigue" had become the aging malady of the moment; diagnosis of it usually involved a physician prescribing hydrocortisone (which carried its own health risks). "Heavy-metal toxicity" was almost as trendy a diagnosis; flushing the buildup of mercury and other metals out of the body required many costly procedures that were also dangerous. As with cosmeceuticals, a good number of doctors had launched their own lines of nutraceuticals, another way to make big bucks. The profit margin on these antiaging supplements was "better than what cocaine dealers get," quipped Thomas Perls, an associate professor of medicine at Boston University. Even better, the business was totally legal.[43]

## Eternity Soup

Not just physicians but also companies with lots of cash on hand were now flocking to the antiaging industry because of the potential profits to be had. Google entered the longevity research arena in 2013 by launching Calico (short for California Life Company), a firm focusing on how technology could lead to a better understanding of life span. Not surprisingly, Google revealed few details about Calico, leaving many wondering how an Internet-based company was going to help people live longer, healthier lives. (A *Time* magazine cover story with the headline "Can Google Solve Death?" further piqued people's interest.)[44] A couple of years later, Google announced a partnership between Calico and the Buck Institute for Research on Aging to search for a biotech fountain of youth.[45] (The Buck Institute had recently made headlines by announcing that ibuprofen could possibly slow aging.)[46] Pharmaceutical companies were also looking for ways to enter the field; the Swiss firm Novartis had already announced that the development of longevity drugs (called "geroprotectors") was a priority.[47]

Indeed, the entry of Google-funded companies into the antiaging arena was the impetus for drug companies large and small to escalate their efforts. The clinical and regulatory obstacles were enormous, but the chase was now on for a marketable drug promising to fight the physical process of aging in some manner. In 2014, Google decided to partner Calico with U.S. drug manufacturer AbbVie (a spin-off of Abbott Laboratories), pushing other pharmaceutical companies such as Denmark's Novo Nordisk to determine if any of its existing products might have antiaging applications. The pharmaceutical industry was clearly embracing the new biology-of-aging approach. For example, diabetes and dementia were just two illnesses that would balloon worldwide over the next few decades, the World Health Organization forecast, but biotech execs were now inclined to shift their research spending from treatment of particular diseases to both prevention and, on a grander scale, slowing down aging itself. Not only did the introduction of drugs that prevented the onset of age-related diseases and aging itself make more sense for individuals, thought Big Pharma, such an approach was far less likely to exhaust the health care system through exorbitantly expensive end-of-life care.[48]

The interest among pharmaceutical companies in developing antiaging drugs was not at all a surprise, but the entry of both tech companies and venture capitalists was an unexpected and interesting twist. Like Google, more wealthy entrepreneurs were taking on the ultimate challenge of making aging and possibly death a thing of the past. In 2014, human genome expert and venture capitalist J. Craig Venter announced he was starting a new company called Human Longevity, whose mission was to learn how people could live longer and healthier lives. By creating what would be the largest human DNA sequencing operation in the world, Venter and his cofounders believed their new company could determine the molecular causes of illnesses related to aging, such as cancer and heart disease. Again, rather than try to cure one disease at a time, Venter hoped to figure out how to slow the aging process in order to delay the onset of various chronic diseases, thus adding decades to the average human life span. Making "100 years old the next 60," was the goal of Human Longevity, said one of the cofounders of the company, which had already attracted tens of millions of dollars from other venture capitalists.[49]

By investing in antiaging, millionaires and billionaires appeared to be intent on buying one of the few things that could not be currently purchased regardless of how rich one was: more time on the planet. Months after Venter's announcement, Menlo Park investor and radiologist Joon Yun revealed that he was sponsoring a science competition with a $1,000,000 prize to go to the team that came closest to curing aging, or at least one important aspect of it. Eleven teams quickly signed up for the competition, with the Palo Alto Longevity Prize to be awarded to the group that was successful in improving "homeostatic capacity" (the ability of an organism to return to normal after undergoing stress). Every day, Yun claimed, a hundred thousand people died unnecessarily due to an age-related illness, something he intended to do something about. The radical life extension community was of course ecstatic as wealthy individuals and companies with billions in cash made the adding of decades to human longevity a cause célèbre. "Ultimately, I think we'll crack the age code and we'll hack aging," said Yun, his ultimate goal being to "unlock human capacity."[50]

Unlocking human capacity by cracking the code of aging was assuredly a bold proposition given how little was still really known about getting older. Professionals working in some aspect of the field of aging were apt to make the usual recommendations—exercise regularly, stay active, engage socially, and do things one likes with people one likes—when advising people how to remain physically and mentally healthy and live as long as one's genetic profile would allow. Beyond that, however, even experts were at a loss of what to tell people wishing to live a long, healthy life. Along with the lack of knowledge about how to become old was a parallel illiteracy of how to be old. "We don't know how to be old because old age is relatively young," explained University of Illinois psychology professor Elizabeth Stine-Morrow in 2014; "it's something new to us." The average life span of humans had jumped dramatically over the course of the twentieth century due to major advances in medicine, in other words, but it was fair to say that equivalent strides in the social and psychological aspects of aging had not been made.[51]

Judging by the quantity of books being published about both aging and antiaging over the past few years, it appears evident that the subject has entered a new orbit. Making aging a thing of the past is clearly one central theme. Like Mark Benecke's *Dream of Eternal Life* (2002) and Stephen Hall's *Merchants of Immortality* (2005), Greg Critser's *Eternity Soup: Inside the Quest to End Aging* (2010) offered a contemporary overview of the disparate attempts being made to dramatically increase human longevity or, perhaps, extend it indefinitely. In *The Longevity Seekers* (2013), Ted Anton also examined the peculiar universe of "longevity science," finding it to be very big business despite the lack of applicable results.[52] Jonathan Weiner's *Long for This World: The Strange Science of Immortality* (2010), meanwhile, raised the many ethical and moral questions that were indelibly linked to the effort to end aging as we knew it. A divide between the haves (who could afford to live long lives) and the have nots (who could not) was just one problematic scenario, Weiner pointed out, warning antiagers to be careful about what they wished for.[53]

With time running out for those who have no intention to get old, antiaging is going from the sublime to the ridiculous. In his 2015 *Spring Chicken: Stay Young Forever (or Die Trying)*, Bill Gifford explored the various ways in which people were pursuing youth, sometimes literally at all costs. One of the odder stories Gifford tells is of the sixty-eight-year-old actress and health and beauty entrepreneur Suzanne Somers. Somers has every intention to live to 110, something she believes will be achieved by her taking forty supplements every morning, swallowing another twenty pills at night, and, to boot, injecting herself daily with estrogen (directly into her vagina). "I have a sex drive," Somers proudly announced at an antiaging conference, something she claimed none her friends enjoyed.[54] Somers was an easy target for antiaging skeptics, especially after reading Jerrold Winter's *Optimal Aging: A Guide to Your First 100 Years* (2015). Winter took a decidedly critical view of the dietary supplement industry, especially where the elderly were involved. Older people were already overmedicated, he argued, and consuming large quantities of nonregulated "natural" supplements for their alleged ability to prevent diseases, delay the onset of Alzheimer's, increase bone density, or boost energy was only adding to the problem.[55]

Essays and articles about aging and antiaging also have recently been abundant, with no shortage of positions taken on the subject. For pro-antiaging people like David Harsanyi, the quest to add decades or centuries to the human life span could not be more aggressive. "I want to live forever," he made plainly clear in an essay in *National Review*, adding that if that were impossible, then for "as long as science can keep me operational." Harsanyi, senior editor of the conservative magazine the *Federalist*, couldn't care less about how researchers in the field achieved the dream of eternal life; he is interested only in the prospect of staying alive as long as possible. Harsanyi was reacting to an essay in the *Atlantic* written by Ezekiel Emanuel that had received much attention and criticism. In his 2014 essay entitled "Why I Hope to Die at 75," Emanuel, who was director of the Clinical Bioethics Department at the National Institutes of Health, took the position that life after that age was typically one of physical and cognitive decline. Both individuals and society would be better off if people died by that age, he truly believed, seeing those older than that as "feeble, ineffectual, even pathetic."[56] While Emanuel

may have had a political agenda attached to his wish—old age was a waste
of valuable national resources, leftists like him commonly argued—Harsanyi
unapologetically had only his own interests in mind. "My selfish hope is that
we make tremendous strides in this department in, say, the next 30 years," he
declared, fully expecting science and technology to allow him to become a
"supercentenarian."[57]

## Love Your Age

Happily, against the backdrop of this fast and furious chasing of Methuselah
is an acceptance and even welcoming of the arrival of aging. Writing in *Prevention* in 2013, sixty-one-year-old Susan Crandell made it known she was
having "the time of [her] life," quite proud of what she called her generation's
"Peter Pan attitude." For her, the absence of what constituted "oldness" was
a good thing, as there were no rules regarding how one looked or what one
could do. Crandell had just finished hiking up a mountain with a few friends
close to her own age, something that would probably have been considered
noteworthy a generation or two earlier but no longer. While she was not
particularly happy about the physical signs of aging that she had acquired,
Crandell felt it was not the outside that mattered but rather the inside. "The
packaging may be getting a little tattered, but we've never felt more confident,
more sure of who we are," she wrote, a wonderfully positive view of getting
older. Crandell was a perfect example of hard research showing that happiness and well-being climbed around the age of fifty, a natural byproduct of
knowing who one was at that point in life. "Love your age," she advised fellow
boomers, wholeheartedly rejecting the pervasive idea that people over sixty
had their best years behind them.[58]

One might have thought that it would be impossible to find a pro-aging
article in an overtly beauty- and fashion-conscious magazine, but that was
not the case. Writing in *Harper's Bazaar* in 2012, Dominique Browning elo-
quently described, as her piece was called, "Why I Like Getting Older." Declaring war on aging with increasing intensity as one got older was not just
futile but considerably less joyful than accepting the march of time, Browning
told other women, thinking that many were missing the whole point of life.
The simple recognition that one was alive was "the most youthful state of
mind a person can have," she felt, not about to worry about her weight or less
than perfect features (as she ironically did when she was young). Along with
her wrinkles, Browning had gained a kinder disposition, just one reason why

she felt aging was a positive experience. A greater appreciation for the beauty to be found in the world was another, something she urged other women of a certain age to prioritize over how the latest youth serum could possibly erase some of the lines on their faces.[59]

Researchers such as Stanford University psychologist Laura Carstensen were finding evidence that experiences like those of Browning and Crandell had their basis in the way the human mind worked. Carstensen, who now applies her work to social-oriented projects under John Rowe at Columbia University, found that a "positivity effect" enabled many older people to gain a great degree of emotional satisfaction from the activities in which they chose to be involved. Seniors invested more of their cognitive resources in pursuits they found emotionally meaningful through "socio-emotional selectivity," according to Carstensen, a means perhaps of making the most of their limited time. There was thus a paradox attached to aging, she argued, as it was those most likely to be facing physical and cognitive loss who were, at the same time, realizing what they perceived as more positive life experiences.[60]

More so than men, women seem to be in tune with their advancing age, a function perhaps of the greater social pressures they face. Reaching the age of sixty-five was an appropriate time for Emily Fox Gordon to reflect on her personal experience of aging, finding mixed emotions in the process. Writing in the *American Scholar* in 2013, Gordon noted how she had physically aged considerably over the past few years, but it was how she was perceived (or in her case not perceived) that bothered her most. Gordon felt she had become invisible to strangers, with her entry into seniority the reason for this new, disturbing kind of anonymity. For most of her life, Gordon never cared much for making herself more beautiful, but now she did, in an attempt to make her presence known. That aside, Gordon liked being her age, finding common ground with others who had realized a greater sense of contentedness in their later years. "I've finally worked free of the agitation and misery of youth, which in my case extended well into middle age," she wrote, concluding that the emotional benefits outweighed the physical burdens.[61]

Elements of such personal narratives could be detected in the storylines of some movies and television shows. In much part due to the aging of the nation and the world, popular culture appeared to be more receptive in general to including older people in various avenues of entertainment. Not just audiences but also producers of films and television shows were collectively getting older, after all, which was likely playing a part in a new appreciation for actors who a generation earlier would have been considered well past their prime. "Once a movie star reached a certain age," observed Brian D. Johnson in *Maclean's,* "it was time to shuffle off into minor character parts—various grandparents, coots and crones—leaving the lead roles to less wrinkled faces." While Hollywood had not given up its reliance on youthful stars for blockbuster movies (and both television and pop music were primarily targeted to younger audiences), quite a few actors in their sixties and seventies could be found on the silver screen.[62]

With respect to aging, the turning point in film was arguably in 2010, when two of that year's most popular action movies—*The Expendables* and *Red*—featured a cast of characters over the age of fifty-five. *Barney's Version, Get Low,* and *True Grit* were other 2010 films that starred older actors (Paul Giamatti, Robert Duvall, and Jeff Bridges, respectively).[63] The trend continued over the next few years, with Arnold Schwarzenegger (sixty-five years old in 2013), Sylvester Stallone (sixty-six), Christopher Walken (sixty-nine), Al Pacino (seventy-two), and Alan Arkin (seventy-eight) just a handful of actors still making their presence known in quasi-action movies (much to critics' dismay). A "codger comedy" like *The Best Exotic Marigold Hotel* starring Maggie Smith and Judi Dench (each seventy-eight) was an unexpected hit, and the senior-filled *Quartet* also did relatively well at the box office.[64] Other films celebrating or at least acknowledging older age include a sequel to *The Best Exotic Marigold Hotel, Last Vegas* starring Michael Douglas (sixty-nine in 2013), Robert De Niro (seventy), Morgan Freeman (seventy-six), and Kevin Kline (sixty-six), *Grandma* starring Lily Tomlin (seventy-five in 2015), and *I'll See You in My Dreams* starring Blythe Danner (seventy-two in 2015), Sam Elliott (seventy-one), and Rhea Perlman (sixty-seven).

Some of the country's best-known directors were also getting up in years, making a number of critics wonder if their films were still relevant and inventive. Woody Allen (seventy-seven in 2013) and Clint Eastwood (eighty-three) were two of the more notable, as each director continued to be as prolific as ever. It was not uncommon to note some repetitiveness and a formulaic quality in movies made by filmmakers in their seventies and eighties, something that was considered apropos to both Allen and Eastwood. Robert Altman had made *Gosford Park* when he was seventy-six, and Sidney Lumet had directed *Before the Devil Knows You're Dead* when he was eighty-three, however, proof that creative vitality in filmmaking need not decline with age. Certain novelists and painters had famously done some of their best work in their later years, reason to believe that excellent films would continue to be made by other directors as they aged.[65]

As the movies already had, television was now becoming somewhat grayer due to changing demographics. *The Millers* on CBS starring Beau Bridges (seventy-two in 2014) was one recent attempt by the networks to appeal to the growing audience of older folks, a break from the standard broadcast strategy to target young viewers. (The show was cancelled during its second season.) Sixty-six-year-old Ted Danson could be seen on *CSI*, as could Tom Selleck (sixty-nine) on *Blue Bloods* and Mark Harmon (sixty-two) on *NCIS*. The median age of a broadcast (versus cable or Internet) television viewer was fifty-four in 2014—the highest in history—making it no wonder that the networks had finally decided to create shows that featured older actors and thus presumably had a decent chance of attracting baby boomers and seniors. Advertising was of course the motive for the new effort, as network ad rates were primarily based on viewership. Research showed that consumers over fifty spent about $90 billion a year on cars alone, and by 2017 would control 70 percent of the nation's disposable income, more justification to advertise to them on network television.[66]

## Age of Disruption

Hollywood might recently have become less ageist, but Silicon Valley was as youth-obsessed as ever despite the sudden interest in antiaging among certain tech companies and individuals. In his 2014 essay for the *New Republic*, Noam Scheiber described why he was, as the piece was called, "Over the Hill in Silicon Valley." Scheiber had years of experience and plenty of talent but was considered completely obsolete, something not usual for anyone over forty in the tech industry. "Silicon Valley has become one of the most ageist places in America," he wrote, something not surprising given managers' desire to avoid hiring those middle-aged or over like the plague. ("Young people are just smarter," Facebook CEO Mark Zuckerberg had said in 2007.) Usage of Botox was booming in the Bay Area as men and women on the forty-ish bubble tried to look younger than their years in order to keep their jobs. Token graybeards could often be found in tech companies so that the offices didn't look completely like a college dorm room, but that was little consolation to professionals like Scheiber, who faced overt discrimination because of his age.[67]

Stories like Scheiber's were the impetus for aging activists to try to change things. Conquering America's worship of youth and contempt for aging had become the mission of a number of gerontologists and geriatricians, notably

Bill Thomas. Thomas, the geriatrician who had followed up his *What Are Old People For?* with *Second Wind: Navigating the Passage to a Slower, Deeper, and More Connected Life,* was now one of the more passionate ambassadors of older people; his goal was to change the perception of aging from a medical condition to a natural stage of life. Celebrating remarkable achievements of octogenarians, nonagenarians, and centenarians was all well and good, he maintained, but at the same time it reinforced the adoration of youth. Rather, it was "elderhood," as Thomas referred to the second half of life, that should receive more respect in American society.[68]

Thomas was not content just to write about ageism in America. In 2015, he hit the road to deliver his antiageism message to audiences in thirty cities via what he called an "Age of Disruption" tour. "It is time for us to start challenging and questioning and overcoming some of society's misconceptions about aging," he told a group in Pittsburgh, taking special aim at nursing homes. Such places were like "penitentiaries for the elderly," he felt, a means of excluding older people from the rest of the population. The intense and escalating endeavor to reverse chronic diseases in order to radically extend longevity was also misguided, he believed, as that too made aging appear to be like an unwelcome guest at the party of life. "It's time we shake ourselves out of the misery of aging and repurpose and restore the wonders and integrity of the second half of our lives," Thomas insisted, precisely what was needed if ageism was to be defeated and older people be allowed to fulfill their potential.[69]

Others well acquainted with the image problem of aging in America saw the idea of "disruption" as a useful one. Since becoming the CEO of AARP in 2014, Jo Ann Jenkins has been on a self-described "mission to disrupt aging," as she explained in 2015 in *Generations—Journal of the American Society on Aging,* meaning she intended to "change the conversation around what it means to get older." Rather than pretend aging didn't exist or take the position that being fifty was like being forty or even thirty, Jenkins believed people should embrace whatever age they actually are. Taking pride in one's age was an act of self-empowerment, she understood, and not unlike the process other marginalized groups had experienced in order to gain greater self-respect and social power. As with race, gender, or class, being defined by one's age was a silly and ignorant practice, and something that had to change if older Americans were to realize their deserved equal rights in everyday life.[70]

In the very same 2015 issue of *Generations,* Charlotte Yeh echoed Jenkins's spot-on philosophy of aging in the United States. Yeh, chief medical officer at AARP, noted how "stubborn" the myths surrounding aging were despite all the research showing that the later stage of life was ripe for well-being. It was the persistency of these myths and stereotypes that diminished the possibilities of Americans aged fifty or older, she maintained, serving as a device that placed restraints on older people along many dimensions. It was steadily downhill after reaching the "prime of life," the basic story went, that long slide bringing on a continuous shrinking of physical, mental, social, and romantic powers. And because aging was seen as something that unfortunately "happened" to us, Yeh continued, it forced the oldest members of society into a victim-like role, a mindset that demands rethinking as baby boomers rush headlong into their senior years.[71]

# Conclusion

Getting old isn't about an end, but a beginning—a time to fulfill old dreams and make new ones a reality. So join us and Get Old with a new attitude. Get Ready. Get Set. Get Old.

—GetOld.com

In 2011, Pfizer launched a marketing campaign that was remarkable in its approach to aging. In its campaign, which is still running, the giant pharmaceutical company drew upon findings of a Pew Research Center study that illustrated the negative views about aging that many Americans held. Older age was a stage of life defined by a loss of physical and cognitive abilities, those surveyed tended to say; the reluctance of young adults to even discuss aging was also confirmed in the study. Pfizer started Get Old to "challenge misperceptions of aging and drive new conversations that inspire people of all ages to take action on their own health," its website stated, knowing that a new and more accurate understanding of getting older would likely be good for business. If aging was as good a time as any to "begin new dreams and adventures," the company's thinking went, more people might be interested in therapies and medicines that could help them pursue such experiences by living longer, healthier lives.[1]

While Pfizer's message is encouraging, aging in America faces an uphill battle when it comes to negative views of older people. The very concept of aging remains a social taboo, eliciting fear and dread despite all the research showing that getting older is usually an enjoyable part of life. Other countries appear to be ahead of the United States in disrupting the prevailing, unhealthy view of aging. In 2014, for example, Britain appointed its first "older workers' champion," whose task was to change that country's antiquated view of the elderly and to reinvent the idea of retirement. An individual's abilities do not automatically switch off at the age of sixty-five, the new appointee told employers and workers, a message that had the potential of reestablishing older people as valuable members of any society. Britain was one of thirteen emerging "super-aged" nations, according to a new report by Moody's, the credit rating agency, meaning a country that was forecast to have more than one in five people sixty-five or older by 2020. There would be thirty-four such countries by 2030, an interesting metric of how to measure global aging.[2]

One might think that with so many older people around, any and all forms of ageism should disappear. With more older people on the planet than ever before in history, this line of thought goes, it makes sense that "age-friendly" societies should emerge, with no need for champions for the elderly. But there is currently little evidence to support this sanguine vision of the future. Youth still rules the day in many countries, particularly the United States, making it difficult to overturn prevailing views about older citizens. The millennial generation (a.k.a. Generation Y) is enormous too, after all, and today's young adults are echoing baby boomers' capacity to dictate cultural norms through their sheer numbers and consumer power. In addition to the demographic and economic factors, there's little doubt that a psychological component is also at play in persistent ageist attitudes and behavior. Our discomfort with age is directly related to fears about physical decline and death, with older people being reminders that all of us are subject to the ways of the march of time. Fears about becoming a victim to Alzheimer's disease are especially fierce these days, fostering a more general dread about approaching old age.

The ever-growing antiaging industry is only advancing our trepidation of getting older and reinforcing our ageist inclinations. Precious little evidence has been produced to indicate that any therapy or technique slows or reverses the aging process, yet, much to marketers' delight, consumers seem determined to find a fountain of youth. Modern-day Ponce de Leóns are following the tradition of many in the past in search of some magical treatment with purported rejuvenating powers. (In the thirteenth century, one of the great minds of the day, British mathematician and scientist Roger Bacon, maintained that sleeping next to a young virginal female in order to breathe in her wholesome air would restore youth.) Twenty-first-century versions of such therapies are nearly as silly, and carry much greater potential health risks.

The radical life extension movement that has been around now for a few decades is a more extreme attempt to follow in the footsteps of Methuselah. The recent entry of tech company executives, dot-com billionaires, and venture capitalists to the antiaging scene has taken the effort to an entirely new level. Wild success in this mortal world is not enough for these captains of industry who believe they can conquer nature through science and technology not unlike the way they conquered the universe of information. Billions will be spent by these techies on finding a solution to the problem of aging and, upon realizing it is a far more difficult undertaking than building a better browser or search engine, I believe they will return to doing what they do best—making money.

Along with the bad news about the future of aging in America is some good news. One reason to be optimistic is the growing number of organizations that collectively compose a new movement of study in the field. One such organization is the North American Network in Aging Studies (NANAS), which was founded in 2013 by a handful of humanities and social science scholars whose research focuses on the larger, more existential issues of aging. NANAS uses the European Network in Aging Studies (ENAS) as inspiration for its work and shares its mission to "facilitate sustainable, international and multi-disciplinary collaboration among all researchers interested in the study of cultural aging." NANAS publishes *Age, Culture, Humanities*, an interdisciplinary journal that points to where the study of aging is headed. Via critical investigations of the experiences of aging as expressed in the humanities and arts, contributors have the opportunity to examine age as a source of identity and further our knowledge of the physical and cognitive dynamics of getting older. More broadly, the journal addresses cultural articulations of aging and old age, precisely where I believe the field should now be directed (www.agingstudies.org).

Exploring the cultural dimensions of aging, particularly those related to baby boomers, leads to other reasons one should not be despondent about the graying of the United States and much of the world. Though boomers are clinging to the remnants of their rapidly fading youth rather than leading a social revolution dedicated to achieving equality for older people, it's fair to say they are redefining the concept of aging for the better. The model of aging forged in the postwar era when boomers were children is a shadow of what it used to be, particularly when it comes to retirement. Rather than end one's career at a predetermined age, usually sixty-five, to embark on a life of leisure in a sunny, warm place, most of today's sexagenarians and septuagenarians are working as long as they can and are staying put in their homes. For them, their third act is not all that different from their second, a lifestyle choice that is serving to blur the lines of age. Although some are suffering from a kind of identity crisis, not quite sure of their mission in life, this blending of middle age with seniority is helping to reintegrate older people back into the mainstream. This is a wonderful development whose significance cannot be underestimated; the transformation of one's latter years from a distinct stage of life to one that is fully incorporated into the full life span represents a historic change that bodes well for aging in America.

Best of all, perhaps, the assimilation of older Americans into the sweep of everyday life offers the possibility of lessening ageism. As the "Golden Girls"–like image of seniors further recedes into our memory, the divisions between young and old will likely shrink, bridging generations. Discrimination based on age in both the workplace (try getting a good job or even an interview if you're past fifty) and in social arenas (such as the cultural invisibility that Germaine Greer and Emily Fox Gordon each documented) may very well diminish as older folks are not seen as being a separate, less competent part of the population. It is highly unlikely that the reverence for older citizens that reigned from the nation's founding through the early decades of the twentieth century will ever return, but there is a good chance that boomers will gain more respect in their later years as they normalize the aging experience.

Part of the reason I expect there to be a renaissance of sorts for older Americans is that they will collectively change and improve the nation's employment landscape. Although they are not yet planning (or even thinking about) it, tens of millions of baby boomers will eventually require a host of services that will exponentially expand the elder care industry. Most octogenarians or nonagenarians will require assistance in health care, housing, transportation, and other basics of daily life as they age in place, making each of them a prime job opportunity for millions of younger people. (Nearly 90 percent of those over the age of sixty-five want to stay in their residence for as long as possible, and 80 percent say they believe their current home is where they will always live, according to an AARP survey.)[3] "Debunking assumptions about aging does not enable anyone to escape its physical, psychological, and spiritual challenges," wrote Amy Hoffman in the *Women's Review of Books* in 2003, meaning the later years of life will not be easy ones for most older boomers even in a friendlier environment.[4] Because of their heavy contribution to the economic well-being of the country, I suggest, today's older Americans—the wealthiest and most consumer-savvy generation of seniors in history—will be treated in a kinder, gentler way than they are today. Until they go off to the big Woodstock in the sky, boomers will continue to drive the American economy; this power will literally buy them some insurance protecting them against overt forms of discrimination in the years ahead.

Boomers' economic clout will also serve as a buffer against the so-called aging crisis as they strain government resources due to their numbers. The system will not crash as many pundits predict, primary because it is in the government's best interests for it not to. (The idea of a coming aging crisis has even entered the world of fiction; in Albert Brooks's 2011 novel *2030*, he imagines a postcancer world in which aging baby boomers—"the olds"—monopolize the nation's economy through their entitlements.)[5] In the real world, local, state, and the federal government adapt all the time to social change, and the coming age wave, despite its enormity, will be no different. Politicians will become increasingly friendly to older voters over the course of the next few decades, knowing that their careers rely heavily on appealing to "gray power." Again, the fact that aging boomers will be a source of millions of jobs will be additional incentive for elected officials to ensure that laws and policies are enacted that cater to that constituency. Hillary Clinton's recent call for an $18 billion, nine-year "war" against Alzheimer's is a good example of how politicians will rally around the interests of aging boomers, fueling the economy in the process. The Alzheimer's Association (cofounded by Robert Butler) has not reached the visibility or war chest mustered by the American Cancer Society or the American Health Association, but this will likely change in the years ahead.[6]

One could even argue, in fact, that the age wave represents not a coming apocalypse but rather an approaching golden age in American history. (Most Americans are actually not worried about the economic consequences of our aging population: just 26 percent of those surveyed by the Pew Research Center in 2014 considered the graying of the nation to be a problem.)[7] From a historical perspective, the United States does best when it has a singular, grand cause of some kind; these causes (notably the two world wars, the Great Depression, and the Cold War) function as a vehicle for our normally divisive population to temporarily put our differences aside to pull together. A massive wave of older citizens could be that cause, with Americans of all social divisions more or less united in the noble mission of caring for that group of people. Most younger Americans will have some personal connection to at least one older person, usually a family member, making the idea of an emerging senior-friendly society not that far-fetched. Many Asian cultures are such societies, suggesting that our own aging population may act to bridge generations rather than to divide them.

Finally, and perhaps most important of all, I believe that finding a cure for aging will remain an elusive enterprise, making the quest for a giant leap in longevity an unfulfilled wish. Although scientists are a lot closer to identifying the biological basis for aging, they may never really completely understand the reasons why our bodies become older and eventually die. One hopes that more people will embrace the idea that aging is a natural part of life, and that attempts to make the clock run backward are counter to the most basic laws of biology. The ethics and morality of antiaging are equally perverse, I contend, although I confess the age-old dream of discovering a fountain of youth is a compelling one that may never go away. Legitimate efforts to extend life are likely to lead to real progress in ameliorating chronic diseases, however, a positive outcome of what is for the most part a misguided enterprise. It is fortunate we can end this story on such a happy note as we embark on what will no doubt be an interesting next chapter in American history.

# Notes

## Introduction

1. Leilani Doty, *Communication and Assertion Skills for Older Persons* (New York: Hemisphere, 1987), 213.

2. Ram Dass, *Still Here: Embracing Aging, Changing, and Dying* (New York: Riverhead, 2000), 25.

3. Martha Holstein, *Women in Late Life: Critical Perspectives on Gender and Age* (Lanham, MD: Rowman & Littlefield, 2015), 1–3.

4. Sandra L. McGuire, "Promoting Positive Attitudes Toward Aging: Literature for Young Children," *Childhood Education,* Summer 1993, 204.

5. Dale Dannefer, Peter Uhlenberg, Anne Foner, and Ronald P. Abeles, "On the Shoulders of a Giant: The Legacy of Matilda White Riley for Gerontology," *Journals of Gerontology Series B: Psychological Sciences and Social Sciences,* 2005, 1.

6. W. Andrew Achenbaum, *Robert N. Butler, M.D.: Visionary of Healthy Aging* (New York: Columbia University Press, 2013), 1–23.

7. Peter Laslett, *A Fresh Map of Life: The Emergence of the Third Age* (London: Weidenfeld & Nicolson, 1989).

8. Bernice L. Neugarten, *Middle Age and Aging: A Reader in Social Psychology* (Chicago: University of Chicago Press, 1968).

9. Paul Higgs and Chris Gilleard, *Rethinking Old Age: Theorising the Fourth Age* (London: Palgrave Macmillan, 2015).

10. David G. Troyansky, *Aging in World History* (London: Routledge, 2015). Recently published textbooks dedicated to the subject of aging and designed for students, researchers, and policy makers also tend to take a global approach. There are today vast inequalities regarding aging on a global level, with regional gerontological efforts strongly shaped by social, political, economic, and health-related factors. Also, social relationships and differences, individual characteristics and change in later life, and policy issues are just a few gerontological factors that vary dramatically by continent and country. See, for example, Jan Baars, Dale Dannefer, Chris Phillipson, and Alan Walker, eds., *Aging, Globalization and Inequality: The New Critical Gerontology* (Amityville, NY: Baywood, 2006), and Dale Dannefer and Chris Phillipson, eds., *The SAGE Handbook of Social Gerontology* (Thousand Oaks, CA: SAGE, 2010).

11. David Hackett Fischer, *Growing Old in America* (New York: Oxford University Press, 1978), 27, 101.

12. W. Andrew Achenbaum, *Old Age in the New Land: The American Experience Since 1790* (Baltimore: Johns Hopkins University Press, 1978). Social historians of aging in America have ably traced the roots of our problematic view of aging in this country by (1) challenging various popular beliefs about older people that have long prevailed in America (e.g., that later life has typically been a period of impoverishment), (2) arguing that old people have always been undervalued, assigned relatively low social status, and considered a burden, and (3) linking the sweeping social and economic changes taking place in the nation to the reorientation of the elderly in everyday life. See Carole Haber and Brian Gratton, *Old Age and the Search for Security: An American Social History* (Bloomington: Indiana University Press, 1994); David Van Tassel and Peter N. Stearns, eds., *Old Age in a Bureaucratic Society: The Elderly, the Experts, and the State in American Society* (Westport, CT: Praeger, 1986); and Carole Haber, *Beyond Sixty-Five: The Dilemma of Old Age in America's Past* (Cambridge: Cambridge University Press, 1983).

13. W. Andrew Achenbaum, *Crossing Frontiers: Gerontology Emerges as a Science* (Cambridge: Cambridge University Press, 1995). The GSA created membership categories in biology, medicine, psychology, and other disciplines in the late 1940s. There are now four groupings, with changes in nomenclature and shifts in member preferences over time revealing much about how the society's sense of itself reflects the field.

14. Achenbaum, *Old Age in the New Land*.

15. Fernando Torres-Gil, *The New Aging: Politics and Change in America* (Santa Barbara, CA: Praeger, 1991).

16. A. Barry Rand, "Society is Aging: What Are We Going to Do About It?" *Vital Speeches of the Day*, June 2013, 175.

17. Thomas R. Cole, "Aging in American Culture," *Tikkun*, May 2002, 50.

18. Elaine Cumming and William E. Henry, *Growing Old* (New York: Basic Books, 1961).

19. Dennis Thompson, John D. Hogan, and Philip M. Clark, *Developmental Psychology in Historical Perspective* (Malden, MA: Wiley-Blackwell, 2012), 207; see Bernice Neugarten, Robert Havighurst, and Sheldon Tobin, "Personality and Patterns of Aging," in Neugarten, *Middle Age and Aging* (173–78).

20. Tanya Fusco Johnson, "Aging Well in Contemporary Society," *American Behavioral Scientist*, November–December 1995, 120.

21. Thomas R. Cole, *The Journey of Life: A Cultural History of Aging in America* (Cambridge: Cambridge University Press, 1991), xix.

## Chapter 1

1. Nick Thimmesch, "An Aging Nation Worships Youth," *Chicago Tribune*, August 19, 1976, A4.

2. "Study Urged to End Aging," *Baltimore Sun*, March 25, 1966, A6.

3. Harry Nelson, "Delaying Old Age Seen as Science Goal," *Los Angeles Times*, August 1, 1966, A1.

4. John A. Osmundsen, "Science Is Urged to Combat Aging," *New York Times*, February 2, 1966, 18.

5. "Scientists Are Making a Study of Aging Process," *New Journal and Guide*, July 24, 1965, 5.

6. Nelson, "Delaying Old Age Seen as Science Goal."

7. Ronald Kotulak, "Unlock Secrets of Processes in the Aging of Man," *Chicago Tribune*, January 23, 1966, 1.

8. "NIH Dedicates Center on Aging," *Washington Post*, June 16, 1968, A3.

9. "Life Span of 100 Years, Aging Probed by Series," *Hartford Courant*, March 24, 1968, 5H.

10. Walter C. Alvarez, "Anti-Clotting Drug May Help Delay Aging," *Newsday*, March 12, 1969, 7A.

11. "Scientist Sees Curbs on Aging," *Chicago Tribune*, May 12, 1971, A9.

12. Alex Comfort, "The Ravages of Age: Slowdown in Sight," *Los Angeles Times*, December 10, 1972, E1.

13. Barbara Gold, "Age Vs. Youth," *Baltimore Sun*, September 7, 1969, C1.

14. Kathleen Saluk, "'Gray Panther' Says Aging Hits Women Hard," *Hartford Courant*, October 29, 1976, 27.

15. Jean Dietz, "Treating Aging as Disease Called Harmful," *Boston Globe*, June 30, 1971, 36.

16. Alex Comfort, "No Country for Old Men," *Washington Post*, May 25, 1975, 174.

17. Bill Fripp, "Hopeful Note on Aging," *Boston Globe*, December 9, 1971, 44.

18. Comfort, "No Country for Old Men."

19. Leroy H. Jones, "Today: Facing the Realities of Aging," *Chicago Tribune*, January 31, 1972, 18.

20. Curtin quoted in Hal Burton, "Raging About Aging," *Newsday*, January 24, 1973, 9A.

21. "'A Bad Press,'" *Los Angeles Times*, April 2, 1974, 2.

22. Lynne Olson, "U.S. Commissioner on Aging Calls Forced Retirement a Serious Bias," *Baltimore Sun*, May 11, 1977, A8.

23. Leonard Silk, "Economic Scene," *New York Times*, November 22, 1978, D2.

24. "Agency on Aging Voted by House," *New York Times*, April 1, 1965, 1. While the Administration on Aging (AoA) intended to provide categorical services, it has been chronically underfunded from the outset and was in recent years merged with federal support efforts for disability groups.

25. "Envelope Will Honor Conference on Aging," *Christian Science Monitor*, November 11, 1971, B13.

26. Penelope McMullan, "When the White House Looks at Aging . . . ," *Newsweek*, November 29, 1971, 3A.

27. Bob Walton, "Aging Eye 2d Conference," *Chicago Tribune*, November 21, 1971, N4.

28. "The White House Conference on Aging," *Washington Post*, November 27, 1971, A12.

29. Walton, "Aging Eye 2d Conference."

30. "As Aging Meet Looms, Political Oratory Starts," *Boston Globe*, November 10, 1971, 48.

31. Joseph Levin, "Nixon Vetoes Bounce $200 Million Aging 'Check,'" *Boston Globe*, November 15, 1972, 68.

32. Jean Dietz, "Nixon Promises the Aging Most of What They Seek," *Boston Globe*, December 3, 1971, 2.

33. Joseph Levin, "Nixon Message on Aging . . . His Aims, or Strategy?" *Boston Globe*, April 12, 1972, 62.

34. "Nixon Asks New Attitude on Aging," *Chicago Tribune*, October 31, 1972, 14.

35. T. R. Van Dellen, "Fighting Aging's Double Standard," *Chicago Tribune*, October 27, 1974, E3.

36. Ronald Kotulak, "Aging Process Gets an 'Ally' in Estrogen Therapy," *Chicago Tribune*, January 30, 1974, B4.

37. G. Timothy Johnson, "Romanian Drug to Slow Aging Proved Ineffective," *Chicago Tribune*, April 10, 1979, A4.

38. Walter Sullivan, "Rumanian Mixes 'Youth Cocktail,'" *New York Times*, May 14, 1967, 34.

39. Muriel Dobbin, "For Aging Americans, Surgery Is the Price of Doing Business," *Baltimore Sun*, October 30, 1979, B3.

40. Beverly Beyette, "From Rocking Chair to Joy of Aging," *Los Angeles Times*, October 12, 1979, E1.

41. "No Country for Old Men"; Robert N. Butler, *Why Survive? Being Old in America* (New York: Harper & Row, 1975).

42. Ronald Gross, Beatrice Gross, and Sylvia Seidman, eds., *The New Old: Struggling for Decent Aging* (New York: Anchor Press, 1978).

43. Maureen M. Gallagher, "Geriatric Nurse Says Elderly Fear Ills, Not Aging Process," *Hartford Courant*, May 14, 1977, 16.

44. T. R. Van Dellen, "Aging 'Problems' Are Exaggerated," *Atlanta Constitution*, October 6, 1971, 4C.

45. Maureen Gallagher, "Major Aging Problem Termed Inability to Accept Its Reality," *Hartford Courant*, October 28, 1977, 27.

46. Gallagher, "Geriatric Nurse Says Elderly Fear Ills, Not Aging Process."

47. Michael Kernan, "Stacking the Deck in Favor of Aging Americans," *Washington Post*, June 2, 1976, B1.

48. Tom Greening and Dick Hobson, *Instant Relief: The Encyclopedia of Self-Help* (New York: Seaview Books, 1979), 8.

49. "Med Students 'Insensitive' to Aging?" *Atlanta Constitution*, September 19, 1976, 13C.

50. "Biologists Will Probe Aging Cause," *Atlanta Constitution*, July 2, 1972, 13B. Congress had created NICHD in 1962 in response to a request by President Kennedy, whose sister, Eunice Kennedy Shriver, was working with family pediatrician Robert E. Cooke

to pursue research in the area of developmental disorders among children. The mission of the institute broadened over the course of its first decade to accommodate related health initiatives, such as age-based research.

51. T. R. Van Dellen, "How to Keep Well," *Chicago Tribune*, September 7, 1972, 24.

52. Brian Sullivan, "Hormone Linked to Aging," *Boston Globe*, April 17, 1973, 22.

53. "Scientists Get Insight on Aging," *Hartford Courant*, March 4, 1973, 20A.

54. Lawrence K. Altman, "Protein Found in Elderly Studied for Link to Aging," *New York Times*, October 22, 1973, 1.

55. Walter Sullivan, "Science Seeks to End the Miseries of Aging," *New York Times*, November 6, 1975, 21.

56. Earl Lane, "Probing Mysteries of Aging," *Newsday*, April, 11, 1977, 4.

57. Albert Rosenfield, *Prolongevity: A Report on the Scientific Discoveries Now Being Made About Aging and Dying, and Their Promise of an Extended Human Life Span—Without Old Age* (New York: Knopf, 1976).

58. Lawrence K. Altman, "Gain Reported in Halting Aging in Cells," *New York Times*, September 20, 1974, 16.

59. http://demog.berkeley.edu.

60. "More Study of Causes of Aging Urged," *Hartford Courant*, March 4, 1974, 17.

61. "Biochemist Says Science May Delay Aging Process," *Hartford Courant*, September 16, 1976, 33.

62. "Cell Processes Under Study," *Chicago Tribune*, September 30, 1978, N1.

63. "Scientist Striving to Retard Aging," *Hartford Courant*, March 3, 1977, 76.

64. "Aging Reversal Is Called Near," *Atlanta Constitution*, September 3, 1976, 2A.

65. Elizabeth M. Fowler, "New Field: Problems of Aging," *New York Times*, May 30, 1979, D17.

66. Ed Meagher, "Research into Aging Needed, Doctor Says," *Los Angeles Times*, April 15, 1973, 24.

67. "Aging: 'A Time Bomb,'" *Los Angeles Times*, January 18, 1976, D13.

68. Philip Shabecoff, "A Fast-Aging Population," *New York Times*, July 30, 1978, F16.

### Chapter 2

1. "Clinique Daily De-Aging Comes to Rich's June 26," *Atlanta Daily World*, June 23, 1983, 5.

2. Matthew Tayback, "Housing to Medicare: '81 Aging Parley Topics," *Baltimore Sun*, March 2, 1980, TR9.

3. Nancy J. Schwerzler, "Aging Conference Opens Amid Protests Over Rules," *Baltimore Sun*, December 1, 1981, A5. Most scholars of the history of aging agree that the 1961 and 1971 conferences were the best, with the last two managed so that delegates had little time to rally around speakers' ideas.

4. "Aging Conference Draws to a Close," *Boston Globe*, December 3, 1981, 1.

5. Elizabeth Mehren, "Delegates Question Conference Value," *Los Angeles Times*, December 1, 1981, F1.

6. "Sorting Out Ways To Help the Aging," *Newsday*, December 8, 1981, 46.

7. Jack Anderson, "White House Rigged Conference on Aging on Political Grounds," *Newsday*, March 8, 1983, 46.

8. Joann Ball, "36 States Urge Non-Political Conference on Aging," *Hartford Courant*, November 18, 1981, B1.

9. Jack Anderson, "Strong-Arm Tactics Kept Conference on Aging in Line," *Newsday*, March 9, 1983, 54.

10. Dorothy Collin, "Parley on Aging Was 'Gray Power' in Action," *Chicago Tribune*, December 6, 1981, A1.

11. Cy Brickfield, "Conference on Aging Scores Successes," *Hartford Courant*, February 10, 1982, E16.

12. Sandy Rovner, "Reagan Recovery Role Model for Aging," *Los Angeles Times*, June 7, 1981, B10

13. "German Scientist's Oxygen Therapy Seems to Slow Down Aging Process," *Baltimore Sun*, October 29, 1980, A3.

14. Harold M. Schmeck, "Aging Goes On," *New York Times*, May 3, 1981, A7.

15. Charles Seabrook, "Colorful Changes," *Atlanta Constitution*, October 7, 1984, 34.

16. Erik Eckholm, "Aging," *New York Times*, June 10, 1986, C1.

17. "Pot May Have Aging Effect on Brain, Researcher Finds," *Chicago Tribune*, September 26, 1986, 4.

18. "Space Travel May Slow Aging," *New York Times*, July 11, 1983, B4.

19. "Books About Aging Keep Presses Busy," *Hartford Courant*, May 4, 1983, C7.

20. Robin Henig, "Can—or Should—We Conquer Aging?" *Washington Post*, November 24, 1987, Z10.

21. UCLA/USC Long Term Care Gerontology Center, "Centenarians: Growing Trend in Longevity," *Los Angeles Times*, August 2, 1987, D8.

22. Jane E. Brody, "Hope Grows for a Vigorous Old Age," *New York Times*, October 2, 1984, C1.

23. Jean Mayer and Jeanne Goldberg, "'Anti-Aging Products Just Won't Do It," *Chicago Tribune*, August 29, 1985, 9.

24. Paddy Calistro, "Controversy at the Cosmetics Counter," *Los Angeles Times*, July 26, 1987, 29.

25. Ellen Goodman, "Fighting Aging with a Full Arsenal," *Boston Globe*, April 28, 1988, 25.

26. Sandy Banisky, "U.S. Aide Urges Change in Perceptions of Aging," *Baltimore Sun*, February 13, 1980, C3.

27. Carroll L. Estes, "The Myths, Realities of Aging," *Chicago Tribune*, April 10, 1981, B4.

28. Enid Nemy, "Aging: Is Our View Distorted?" *New York Times*, September 20, 1982, B14. Dobrof was and remains a leader in the field of gerontological social work, having created Hunter College's Brookdale Center on Aging. With Robert Butler, she co-directed the Hunter/Mount Sinai School of Medicine Geriatric Education Center, where they developed that institution's curricula and taught hundreds of students.

29. Walter Goodman, "Our Aging Country Creates a New Audience," *Chicago Tribune*, December 4, 1986, 14H.

30. Richard Worth, *You'll Be Old Someday, Too* (London: Franklin Watts, 1986).

31. Barbara Cartland, "Getting Older, Growing Younger," *Saturday Evening Post*, January/February 1985, 62.

32. Misti Snow, *Minneapolis Star Tribune*, February 2, 1988, 1E.

33. Dave Alexander, "With the Help of Seniors, Grade School Pupils Learn That Aging Is Nothing to Fear," *Minneapolis Star Tribune*, December 10, 1987, 8Y.

34. Alexander, "With the Help of Seniors, Grade School Pupils Learn That Aging Is Nothing to Fear."

35. Kathryn A. Johnson, "A Better Understanding of Aging," *Austin American Statesman*, July 30, 1989, E8. The Gray Panthers lost visibility and members when founder Maggie Kuhn died in 1995.

36. Don Colburn, "Beyond Aging as a Disease," *Washington Post*, May 29, 1985, WH7.

37. "Study Finds Life's Jolts Speeds Process of Aging," *Los Angeles Times*, December 10, 1989, 4.

38. Peg Meier, "Exhibit Looks at Aging as Change," *Minneapolis Star and Tribune*, March 22, 1986, 1C.

39. Walter Goodman, "Our Aging Country Creates a New Audience," *Chicago Tribune*, December 4, 1986, 14H.

40. Betty Ommerman, "The Aging of America," *Newsday*, July 28, 1986, A19.

41. Elizabeth Mehren, "Plotting Course for an Aging Population," *Los Angeles Times*, June 13, 1986, 1.

42. Leslie Kenton, *Ageless Aging: The Natural Way to Stay Young* (New York: Grove Press, 1986).

43. Anne C. Averyt, *Successful Aging: A Sourcebook for Older People and Their Families* (New York: Ballantine Books, 1987); Isadore Rossman, *Looking Forward: The Complete Guide to Successful Aging* (New York: Dutton, 1989).

44. Daniel Goleman, "Despair Over Aging Strikes Hardest at 50," *Austin American Statesman*, April 8, 1989, F12.

45. Leo F. Buscaglia, "Discovering the Wisdom That Comes with Aging," *Los Angeles Times*, December 14, 1984, M8.

46. Rochel U. Berman, "Many in Their 50's Tend Aging Parents," *New York Times*, March 5, 1989. E22. Fifty had been a principal aging marker since the colonial era, but Howard P. Chudacoff argues in *How Old Are You?* that in the beginning of the twentieth century the age of sixty-five or seventy emerged as the onset of old age due to the institutionalization of retirement and spread of "old-age" homes. (Howard P. Chudacoff, *How Old Are You? Age Consciousness in American Culture* [Princeton: Princeton University Press, 1989], 108.) I believe, however, that the rise of youth culture in the twentieth century lowered, rather than raised, the perceived beginning of old age. Fifty year olds are considered positively ancient by today's millennials.

47. Aristides, "An Older Dude," *American Scholar*, Autumn 1986, 439.

48. Avery Corman, *50* (New York: Simon & Schuster, 1987).

49. Bill Case, *Life Begins at Sixty* (New York: Stein & Day, 1986).

50. Paula Brown Doress et al., *Ourselves, Growing Older: Women Aging with Knowledge and Power* (New York: Simon & Schuster, 1987).

51. "Jong Novel Deals with New Fear: Aging," *Baltimore Sun*, July 5, 1987, 3C.

52. Molly Sinclair, "A Feminist Confronts Aging," *St. Petersburg Times*, March 5, 1989, 8F.

53. Bowen Northrup, "Gray Matters: An Aging Population Grows Younger and Shatters Stereotypes of What's 'Old,'" *Wall Street Journal*, April 24, 1987, 1.

54. Carol Tavris, "You're Only as Old as You Feel," *Sun Sentinel*, February 8, 1988, 3D.

55. Marj Jackson Levin, "Aging," *St. Louis Post-Dispatch*, January 17, 1988, accessed online

56. Phillip Longman, *Born to Pay: The New Politics of Aging* (New York: Houghton Mifflin, 1987).

57. Fernando Torres Gil, "The Latinization and Aging of America: Tension or Partnership?" *Los Angeles Times*, February 4, 1987, C5.

58. "Crime off 7 Percent; Biggest Drop in 23 Years," *Los Angeles Times*, April 19, 1984, A2.

59. Marilyn Kalfus, "Aging Baby Boomers Now Outnumber Young Adults," *Orange County Register*, July 21, 1988, A1; George Sternlieb and James W. Hughes, "Aging 'Baby Boomers' Buoy Co-op and Condo Outlook," *New York Times*, September 22, 1985, R7.

60. Thomas R. King, "A Centennial View: Changing Markets," *Wall Street Journal*, June 23, 1989, 1.

61. Julie Amparano, "Marriott to Build Complexes Aimed at Aging America," *Wall Street Journal*, December 8, 1988, 1.

62. Ken Dychtwald and Joe Flower, *Age Wave: The Challenges and Opportunities of an Aging America* (New York: Tarcher, 1989).

63. Jan Hofmann, "Caring for an Aging Parent Can Bring Crushing Responsibility," *Los Angeles Times*, December 12, 1987, 7.

64. Dorothy A. Miller, "The 'Sandwich' Generation: Adult Children of the Aging," *Social Work*, September 1981, 419–23.

65. Judith E. Dobson and Russell L. Dobson, "The Sandwich Generation: Dealing with Aging Parents," *Journal of Counseling and Development*, May 1985, 572–74.

66. Jane Mayer and Judith Jacovitz, "Handling Pain of Caring for Aging Parents Is No Easy Job," *Los Angeles Times*, June 9, 1988, B20.

67. Barbara Silverstone and Helen Kandel Hyman, *You and Your Aging Parent: A Family Guide to Emotional, Physical, and Financial Problems* (New York: Pantheon, 1989).

68. "Elderlaw Helps Aging America," *Sun Sentinel*, January 22, 1989, 8A.

69. Susan Levine, "Young and Old Study Aging, Aged," *Hartford Courant*, March 14, 1983, C1.

70. Diane Lade, "Aging as College Curriculum," *Sun Sentinel*, December 7, 1987, 3D.

71. Lade, "Aging as College Curriculum."

72. Bill Billiter, "Cal State Fullerton Breaks Ground for Center on Aging," *Los Angeles Times*, May 23, 1986, 4.

73. Ursula Vils, "USC Professor Probes the Riddle of Aging," *Los Angeles Times*, January 12, 1986, 1.

74. Patricia McCormack, "Comfort Says Society Undermines the Joy of Aging," *Newsday*, March 23, 1981, B2.

75. David Steinberg, "Aging as a Self-Fulfilling Prophecy," *Sun Sentinel*, December 9, 1985, 3C.

76. Lucia C. Grassi, "Is Aging a Disease?" *Nursing Homes/Long Term Care Management*, October 1988, 20.

77. Grassi, "Is Aging a Disease?"

78. Jean Dietz, "A New Interest in Therapy for the Aging," *Boston Globe*, February 28, 1988, A15.

79. Philip G. Weiler, "The Public Health Impact of Alzheimer's Disease," *American Journal of Public Health*, September 1987, 1157–58.

80. Weiler, "The Public Health Impact of Alzheimer's Disease."

81. Weiler, "The Public Health Impact of Alzheimer's Disease."

82. Weiler, "The Public Health Impact of Alzheimer's Disease."

### Chapter 3

1. Dave Barry, *Dave Barry Turns Forty* (New York: Crown, 1990), 3.

2. Peter Gorner and Ronald Kotulak, "Do We Want to 'Cure' Aging?" *Chicago Tribune*, December 15, 1991, C1.

3. Gorner and Kotulak, "Do We Want to 'Cure' Aging?"

4. Nicholas Wade, "Can Life Span Be Extended? Biologists Offer Some Hope," *New York Times*, January 13, 1998, F1.

5. Marlene Cimons, "More Funds Urged for Research on Aging," *Los Angeles Times*, June 13, 1991, A22.

6. "Savings Seen by Using Millions to Study Aging," *New York Times*, June 12, 1991, B12.

7. Sharon Begley and Mary Hager, "The Search for the Fountain of Youth," *Newsweek*, March 5, 1990, 44.

8. Rick Weiss, "Hormone Hailed as Anti-Aging Drug Stirs Controversy," *Washington Post*, June 27, 1995, 7.

9. Marvin Cetron and Owen Davies, "Extended Life-Spans," *Futurist*, April 1998, 17.

10. "Melatonin Has Yet to Show Effect Against Aging in People," *Washington Post*, February 24, 1998, 17.

11. "Alzheimer's Disease Linked to Aging in Normal Genes," *Washington Post*, July 25, 1990, A12.

12. Monte Peterson, "Physical Aspects of Aging: Is There Such a Thing?" *Geriatrics*, February 1994, 45.

13. Constance L. Hays, "Woman Files Age-Bias Suit Against Agency for the Aging," *New York Times*, October 3, 1991, B5.

14. Don van Natta Jr., "Department for the Aging Loses Age-Bias Lawsuit," *New York Times*, December 2, 1995, 25.

15. Katharine Graham, "Aging," *Vital Speeches of the Day*, August 1, 1995, 639.

16. Gail Sheehy, *The Silent Passage* (New York: Random House, 1992).

17. Germaine Greer, *The Change: Women, Aging and the Menopause* (New York: Alfred A. Knopf, 1992).

18. Alice V. Luddington, "Betty Friedan," *Geriatrics*, December 1993, 52.

19. Kathy Keeton, "Mental Muscle," *Omni*, May 1992, 40.

20. Mark Clements, "What We Say About Aging," *Washington Post*, December 12, 1993, N4.

21. Erica Goode, "Happiness May Grow with Aging, Study Finds," *New York Times*, October 27, 1998, F7.

22. Lynne Ames, "Aging That Brings Honor to Those Who Grace Others' Lives," *New York Times*, December 27, 1998, WE2.

23. Ames, "Aging That Brings Honor to Those Who Grace Others' Lives.

24. Thomas H. Maugh II, "Studies Show Mental Effect of Aging," *Los Angeles Times*, February 16, 1991, A31.

25. Bradley J. Fisher and Diana K. Specht, "Successful Aging and Creativity in Later Life," *Journal of Aging Studies*, Winter 1999, 457.

26. Gabriella Stern, "Aging Boomers Are New Target for Maybelline," *Wall Street Journal*, April 13, 1993, B1.

27. Stern, "Aging Boomers Are New Target for Maybelline."

28. Michael Mason, "Why Anti-Aging Creams are Hot," *Health*, October 1994, 36.

29. Deirdre Carmody, "Magazines," *New York Times*, December 26, 1994, 57.

30. Chalmers M. Roberts, "'Generations Aging Together,'" *Washington Post*, May 9, 1995, 8.

31. For a good summary of this shift and subsequent developments, see Robert H. Binstock, "From Compassionate Ageism to Intergenerational Conflict?" *Gerontologist*, 2010, volume 50, issue 5, 574–85.

32. Spencer Rich, "Conferees Defend Social Security, Medicare," *Washington Post*, May 6, 1995, A7.

33. Susan Levine, "One in Four U.S. Families Cares for Aging Relatives," *Washington Post*, March 24, 1997, A13.

34. Jill Smolowe and Sam Allis, "Older, Longer," *Time*, Fall 1996 Special Issue, 76.

35. Denise M. Topolnicki and Roberta Kirwan, "How to Care for Your Aging Parents (Without Going Broke)," *Money*, May 1996, 128.

36. Kenneth N. Gilpin, "21 Companies to Expand a Dependent-Care Project," *New York Times*, September 14, 1995, D4.

37. Cathy Booth, "Taking Care of Our Aging Parents," *Time*, August 30, 1999, 48.

38. Karin Horgan Sullivan, "Aging with Soul," *Vegetarian Times*, February 1997, 68.

39. Marc Freedman, "Coming of Age," *American Prospect*, November 23, 1999, 66.

40. Robert N. Butler, "Older Astronauts: Next Giant Leap for Mankind," *Geriatrics*, April 1997, 14.

41. Joseph P. Shapiro, "John Glenn's Mixed Message on Aging," *U.S. News & World Report*, November 16, 1998, 69.

42. Shapiro, "John Glenn's Mixed Message on Aging."

43. Gayle Olinekova, *Power Aging: Staying Young at Any Age* (New York: Thunder Mouth Press, 1998).

44. Helen Kerschner and Jo Ann M. Pegues, "Productive Aging: A Quality of Life Agenda," *Journal of the American Dietetic Association*, December 1998, 1445.

45. Freedman, "Coming of Age."

46. Freedman, "Coming of Age.

47. Freedman, "Coming of Age.

48. Robert J. Samuelson, "Off Golden Pond," *New Republic*, April 12, 1999, 36–44.

49. Samuelson, "Off Golden Pond."

50. Jeffrey Kluger and Elaine Lafferty, "Can We Stay Young?" *Time*, November 25, 1996, 88.

51. Kluger and Lafferty, "Can We Stay Young?"

52. Geoffrey Cowley, "How to Live to 100," *Newsweek*, June 30, 1997, 56.

53. Karen F. Schmidt, "Old No More," *U.S. News & World Report*, March 8, 1993, 66.

54. Nancy Shute, "Why Do We Age?" *U.S. News & World Report*, August 18, 1997, 55.

55. Robert Goldman, "Anti-Aging Therapy Is Here to Stay," *Total Health*, May/June 1997, 26.

56. Goldman, "Anti-Aging Therapy Is Here to Stay."

57. Ronald M. Klatz, "Anti-Aging Medicine Comes of Age," *Total Health*, April/May 1999, 50.

58. Ronald Klatz, "The Dawning of a New Medicine for the Next . . . ," *Total Health*, October 1996, 20.

59. Ronald Klatz, "Anti-aging & Longevity," *Total Heath*, March/April 1997, 25.

60. David Stipp, "The Hunt for the Youth Pill," *Fortune*, October 11, 1999, 199–218.

61. Susan V. Seligson, "Anti-Aging Comes of Age," *Health*, April 1998, 62.

62. Lawrence A. Armour, "Better (And Fun!) Aging," *Fortune*, October 25, 1999, 403–6.

63. David Stipp, "Live a Lot Longer," *Fortune*, July 5, 1999, 144–60.

64. Michael Fossel, "Reversing Human Aging," *Futurist*, July–August 1997, 25.

65. Victoria Dolby Toews, "8 Steps to Age Without 'Aging,'" *Better Nutrition*, July 1999, 58.

66. "Blueberries May Reduce Effects of Aging," *New York Times*, September 21, 1999, F8.

67. Judy McBride, "Can Foods Forestall Aging?" *Agricultural Research*, February 1999, 14.

68. Doug Stewart and Brad Trent, "Solving the Aging Puzzle," *Smithsonian*, January 1998, 36.

69. Parris M. Kidd, "The Aging Clock," *Total Health*, October 1996, 17.

## Chapter 4

1. Soo Youn, "Anti-Aging Biz Boom," *New York Daily News*, May 24, 2004, 54.

2. Benedict Carey, "Can Doctors Really Turn Back Time?" *Los Angeles Times*, May 8, 2000, S1.

3. Carey, "Can Doctors Really Turn Back Time?"

4 Youn, "Anti-Aging Biz Boom."

5. Jane E. Allen, "Fine Lines Between Hype and Hope," *Los Angeles Times*, February 19, 2001, S1.

6. Virginia Linn, "Fountains of Youth Creams More and Pricier," *Pittsburgh Post-Gazette*, May 18, 2004, D1. In 2004, the Carlyle Hotel in Manhattan began putting complimentary jars of Kiehl's new Abyssine restorative face cream in its rooms; that product was all the rage among celebrities such as Demi Moore. (Kitty Bean Yancy, "Turn Back Time," *USA Today*, March 5, 2004, D1).

7. Jennifer Saranow, "The New Face of Plastic Surgery," *Wall Street Journal*, April 15, 2003, D1.

8. Maria Elena Fernandez, "On Pins 'n' Needles to Look Younger," *Los Angeles Times*, December 8, 2000, E1.

9. Joanne Omang, "Older and So Much Better," *Pittsburgh Post-Gazette*, March 12, 2003, E2.

10. Abigail Trafford, "Aging: The View from Below," *Washington Post*, November 23, 2004, F1.

11. "Aging: The View from Below." See Margaret Morganroth Gulette, *Aged by Culture* (Chicago: University of Chicago Press, 2004), for more on this fascinating case study, as well as her equally interesting *Declining to Decline: Cultural Combat and the Politics of the Mid-life* (Charlottesville: University of Virginia Press, 1997).

12. Margo Harakas, "In Praise of Wrinkles," *South Florida Sun-Sentinel*, November 16, 2004, 1E.

13. Marilyn Elias, "'Anti-aging Ads Are Getting Old," *USA Today*, November 14, 2002, D10.

14. David Wikenheiser, "Herbal Antioxidants and Biological Aging," *Total Health*, July/August 2000, 44.

15. Dharma Singh Khalsa, "Meditation as Anti-aging Medicine," *Total Health*, March/April 2001, 26.

16. Andrea Petersen, "Finding a Cure for Old Age," *Wall Street Journal*, May 20, 2003, D1. See Evans's *Biomarkers: The 10 Determinants of Aging You Can Control* (Simon & Schuster, 1991) for more on that subject.

17. Petersen, "Finding a Cure for Old Age.

18. Rick Weiss, "Age-Addled Genes Key to Aging Research with Microchips," *Pittsburgh Post-Gazette*, March 31, 2000, A3.

19. Robert Lee Hotz, "Alterations in Cells Cause Aging, Study Finds," *Los Angeles Times*, March 31, 2000, A1.

20. Jocelyn Selim, "The Genetic Secrets of Aging," *Discover*, December 2001, 16.

21. Rick Weiss, "Enzymes Found to Delay Aging Process," *Washington Post*, August 25, 2003, A2.

22. Andrew Pollack, "Forget Botox, Anti-Aging Pills May Be Next," *New York Times*, September 21, 2003, BU1. See Lenny Guarente's *Ageless Quest: One Scientist's Search for Genes That Prolong Youth* (Cold Spring Harbor, NY: Cold Spring Harbor Laboratory Press, 2002) for more on the pursuit of a "longevity gene."

23. Marsha Austin, "Venture Aiming for a Long Life," *Denver Post*, December 7, 2003, K1.

24. Michael R. Rose, "Will Human Aging Be Postponed?" *Scientific American*, June 2004, 24–29.

25. Catherine Arnst, "Aging Is Becoming So Yesterday," *Business Week*, October 11, 2004, 148.

26. Joao Pedro de Magalhaes, "Winning the War Against Aging," *Futurist*, March/April 2003, 48, 50.

27. www.undesadspd.org. The United Nations later rejected several petitions to stipulate that older people were to be especially designated for inclusion under the 1948 Declaration for Human Rights, however.

28. Betsy McCaughey, "Aging in America: The Path Ahead," *New York Times*, September 20, 2000, A26.

29. Joan Axelrod-Contrada, "Career Path Grows Out of an Aging US," *Boston Globe*, January 26, 2003, G1.

30. Jane Glenn Haas, "The Middle-Aging of the Boomer Generation," *Washington Post*, March 27, 2001, C4.

31. Margo Hammond, "Baby Boomers Rewrite Aging," *St. Petersburg Times*, March 4, 2001, 7D.

32. Terence Samuel, "The Aging of America has Experts Wondering How the Nation Will Adjust," *St. Louis Post-Dispatch*, June 11, 2000, A14.

33. Zorba Paster, *The Longevity Code: Your Personal Prescription for a Longer, Sweeter Life* (New York: Clarkson Potter, 2001); Deepak Chopra, *Grow Younger, Live Longer: Ten Steps to Reverse Aging* (New York: Harmony, 2002).

34. David Snowden, *Aging with Grace: What the Nun Study Teaches Us About Leading Longer, Healthier, and More Meaningful Lives* (New York: Bantam, 2001).

35. Ram Dass, *Still Here: Embracing Aging, Changing, and Dying* (New York: Riverhead Books, 2000).

36. Jocelyn Y. Stewart, "Few Plan for the Hard Realities of Infirm Parents' Care," *Los Angeles Times*, April 2, 2000, A1.

37. Janet Kornblum, "Now Is the Time to Discuss Crucial Details with Elders," *USA Today*, December 17, 2003, D10.

38. Raenn Berman and Bernard H. Shulman, *How to Survive Your Aging Parents* (Chicago: Surrey Books, 2001).

39. Jenny Deam, "Nursing Homes Changing to Ease Aging Boomers' Qualms," *Denver Post*, April 2, 2001, E1.

40. Deam, "Nursing Homes Changing to Ease Aging Boomers' Qualms."

41. Cathryn J. Prince, "Nursing Homes Reach Out," *Christian Science Monitor*, July 19, 2000, 15.

42. Jeffrey Zaslow, "Moving On: Face It, Baby Boomers, You've Peaked," *Wall Street Journal*, December 5, 2002, D1.

43. Christina Crews, "Research Acknowledges Male Menopause," *Philadelphia Tribune*, July 11, 2000, 12E.

44. Crews, "Research Acknowledges Male Menopause."

45. Sara Schaefer Munoz, "Men Shouldn't Use Testosterone to Ward Off Aging, Panel Warns," *Wall Street Journal*, November 13, 2003, D3.

46. Noel C. Paul, "Selling to Seniors," *Christian Science Monitor*, March 19, 2001, 11.

47. Marilyn Elias, "Boomers Generate New Business," *USA Today*, February 28, 2001, D6.

48. Hal Boedeker, "TV's Old Story," *South Florida Sun-Sentinel*, September 5, 2001, 1E.

49. Marc Freedman, *Prime Time: How Baby Boomers Will Revolutionize Retirement and Transform America* (New York: PublicAffairs, 2002).

50. Elias, "Boomers Generate New Business."

51. "Retired but Relevant," *Pittsburgh Post-Gazette*, February 18, 2004, C2.

52. Jocelyn Y. Stewart, "Retirees Reinvent the Concept," *Los Angeles Times*, April 3, 2000, A1.

53. Kris Axtman, "Retirees Not Just After Fun in the Sun," *Christian Science Monitor*, January 23, 2001, 1.

54. Craig Savoye, "More People Are Staying Put for Retirement," *Christian Science Monitor*, April 3, 2001, 3.

55. Marilyn Gardner, "Boomers Refuse to Fade into the Sunset," *Christian Science Monitor*, May 16, 2001, 11.

56. Esther "Tess" Canja, "Aging in the 21st Century: Myths and Challenges," *Executive Speeches*, December 2001/January 2002, 24.

57. Michelle Maltais, "Probing Our Fear of Aging," *Los Angeles Times*, August 30, 2002, F29.

58. A. Scott Walton, "What, Me Get Old?" *Atlanta Journal-Constitution*, May 19, 2002, M6.

59. Barry Koltnow, "The Small Picture," *Orange County Register*, January 3, 2003, Movies 1.

60. Sara Terry, "Older Women's Newer Models: Gray is Glam," *Christian Science Monitor*, June 9, 2000, 1.

61. Richard O'Mara, "Sky-diving Seniors? Not Me!" *Christian Science Monitor*, December 11, 2001, 9.

62. Marilyn Gardner, "Stereotypes Tarnish 'Golden Years,'" *Christian Science Monitor*, November 22, 2000, 15.

63. Marjorie Miller, "Mick Jagger: Cover Boy for the Over-50 Set," *Los Angeles Times*, August 27, 2001, E1.

64. Vicki Goldberg, "The Effects of Aging," *New York Times*, January 2, 2000, AR43.

65. Cate McQuaid, "Portraits of Aging at Gallery NAGA," *Boston Globe*, July 5, 2001, E2.

66. John Petrakis, "Silver Images Continues Its 'Reimagine Aging' Tradition," *Chicago Tribune*, April 28, 2000, 7H.

67. Cassie J. Moore, "Faces of Aging, Faces of Charity," *Chronicle of Philanthropy*, April 1, 2004, 13–15.

68. Aviv Shahar, "The Holistic Future of Aging," *Futurist*, September–October 2003, 8.

69. Laura Tangley, "Aging Brains Need Fresh Challenges to Stay Agile," *U.S. News & World Report*, June 5, 2000, 90.

70. Jane E. Allen, "A Positive Outlook on Aging May Mean a Longer Life," *Los Angeles Times*, July 29, 2002, S3.

71. Alice Dembner, "Over-50 Women Say Aging's Not So Bad," *Boston Globe*, November 19, 2002, C4.

72. Jane Glenn Haas, "Survey: We're Older but Not Old," *Orange County Register*, April 25, 2000, E6.

73. Maura Lerner, "'Aging Game' Brings Wisdom," *Minneapolis Star Tribune*, May 9, 2000, 1B.

74. Warren Wolfe, "Class on Aging Yields Insights Overnight," *Minneapolis Star Tribune*, February 8, 2002, 1B.

75. Warren Wolfe, "Advances to Extend Human Life Have Age Limit, Biologist Says," *Minneapolis Star Tribune*, April 29, 2000, 3B.

76. See Gerald J. Gruman, *A History of Ideas About the Prolongation of Life* (New York: Springer, 2003), a reissue of his essay, which traced the evolution of prolongevity hypotheses to 1800.

77. Patricia Guthrie, "Forget Fountain of Youth, Expert Advises," *Atlanta Constitution*, October 3, 2000, C5.

78. "Don't Fall for Anti-Aging Claims, Study Advises," *Los Angeles Times*, May 27, 2002, A13. Charlatans and quacks permeate the annals of gerontology; failed remedies by Russian biologist and Nobel Laureate Elie Metchnikoff (yogurt) and Mauritan physiologist Charles-Edouard Brown-Sequard (dog semen) still discredit the field.

79. Jane Glen Haas, "Anti-Aging Efforts," *Orange County Register*, May 27, 2002, cover.

80. "Silver Fleece Awards Given for Anti-Aging Hype," *NCAHF Newsletter*, March/April 2002, 3.

81. "Silver Fleece Awards Given for Anti-Aging Hype."

82. "Anti-Aging or Successful Aging?" *Tufts University Health & Nutrition Letter*, April 2001, 1.

83. Bob Jackson, "A Backlash Against the Anti-aging Industry," *Pittsburgh Post-Gazette*, May 20, 2003, F7.

84. Valerie Reitman, "A Rift in Business, Science of Aging," *Los Angeles Times*, January 12, 2004, F1.

85. Andrea Petersen, "The Dream Vacation," *Wall Street Journal*, August 13, 2003, D1.

86. Lan N. Nguyen, "'Disease Is Not Normal to the Aging Process,'" *New York Daily News*, June 16, 2004, 11.

87. Geoffrey Cowley and Rachel Davis, "The Biology of Aging," *Newsweek*, Fall/Winter 2001 Special Edition, 12.

88. Martin Miller, "The Doctor Behind the Spartan Diet," *Los Angeles Times*, November 25, 2002, F1. Walford died three years later at the age of eighty.

89. Rob Stein, "Seeking the Low-Calorie Fountain of Youth," *Washington Post*, May 4, 2004, A1.

### Chapter 5

1. Joey Bunch, "A Silver Tsunami," *Denver Post*, June 11, 2007, A1.

2. Bunch, "A Silver Tsunami."

3. David Peterson, "'Burbs to Be Hit with Senior Boom," *Minneapolis Star Tribune*, June 12, 2007, 1A.

4. Jane Adler, "There's No Place Like Home for Aging Boomers," *Chicago Tribune*, December 24, 2006, 4.

5. "Study on Aging Reaches the Half-Century Mark," *Washington Post*, December 9, 2008, F2.

6. "Peering into the Future of Aging," *Nursing Homes/Long Term Care Management*, August 2006, 22.

7. Jane Glenn Haas, "Challenging Old Perceptions," *Orange County Register*, March 16, 2006, 1.

8. Steven Mintz, *The Prime of Life: A History of Modern Adulthood* (Cambridge, MA: Belknap Press of Harvard University Press, 2015) 300.

9. Don Aucoin, "Crisis? What Crisis?" *Boston Globe*, September 7, 2005, C1.

10. Ken Dychtwald and Daniel J. Kadlec, *The Power Years: A User's Guide to the Rest of Your Life* (Hoboken, NJ: Wiley, 2005).

11. http://firstrunfeatures.com/openroad.html.

12. James A. Lomastro, "The White House Conference on Aging: A Positive View," *Nursing Homes/Long Term Care Management*, October 2006, 14.

13. "White House Aging Conference Focuses on Care, Transportation," *Nation's Health*, January/February 2006, 12.

14. "White House Aging Conference Focuses on Care, Transportation."

15. Sue Kirchhoff, "Will Aging Boomers Lose Benefits?" *USA Today*, January 17, 2008, B3.

16. Lyn M. Holley, *"Aging Nation: The Economics and Politics of Growing Older in America* by James H. Schulz and Robert H. Binstock," *Educational Gerontology*, December 2008, 1122–25.

17. Maria L. La Ganga, "Crisis in Healthcare Foreseen," *Los Angeles Times*, April 15, 2008, A8.

18. Suzanne Perry, "Nonprofit Groups Devise Ideas for White House Meeting on Aging," *Chronicle of Philanthropy*, October 27, 2005, 68.

19. Michael J. Stoil, "Should We Retire the White House Conference on Aging?" *Nursing Homes/Long Term Care Management*, February 2006, 12–14.

20. Jennifer L. Huget, "Blogging Through the Ages," *Washington Post*, August 2, 2005, F1.

21. Huget, "Blogging Through the Ages."

22. Anita Manning, "Aging Gracefully is Biggest Concern," *USA Today*, October 24, 2005, A7.

23. Glenn Harlan Reynolds, "The End of Aging?" *Popular Mechanics*, March 2008, 56.

24. Colleen O'Connor, "Aging, and Proud About It," *Denver Post*, December 4, 2005, L1.

25. Maureen Dowd, "Aging in Public," *Pittsburgh Post-Gazette*, December 20, 2007, B7.

26. Nora Ephron, *I Feel Bad About My Neck* (New York: Knopf, 2006).

27. Janet Champ and Charlotte Moore, *Ripe: The Truth About Growing Older and the Beauty of Getting On with Your Life* (Hillsboro, OR: Beyond Words, 2005).

28. Lillian B. Rubin, *60 On Up: The Truth About Aging in America* (Boston: Beacon, 2007).

29. Mark Dolliver, "Mere Aging Can't Quell Their Self-Satisfaction," *Adweek*, April 9, 2007, 41.

30. Amy Gorman, *Aging Artfully: Profiles of 12 Visual and Performing Artists 85–105* (Berkeley: PAL, 2006).

31. Mary Jane Smetanka, "Keeping a Lively Life with the Arts," *Minneapolis Star Tribune*, January 16, 2005, 1B.

32. James Sallie, "Angelou Shares Life Lessons at Conference on Aging," *South Florida Sun-Sentinel*, January 15, 2007, B3.

33. Suzanne Perry, "Topic of Aging Gets New Look with the Support of Foundations," *Chronicle of Philanthropy*, March 8, 2007, 16.

34. Abigail Trafford, "Taking a Fresh Look at Aging," *Washington Post*, March 21, 2006, F4.

35. Trafford, "Taking a Fresh Look at Aging."

36 Mary Brophy Marcus, "The Boom Lowers on Boomers," *USA Today*, September 24, 2007, D4.

37. Sherwin B. Nuland, *The Art of Aging: A Doctor's Prescription for Well-Being* (New York: Random House, 2007).

38. Bernadine Healy, "The Power of the Aging Mind," *U.S. News & World Report*, November 12, 2007, 66.

39. Kay Lazar, "Aging Has Its Benefits," *Boston Globe*, January 12, 2009, A8.

40. Sharon Begley, "The Upside of Aging," *Wall Street Journal*, February 16, 2007, W1.

41. "Aging Well at All Ages," *Washington Post*, August 11, 2009, E1.

42. Robert N. Jenkins, "Stay Young in Spite of the Years," *St. Petersburg Times*, July 29, 2008, S11.

43. Jenkins, "Stay Young in Spite of the Years."

44. Aubrey de Grey and Michael Rae, *Ending Aging: The Rejuvenation Biotechnologies That Could Reverse Human Aging in Our Lifetime* (New York: St. Martin's, 2007). See also Michael R. Rose's almost as ambitious *The Long Tomorrow: How Advances in Evolutionary Biology Can Help Us Postpone Aging* (New York: Oxford University Press, 2005), in which the author recounts his breeding of "Methuselah fruit flies" and other evolutionary biological feats that he believed would soon lead to a significantly longer human life span.

45. mfoundation.org.

46. Reynolds, "The End of Aging?" 56.

47. Kathleen McGowan, "Can We Cure Aging?" *Discover*, December 2007, 58–77.

48. Brian M. Delaney and Lisa Walford, *The Longevity Diet: The Only Proven Way to Slow the Aging Process and Maintain Peak Vitality Through Caloric Restriction* (New York: Da Capo Lifelong Books, 2010).

49. Nicholas Wade, "Aging Drugs: Hardest Test Is Still Ahead," *New York Times*, November 7, 2006, F1.

50. "Aging: The Running Thread," *Total Health*, April/May 2006, 39.

51. Nicholas Wade, "Tests Begin on Drugs That May Slow Aging," *New York Times*, August 18, 2009, D1.

52. Arlene Weintraub, "The Hard Sell on Anti-Aging," *BusinessWeek*, August 10, 2009, 48–50.

53. "Resveratrol in Dark Chocolate & Cocoa Leads to Anti-Aging," *Biotech Business*, March 2009, 7–8.

54. "Let Reason Be Your Guide in Assessing the Growing Anti-Aging Industry," *Electronic Ardell Wellness Report*, May 4, 2007, 2.

55. Martha Irvine, "In the Gym, Trying to Work the Years Off," *Los Angeles Times*, February 15, 2009, A12.

56. Chris Woolston, "The Healthy Skeptic," *Los Angeles Times*, July 13, 2009, E1.

57. "Anti-Aging Aids Aren't Working, A Rigorous Study of Them Finds," *St. Louis Post-Dispatch*, October 19, 2006, A4.

58. Judith Graham, "Legal Dispute over Anti-Aging Medicine Ends," *Chicago Tribune*, November 17, 2006, 2NS.12.

59. Duff Wilson, "Aging: Disease or Business Opportunity?" *New York Times*, April 15, 2007, B1.

60. Laura Petrecca, "Men Arm Themselves with Anti-Aging Weapons," *USA Today*, April 15, 2008, B3.

61. Stacie Stutkin, "Dermatology in a Bottle," *Los Angeles Times*, July 6, 2008, P3.

62. Natasha Singer, "Anti-Aging Makeup: Multitasker in a Jar," *New York Times*, August 18, 2005, G3.

63. Christopher Rowland, "New Wrinkle in Anti-Aging Cosmetics," *Boston Globe*, August 23, 2005, A1.

64. Rowland, "New Wrinkle in Anti-Aging Cosmetics."

65 Jonathan Peterson, "Aging Boomers a Target Audience," *South Florida Sun-Sentinel*, June 4, 2006, 1E.

66. Meg Richards, "Booming Opportunity," *Pittsburgh Post-Gazette*, February 14, 2005, B1.

67. Sara Lin, "The Home Front," *Wall Street Journal*, April 25, 2008, W8.

68. Hiawatha Bray, "At MIT's AgeLab, Growing Old Is a New Frontier," *Boston Globe*, March 23, 2009, B5.

69. Kate Ashford, "How to Help: Your Aging Parents," *Good Housekeeping*, January 2009, 135.

70. Linda Marsa, "Aging Under a High-Tech Eye," *Chicago Tribune*, December 20, 2007, 1.

71. Jonathan Peterson, "Care Across the Miles," *Chicago Tribune*, March 16, 2008, 5.

72. David Crary, "Concerns Rise over Who Will Care for Aging Boomers," *Deseret News*, June 15, 2007, A1. Boomers' distress over how their parents and peers spent their dying days would leave a lasting imprint; already they are rejecting the "industrial" model of death as described by Jessica Mitford in her classic *The American Way of Death* by increasingly preferring cremation and personalizing burial rituals. See my *Death, American Style: A Cultural History of Dying in America* (Lanham, MD: Rowman & Littlefield, 2013) for more on boomers and death.

73. Joan Raymond, "How to Talk About Aging," *Newsweek*, June 18, 2007, 59.

74. Mindy Fetterman, "Your Aging Parents and You," *USA Today*, June 25, 2007, A1.

75. Abi Albrecht, "A Review of: *The Emotional Survival Guide for Caregivers: Looking After Yourself and Your Parent While Helping an Aging Parent*, Barry J. Jacobs," *Journal of Loss and Trauma*, January 2008, 85. See also Cheryl A. Kuba, *Navigating the Journey of Aging Parents: What Care Receivers Want* (New York: Routledge, 2006).

76. Fetterman, "Your Aging Parents and You."

77. Rob Owen, "PBS Special Focuses on Challenges of Caring for One's Aging Parents," *Pittsburgh Post-Gazette*, April 2, 2008, C6.

78. Kathy Segrist, "*The Caregiver—A Life with Alzheimer's* by Aaron Alterra," *Educational Gerontology*, December 2008, 1124.

79. Tom Valeo, "Disease, or Just an Aging Brain?" *St. Petersburg Times*, March 25, 2008, E3.

80. Melissa Healy, "Aging Well," *Los Angeles Times*, October 15, 2007, F4.

81. Catherine Arnst, "Chicken Soup for the Aging Brain," *BusinessWeek*, September 25, 2006, 94–96.

### Chapter 6

1. "Real Age: Live Life to the Youngest," www.sharecare.com/static/realage-sharecare.

2. Phillip Longman, "Global Aging," *Foreign Policy*, November 2010, 52–58.

3. Longman, "Global Aging."

4. "Baby Boomers and the New Aging," *San Diego Business Journal*, November 5, 2012, S24.

5. Jane Kitchen, "New Study Shows Number of Grandparents at Record High and Growing," *KidsToday*, September 2011, 8.

6. "Baby Boomers and the New Aging."

7. Dina ElBoghdady, "Some Aging Baby Boomers Will Upsize, Not Downsize, If They Move at All, Poll Finds," *Washington Post*, October 30, 2014, accessed online

8. Shan Li, "Reshaping the Gym," *Los Angeles Times*, September 8, 2013, B1.

9. Bill Ward, "Boomers Truckin' into Old Age," *Star Tribune*, October 21, 2012, E1.

10. Merrill Goozner, "Demands of an Aging Population Will Have Medicare and Medicaid Fighting for Dollars," *Modern Healthcare*, May 25, 2015, 16.

11. Deborah Kotz, "Get Ready for the Age Wave," *U.S. News & World Report*, February 2010, 18–22.

12. Kotz, "Get Ready for the Age Wave."

13. Matthew Segal, "How to Live a Long Life in LA," *Los Angeles*, November 2014, 156.

14. Oliver Sacks, "The Joy of Old Age. (No Kidding.)" *New York Times*, July 6, 2013, accessed online

15. Philip Moeller, "Celebrating Old Age Should Happen Every Day," *U.S. News Digital Weekly*, July 31, 2013, 9.

16. Oliver Sacks, "My Own Life," *New York Times*, February 19, 2015, A25.

17. Susan Jacoby, "The Myth of Aging Gracefully," *Newsweek*, February 7, 2011, 14.

18. Karen Weintraub, "Number of People with New Joints Top 7 Million," *USA Today*, March 14, 2014, B5.

19. David Templeton, "Ambassador for the Aging to Promote Cause Here," *Pittsburgh Post-Gazette*, May 4, 2015, A7.

20. Ariel Green, "A Young Geriatrician on the Struggles of Alzheimer's Patients—and Their Caretakers," *Washington Post*, September 3, 2013, accessed online

21. "Gerontology: Aging Is a Hard Sell," *Boston Globe*, February 11, 2013, A8.

22. Karen Pennar, "Unafraid of Aging," *New York Times*, June 26, 2012, D1.

23. "Chasing Methuselah," *Christianity Today*, January 2011, 18.

24. Laurence D. Mueller, Casandra L. Rauser, and Michael R. Rose, *Does Aging Stop?* (New York: Oxford University Press, 2011).

25. Michael R. Rose, "Life Begins at 90," *New Scientist*, August 6, 2011, 42–45.

26. T. E. Holt, "The End of Aging," *Men's Health*, November 2010, 164–80.

27. Thomas Kirkwood, "Why Can't We Live Forever?" *Scientific American*, September 2010, 42–49.

28. Rachel Ehrenberg, "DNA Disorganization Promotes Aging," *Science News*, May 30, 2015, accessed online.

29. Jane Glenn Haas, "Research to Slow Aging Gains Momentum," *Orange County Register*, July 7, 2010, accessed online.

30. Christoph Westphal, "Biotechnology's New Frontier," *Boston Globe*, June 14, 2010, A11.

31. Tracey Samuelson, "Science (and Quacks) vs. the Aging Process," *New York Times*, November 19, 2014, F5.

32. Haas, "Research to Slow Aging Gains Momentum."

33. Tara Bahrampour, "To Live a Longer, Healthier Life," *Washington Post*, October 7, 2013, accessed online.

34. David Templeton, "Your Older Years," *Pittsburgh Post-Gazette*, December 9, 2014, E1.

35. Jeremy Olson, "Changing Aging," *Star Tribune*, February 1, 2012, T12.

36. Tiffany Sstrobel, "Is America Addicted to Youth?" *Shape*, September 2013, 200.

37. Nedra Rhone, "Healthy Aging: New Therapies in War on Aging," *Atlanta Journal-Constitution*, September 25, 2012, D1.

38. "Anti-Aging Products," *Consumer Reports on Health*, June 2015, accessed online.

39. "Chasing Methuselah."

40. Kristin Tice Studeman, "Hot Spot: Cryotherapy at the Thermes Marins-Monte Carlo Spa" yahoo.com/beauty, June 15, 2015.

41. Matthew Perrone, "Stem Cell Treatments Take Root in U.S.," *South Florida Sun-Sentinel*, May 23, 2015, A6.

42. Gretchen Voss, "Dying to Be Young," *Health*, December 2011, 110.

43. Voss, "Dying to Be Young."

44. Todd R. Weiss, "Google Launching Health Company to Fight Disease, Aging," *eWeek*, September 19, 2013, 2.

45. Richard Halstead, "Google Partners with Buck Institute in Marin to Search for Biotech Fountain of Youth," *Oakland Tribune*, April 29, 2015, accessed online.

46. Richard Halstead, "Ibuprofen May Slow Aging, Marin-based Buck Institute Study Suggests," *Oakland Tribune*, December 19, 2014, accessed online.

47. Clare Wilson, "Elixir of Youth? It's Already Here," *New Scientist*, October 4, 2014, 6–7.

48. Caroline Copley, "Global Drugmakers Looking to Push Bounds of Aging," *Chicago Tribune*, November 19, 2014, 6.

49. Andrew Pollack, "A Genetic Entrepreneur Sets His Sights on Aging and Death," *New York Times*, March 5, 2014, B1.

50. Aaron Kinney, "Silicon Valley Launches Another Bid to 'Hack' Aging, Cheat Death," *Oakland Tribune*, September 14, 2014, accessed online.

51. "With Folks Living Longer, Science of Aging in Spotlight," *Chicago Tribune*, February 18, 2014, 5.

52. Mark Benecke, *The Dream of Eternal Life* (New York: Columbia University Press, 2002); Stephen Hall, *Merchants of Immortality: Chasing the Dream of Human Life Extension* (New York: Mariner Books, 2005); Greg Critser, *Eternity Soup: Inside the Quest to End Aging* (New York: Harmony/Crown, 2010); Ted Anton, *The Longevity Seekers: Science, Business, and the Fountain of Youth* (Chicago: University of Chicago Press, 2013).

53. Jonathan Weiner, *Long for this World: The Strange Science of Immortality* (New York: Ecco, 2010).

54. Bill Gifford, *Spring Chicken: Stay Young Forever (or Die Trying)* (New York: Grand Central, 2015).

55. Jerrold Winter, *Optimal Aging: A Guide to Your First 100 Years* (Seattle: CreateSpace, 2015).

56. Ezekiel J. Emanuel, "Why I Hope to Die at 75," *Atlantic*, October 2014, 74.

57. David Harsanyi, "Threescore and Fifteen," *National Review*, October 20, 2014, 60.

58. Susan Crandell, "The Time of My Life," *Prevention*, August 2013, 96–97.

59. Dominique Browning, "Why I Like Getting Older," *Harper's Bazaar*, April 2012, 180–83.

60. Brian Bethune, "What It's Really Like to Grow Old," *Maclean's*, November 21, 2011, 58–61.

61. Emily Fox Gordon, "At Sixty-Five," *American Scholar*, Summer 2013, 76.

62. Brian D. Johnson, "You Can Stay—Just Act Your Age," *Maclean's*, February 18, 2013, 1.

63. Steven Zeitchik, "Not Just the Same Old Films," *South Florida Sun-Sentinel*, January 16, 2011, G4.

64. Johnson, "You Can Stay-Just Act Your Age."

65. Stephen Farber, "Are Older Directors Still Making Vital Movies?" *Chicago Tribune*, August 20, 2013, 4.4.

66. Meredith Blake, "For Prime Time, Aging Boomers Are Next Big Thing," *Los Angeles Times*, February 23, 2014, A1.

67. Noam Scheiber, "Over the Hill in Silicon Valley," *New Republic*, April 7, 2014, 20.

68. David Templeton, "Ambassador for the Aging to Promote Cause Here," *Pittsburgh Post-Gazette*, May 4, 2015, A7.

69. Templeton, "Ambassador for the Aging to Promote Cause Here."

70. Jo Ann Jenkins, "Disrupting Aging," *Generations—Journal of the American Society on Aging*, Spring 2015, 6.

71. Charlotte Yeh, "Fostering a New (More Self-Empowering) World View on Aging," *Generations—Journal of the American Society on Aging*, Spring 2015, 10.

## Conclusion

1. "Our Mission: Inspiring New Attitudes on Aging," GetOld.com.

2. "Redefining Age in Aging Societies," *Christian Science Monitor*, August 8, 2014, 12.

3. Kerry Hannon, "An Aging Population Also Poses Opportunities for Retirement Careers," *New York Times*, March 8, 2014, B7.

4. Amy Hoffman, "Special Issue: Women Aging," *Women's Review of Books*, July 2003, 3.

5. Albert Brooks, *2030: The Real Story of What Happens to America* (New York: St. Martin's, 2011).

6. Korin Miller, "Hillary Clinton Shares Plan to End Alzheimer's," *Yahoo News*, December 22, 2015.

7. Tara Bahrampour, "Americans Upbeat on Aging, Study Finds," *Washington Post*, January 31, 2014, A8.

# Selected Bibliography

Achenbaum, W. Andrew. *Crossing Frontiers: Gerontology Emerges as a Science.* Cambridge: Cambridge University Press, 1995.

———. *Old Age in the New Land: The American Experience Since 1790.* Baltimore: Johns Hopkins University Press, 1978.

———. *Robert N. Butler, M.D.: Visionary of Healthy Aging.* New York: Columbia University Press, 2013.

Alterra, Aaron. *The Caregiver—A Life with Alzheimer's.* Hanover, NH: Steerforth Press, 1999.

Anton, Ted. *The Longevity Seekers: Science, Business, and the Fountain of Youth.* Chicago: University of Chicago Press, 2013.

Averyt, Anne C. *Successful Aging: A Sourcebook for Older People and Their Families.* New York: Ballantine Books, 1987.

Baars, Jan, Dale Dannefer, Chris Phillipson, and Alan Walker, eds. *Aging, Globalization and Inequality: The New Critical Gerontology.* Amityville, NY: Baywood, 2006.

Barry, Dave. *Dave Barry Turns Forty.* New York: Crown, 1990.

Benecke, Mark. *The Dream of Eternal Life.* New York: Columbia University Press, 2002.

Berman, Raenn, and Bernard H. Shulman. *How to Survive Your Aging Parents.* Chicago: Surrey Books, 2001.

Brooks, Albert. *2030: The Real Story of What Happens to America.* New York: St. Martin's, 2011.

Butler, Robert N. *Why Survive? Being Old in America.* New York: Harper & Row, 1975.

Carter, Jimmy. *The Virtues of Aging.* New York: Ballantine, 1998.

Carter, Jimmy and Rosalynn. *Everything to Gain: Making the Most of the Rest of Your Life.* New York: Random House, 1987.

Case, Bill. *Life Begins at Sixty.* New York: Stein & Day, 1986.

Champ, Janet, and Charlotte Moore. *Ripe: The Truth About Growing Older and the Beauty of Getting On with Your Life*. Hillsboro, OR: Beyond Words, 2005.

Chopra, Deepak. *Grow Younger, Live Longer: Ten Steps to Reverse Aging*. New York: Harmony, 2002.

Chudacoff, Howard P. *How Old Are You? Age Consciousness in American Culture*. Princeton: Princeton University Press, 1989.

Cole, Thomas R. *The Journey of Life: A Cultural History of Aging in America*. Cambridge: Cambridge University Press, 1991.

Comfort, Alex. *Aging: The Biology of Senescence*. London: Routledge & K. Paul, 1956.

———. *The Process of Aging*. New York: Signet, 1961.

Corman, Avery. *50*. New York: Simon & Schuster, 1987.

Critser, Greg. *Eternity Soup: Inside the Quest to End Aging*. New York: Harmony/Crown, 2010.

Cumming, Elaine, and William E. Henry. *Growing Old*. New York: Basic Books, 1961.

Curtin, Sharon R. *Nobody Ever Died of Old Age*. Boston, MA: Little, Brown, 1972.

Dannefer, Dale and Chris Phillipson, eds. *The SAGE Handbook of Social Gerontology*. Thousand Oaks, CA: SAGE, 2010.

Dass, Ram. *Still Here: Embracing Aging, Changing, and Dying*. New York: Riverhead, 2000.

de Grey, Aubrey, and Michael Rae. *Ending Aging: The Rejuvenation Biotechnologies That Could Reverse Human Aging in Our Lifetime*. New York: St. Martin's, 2007.

Delaney, Brian M., and Lisa Walford. *The Longevity Diet: The Only Proven Way to Slow the Aging Process and Maintain Peak Vitality Through Calorie Restriction*. New York: Da Capo Lifelong Books, 2010.

Doress-Worters, Paula Brown, and Diana Laskin Siegal. *Ourselves, Growing Older: Women Aging with Knowledge and Power*. New York: Simon & Schuster, 1987.

Doty, Leilani Doty. *Communication and Assertion Skills for Older Persons*. New York: Hemisphere, 1987.

Drabble, Margaret. *A Natural Curiosity*. New York: Viking Adult, 1989.

Dychtwald, Ken, and Joe Flower. *Age Wave: The Challenges and Opportunities of an Aging America*. New York: Tarcher, 1989.

Dychtwald, Ken, and Daniel J. Kadlec. *The Power Years: A User's Guide to the Rest of Your Life*. Hoboken, NJ: Wiley, 2005.

Ephron, Nora. *I Feel Bad About My Neck*. New York: Knopf, 2006.

Evans, William. *Biomarkers: The 10 Determinants of Aging You Can Control*. New York: Simon & Schuster, 1991.

Fischer, David Hackett. *Growing Old in America*. New York: Oxford University Press, 1978.

Fossel, Michael. *Reversing Human Aging: A Groundbreaking Book About Medical Advances That Will Revolutionize. . . .* New York: William Morrow, 1996.

Freedman, Mark. *Prime Time: How Baby Boomers Will Revolutionize Retirement and Transform America*. New York: PublicAffairs, 2002.

Gifford, Bill. *Spring Chicken: Stay Young Forever (or Die Trying)*. New York: Grand Central, 2015.

Gillick, Muriel R. *The Denial of Aging: Perpetual Youth, Eternal Life, and Other Dangerous Fantasies*. Cambridge, MA: Harvard University Press, 2006.

Gorman, Amy. *Aging Artfully: Profiles of 12 Visual and Performing Artists 85–105*. Berkeley: PAL, 2006.

Greening, Tom, and Dick Hobson. *Instant Relief: The Encyclopedia of Self-Help*. New York: Seaview Books, 1979.

Greer, Germaine. *The Change: Women, Aging and the Menopause*. New York: Alfred A. Knopf, 1992.

Gross, Ronald, Beatrice Gross, and Sylvia Seidman, eds. *The New Old: Struggling for Decent Aging*. New York: Anchor Press, 1978.

Gruman, Gerald J. *A History of Ideas About the Prolongation of Life*. New York: Springer, 2003.

Guarente, Lenny. *Ageless Quest: One Scientist's Search for Genes That Prolong Youth*. Cold Spring Harbor, NY: Cold Spring Harbor Laboratory Press, 2002.

Gulette, Margaret Morganroth. *Aged by Culture*. Chicago: University of Chicago Press, 2004.

———. *Declining to Decline: Cultural Combat and the Politics of the Mid-life*. Charlottesville: University of Virginia Press, 1997.

Haber, Carole. *Beyond Sixty-Five: The Dilemma of Old Age in America's Past*. Cambridge: Cambridge University Press, 1983.

Haber, Carole, and Brian Gratton. *Old Age and the Search for Security: An American Social History*. Bloomington: Indiana University Press, 1994.

Hall, Stephen. *Merchants of Immortality: Chasing the Dream of Human Life Extension*. New York: Mariner Books, 2005.

Higgs, Paul, and Chris Gilleard. *Rethinking Old Age: Theorising the Fourth Age*. London: Palgrave Macmillan, 2015.

Holstein, Martha. *Women in Late Life: Critical Perspectives on Gender and Age*. Lanham, MD: Rowman & Littlefield, 2015.

Jacobs, Barry J. *The Emotional Survival Guide for Caregivers: Looking After Yourself and Your Parent While Helping an Aging Parent*. New York: Guilford Press, 2006.

Jong, Erica. *Serenissima: A Novel of Venice*. New York: Houghton Mifflin, 1987.

Kashi, Ed, and Julie Winokur. *Aging in America: The Years Ahead*. Brooklyn, NY: Powerhouse Books, 2003.

Katchadourian, Herant. *Fifty: Midlife in Perspective*. New York: W. H. Freeman, 1987.

Kent, Saul. *The Life-Extension Revolution: The Source Book for Optimum Health and Maximum Life-Span*. New York: William Morrow, 1983.

Kenton, Leslie. *Ageless Aging: The Natural Way to Stay Young*. New York: Grove Press, 1986.

Khalsa, Dharma Singh, and Cameron Stauth. *Brain Longevity: The Breakthrough Medical Program That Improves Your Mind and Memory*. New York: Little, Brown, 1997.

Kirkwood, Thomas. *Time of Our Lives: The Science of Human Aging*. London: Weidenfeld & Nicolson, 1999.

Kuba, Cheryl A. *Navigating the Journey of Aging Parents: What Care Receivers Want*. New York: Routledge, 2006.

Lamm, Steven, and Gerald Secor Couzens. *Younger at Last: The New World of Vitality Medicine*. New York: Simon & Schuster, 1997.

Laslett, Peter. *A Fresh Map of Life: The Emergence of the Third Age*. London: Weidenfeld & Nicolson, 1989.

Longman, Phillip. *Born to Pay: The New Politics of Aging*. New York: Houghton Mifflin, 1987.

Mann, John A. *Secrets of Life Extension*. San Francisco: Harbor, 1980.

Mintz, Steven. *The Prime of Life: A History of Modern Adulthood*. Cambridge, MA: Belknap Press of Harvard University Press, 2015.

Mueller, Laurence D., Casandra L. Rauser, and Michael R. Rose. *Does Aging Stop?* New York: Oxford University Press, 2011.

Neugarten, Bernice L. *Middle Age and Aging: A Reader in Social Psychology*. Chicago: University of Chicago Press, 1968.

Nuland, Sherwin B. *The Art of Aging: A Doctor's Prescription for Well-Being*. New York: Random House, 2007.

Null, Gary. *Power Aging: The Revolutionary Program to Control the Symptoms of Aging Naturally*. New York: New American Library, 2003.

Olinekova, Gayle. *Power Aging: Staying Young at Any Age*. New York: Thunder Mouth Press, 1998.

Olshansky, S. Jay, and Bruce A. Carnes. *The Quest for Immortality: Science at the Frontiers of Aging*. New York: W. W. Norton, 2003.

Palmer, Robert. *Age Well!* Cleveland: Cleveland Clinic Guides, 2005.

Paster, Zorba. *The Longevity Code: Your Personal Prescription for a Longer, Sweeter Life*. New York: Clarkson Potter, 2001.

Pearson, Durk, and Sandy Shaw. *Life Extension: A Practical Scientific Approach*. New York: Warner Books, 1982.

Pelletier, Kenneth R. *Longevity: Fulfilling Our Biological Potential*. New York: Delacorte Press, 1981.

Peterson, Peter G. *Gray Dawn: How the Coming Age Wave Will Transform America- and the World*. New York: Crown, 1999.

———. *Will America Grow Up Before It Grows Old? How the Coming Social Security Crisis Threatens You, Your Family, and Your Country*. New York: Random House, 1996.

Pifer, Alan, and Lydia Bronte, eds. *Our Aging Society: Paradox and Promise*. New York: W. W. Norton, 1986.

Rose, Michael R. *The Long Tomorrow: How Advances in Evolutionary Biology Can Help Us Postpone Aging*. New York: Oxford University Press, 2005.

Rosenfield, Albert. *Prolongevity: A Report on the Scientific Discoveries Now Being Made About Aging and Dying, and Their Promise of an Extended Human Life Span—Without Old Age*. New York: Knopf, 1976.

Rossman, Isadore. *Looking Forward: The Complete Guide to Successful Aging*. New York: Dutton, 1989.

Roszak, Theodore. *America the Wise: The Longevity Revolution and the True Wealth of Nations*. New York: Houghton Mifflin, 1998.

Rowe, John W., and Robert L. Kahn. *Successful Aging*. New York: Pantheon, 1998.

Rubin, Lillian B. *60 On Up: The Truth About Aging in America*. Boston: Beacon, 2007.

Samuel, Lawrence R. *Death, American Style: A Cultural History of Dying in America*. Lanham, MD: Rowman & Littlefield, 2013.

———. *Remembering America: How We Have Told Our Past*. Lincoln: University of Nebraska, 2015.

Schulz, James H., and Robert H. Binstock. *Aging Nation: The Economics and Politics of Growing Older in America*. Baltimore: Johns Hopkins Press, 2008.

Segerberg Jr., Osborn. *Living to Be 100: 1,200 Who Did and How They Did It.* New York: Charles Scribner's Sons, 1982.

Sheehy, Gail. *The Silent Passage.* New York: Random House, 1992.

Silverstone, Barbara, and Helen Kandel Hyman. *You and Your Aging Parent: A Family Guide to Emotional, Physical, and Financial Problems.* New York: Pantheon, 1989.

Snowden, David. *Aging with Grace: What the Nun Study Teaches Us About Leading Longer, Healthier, and More Meaningful Lives.* New York: Bantam, 2001.

Stipp, David. *The Youth Pill: Scientists at the Brink of an Anti-Aging Revolution.* New York: Current, 2010.

Thomas, Bill. *Second Wind: Navigating the Passage to a Slower, Deeper, and More Connected Life.* New York: Simon & Schuster, 2014.

———. *What Are Old People For? How Elders Will Save the World.* St. Louis: Vanderwyk & Burnham, 2004.

Thompson, Dennis, John D. Hogan, and Philip M. Clark. *Developmental Psychology in Historical Perspective.* Malden, MA: Wiley-Blackwell, 2012.

Torres-Gil, Fernando. *The New Aging: Politics and Change in America.* Santa Barbara: Praeger, 1991.

Troyansky, David G. *Aging in World History.* London: Routledge, 2015.

Van Tassel, David, and Peter N. Stearns, eds. *Old Age in a Bureaucratic Society: The Elderly, the Experts, and the State in American Society.* Westport, CT: Praeger, 1986.

Walford, Roy L. *The 120-Year Diet: How to Double Your Vital Years.* New York: Simon & Schuster, 1987.

———. *Maximum Life Span.* New York: W. W. Norton, 1985.

Weil, Andrew. *Healthy Aging: A Lifelong Guide to Your Physical and Spiritual Well-Being.* New York: Knopf, 2005.

Weiner, Jonathan. *Long for this World: The Strange Science of Immortality.* New York: Ecco, 2010.

Whitehouse, Peter L. *The Myth of Alzheimer's Disease: What You Aren't Being Told About Today's Most Dreaded Diagnosis.* New York: St. Martin's Griffin, 2008.

Winter, Jerrold. *Optimal Aging: A Guide to Your First 100 Years.* Seattle: CreateSpace, 2015.

Winter, Ruth. *The Anti-Aging Hormones: That Can Help You Beat the Clock.* New York: Three Rivers Press, 2013.

Worth, Richard. *You'll Be Old Someday, Too.* London: Franklin Watts, 1986.

# Index